THE BARBARY WARS

THE BARBARY WARS

AMERICAN INDEPENDENCE IN
THE ATLANTIC WORLD

FRANK LAMBERT

 HILL AND WANG

A DIVISION OF FARRAR, STRAUS AND GIROUX

NEW YORK

Hill and Wang
A division of Farrar, Straus and Giroux
19 Union Square West, New York 10003

Illustrations courtesy of The Mariner's Museum, Newport News, Va.

Library of Congress Cataloging-in-Publication Data
Lambert, Frank, 1943–
    The Barbary wars : American independence in the Atlantic world / by Frank Lambert.—
1st ed.
        p.   cm.
    Includes bibliographical references.
    ISBN-13: 978-0-8090-9533-9
    ISBN-10: 0-8090-9533-5 (hardcover : alk. paper)
    1. United States—History—Tripolitan War, 1801–1805.   2. United States—Relations—
Africa, North.   3. Africa, North—Relations—United States.   4. United States—History—
War with Algeria, 1815.   5. United States—Foreign relations—1783–1815.
6. Pirates—Africa, North—History—19th century.   7. Pirates—Mediterranean Region—
History—19th century.   8. Africa, North—History, Naval—19th century.   9. Mediterranean
Region—History, Naval—19th century.   I. Title.

E335.L36 2005
973.4'7—dc22

                                                                                    2004019361

Designed by Jonathan D. Lippincott
Maps designed by Jeffrey L. Ward

www.fsgbooks.com

1   3   5   7   9   10   8   6   4   2

FOR BETH

CONTENTS

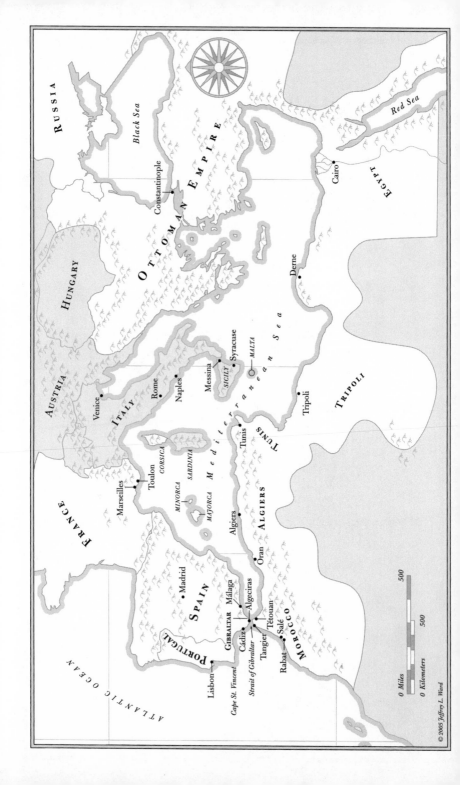

THE BARBARY WARS

INTRODUCTION

On September 3, 1783, Britain recognized American independence by agreeing to terms of the long-awaited peace treaty. Benjamin Franklin, John Adams, and John Jay, commissioners of the U.S. Congress, and David Hartley, minister plenipotentiary for Parliament, signed the accord at Paris. Preliminary articles of peace had been negotiated almost a year earlier, but reaching a final settlement had been a long, contentious process. Arriving in Philadelphia on Saturday, November 22, aboard the French packet *Courier de l'Europe*, John Thaxter, private secretary to John Adams, delivered the treaty to Congress. As word spread, Americans everywhere celebrated. New Yorkers in "prodigious" numbers poured out onto the Bowling Green in the Broad-Way for a grand fireworks display that "exceeded every former exhibition in the United States."[1] The treaty's publication in Providence, Rhode Island, was literally an earth-shaking event: just hours after the treaty appeared, an earthquake leveled a beacon tower erected "at the commencement of the late war."[2] One local commentator saw the act as a providential signal that British oppression had been toppled and American independence was now a reality.

One year after the *Courier de l'Europe* arrived in Philadelphia with the good news of independence, the crew of a Philadelphia brigantine lost their independence when a band of Barbary pirates captured their vessel and took them prisoner. U.S. consul at Madrid William Carmichael sent a terse official dispatch to Benjamin

Franklin in Paris, informing him of this violation of American independence: "In the month of November I received advice from Cadiz of the capture of an American vessel by a corsair of the Emperor of Morocco."[3] As details emerged, Americans learned that the brig *Betsey*, under the command of Captain James Erwin, had been sailing from Cádiz to Tenerife when a band of pirates overtook the ship, swarmed aboard, took the crew captive, and demanded the payment of tribute to prevent future captures. This particular group of pirates was known throughout Europe as Sallee Rovers, so called because they sailed from their base at the Morocco port of Salé on the Atlantic. Of course, the designation "pirate" depended on one's perspective. To Europeans and Americans, the rovers were robbers on the high seas and thus pirates. But to Moroccans they were at worst privateers sailing under the king's flag and at best commercial capitalists seeking profit in the highly competitive Atlantic. By whatever designation, the Moroccans reminded Americans that when they traded overseas, they operated within a "tribute-demanding" world.[4]

That was not the world Americans had envisioned when they severed ties with Great Britain. Long restrained by Britain's Navigation Acts, nearly all Americans wished to be freed from the old colonial trade restrictions, and many embraced the principle of free trade.[5] Indeed, before declaring political independence in July 1776, the Continental Congress had declared commercial independence in December 1775. In direct defiance of Parliament's Restraining Act, which closed American ports to ships from countries other than Great Britain, Congress opened the ports to ships of all nations except Britain. The delegates understood that their actions meant war. As Maryland's Samuel Chase succinctly put it, "When you once offer your trade to foreign nations, away with all hopes of reconciliation."[6]

Though they wanted access to wider markets and freedom from trade restrictions, colonial merchants had enjoyed certain benefits by trading within Britain's closed colonial system. One enormous advantage was the protection of American merchant vessels under treaties that English monarchs had negotiated with the Barbary States and enforced, when necessary, with the British navy. The treaty of "Peace & Commerce" between Charles II and the dey of Algiers, dated April 10, 1682, covered "all the Dominions and Subjects of either side." It provided that English ships "may safely come to the Port of Algiers, or any other Port or Places of that Kingdom, there freely to Buy and Sell." And they would be allowed to "depart from thence whensoever they please, without any stop or hindrance whatsoever." Moreover, all British ships "shall freely pass the Seas, and Traffick without any Search." When an Algerine warship spotted a vessel flying the English flag, the captain would dispatch a boat with two sailors to board and inspect the ship. If the captain of the English ship produced a "Pass under the Hand and Seal of the Lord High Admiral of England," the "said Boat shall presently depart, and the Merchant Ship or Vessel shall proceed freely on her Voyage." The dey further promised that no British subjects would be "Bought or Sold or made Slaves in any part of the Kingdom of Algiers."[7]

Even as Congress boldly declared independence from Britain, the delegates recognized that American merchants, sailors, and shipping became fair game to the pirates from Morocco, Algiers, Tunis, and Tripoli. Accordingly, the wartime Congress sought a new protector and found one in Britain's archenemy France, which promised in the 1778 Treaty of Amity and Commerce to use its good offices to protect American interests against the Barbary pirates.

After the war, the United States tried to reenlist Britain's good offices in protecting American ships in the Mediterranean. The most powerful force in the Atlantic world, England and the Royal Navy exercised more influence over the Barbary States than did any of Europe's other maritime powers. Thus, Congress sought two treaties from Whitehall: one a peace treaty, the so-called Definitive Treaty, recognizing U.S. independence; and the other a commercial treaty, giving American vessels free and equal access to all ports without harassment, including that from the Barbary pirates.

While it was signing the Treaty of Paris, Parliament determined that the proposed commercial treaty was not in Britain's best interest. Indeed, many British merchants and politicians took the view that the Barbary pirates could be useful allies in thwarting the Americans' goal of free trade, which the British viewed as anathema to their existing trade advantages. If the pirates allowed the expanding American merchant fleet to sail unfettered, the British would suffer in two ways: they would lose the carrying trade, and low-cost American produce would take market share at Mediterranean ports. If world demand were unchanging, as mercantilists deemed it to be, then international commerce was indeed a zero-sum game that the upstart United States threatened. Mercantilists imagined a world of nation-states locked in perpetual conflict over the acquisition of wealth. Measured in gold and silver, the world's wealth, they argued, was fixed, and one country's gain was the other's loss. The surest path to riches was for a nation to establish a closed trading system in which colonies shipped valuable commodities only to the mother country and bought manufactured goods exclusively from the mother country. For maximum effectiveness, a nation would buy nothing from another state and would not ship goods in vessels belonging to other countries. Threatening that system and those nations who benefited by it were free-trade Americans who wanted to eliminate protective tariffs and open world markets to every country on an equal basis.

In summer 1785 American troubles with the Barbary pirates took on a much more sinister tone, ending wishful thinking about free trade. On July 25 an Algerine xebec, a small three-masted vessel of fourteen guns, intercepted the Boston schooner *Maria* (Isaac Stephens, master) as it passed Cape St. Vincent on its way to Cádiz and imprisoned its six-man crew. Less than a week later an Algerine corsair captured the ship *Dauphin* of Philadelphia (Richard O'Brien, master), bound from St. Ubes, and took its fifteen crewmen prisoner.

The Moroccan capture of the *Betsey* and the Algerine taking of the *Dauphin* and *Maria* were the opening encounters in the so-called Barbary Wars, a thirty-three-year period of tension between the United States and the Barbary States that included two wars in the Mediterranean: the Tripolitan War (1801–5) and the Algerine War (1815–16). Thomas Jefferson considered the Barbary conflict to be a "sideshow" because, during the same time, the United States faced challenges from much more powerful foes, fighting the Quasi-War with the French (1797–1800) and the War of 1812 with the British (1812–15). Yet their status as a sideshow makes the Barbary Wars an effective window onto the United States' struggle to extend its newly won independence to overseas commerce. If Americans could not trade in the Mediterranean because of "petty tyrants," as Jefferson's Republican Party dubbed the Algerines, then the ideal of free trade would remain a chimera. While the characterization of the Barbary States as "petty" was largely correct, it must be noted that the United States in 1783 was an equally petty presence in the Atlantic world, which was dominated by the great European maritime powers Britain, France, and Spain. The Moroccan and Algerine captures in the 1780s exposed the United States as a weak confederation of minor, jealous states that had neither the will nor the power nor the treasury to protect its merchant ships.

Historians and popular writers have debated the place and meaning of the Barbary Wars in American history, particularly since the September 11, 2001, attacks on the World Trade Center in New York and the Pentagon in Washington. To make sense of current events in the region, journalists and scholars have searched for historical origins and context that would help explain such events as the bombing of Libya (1986), the Gulf War (1991), and the "war on terrorism." Regrettably, much of what we learn from recent works tells us more about the present than about the past. In one scholarly treatment of the Barbary Wars with the United States, the focus is on the "Muslim World" and the "Specter of Islam."[8] Another work views the Barbary Wars as "a holy war of Muslims against the infidel invaders."[9] Several popular writers and commentators emphasize religion as the primary influence shaping hostilities between the United States and the Barbary States. Some chauvinistic books point to the Tripolitan War as an example of American moral, technological, and intellectual superiority in toppling a ruthless enemy. After all, it was that war that inspired the refrain in the U.S. Marine Corps hymn "To the shores of Tripoli."[10]

Certain American religious leaders likewise saw religion as the principal influence guiding the conflicts between America and the Barbary States. While some view Islamic extremists as the principal agents of attacks on Christians and Jews, others consider Islam itself as a militant religion that rewards believers who kill "infidels" under any circumstances, in offensive as well as in defensive warfare. They ascribe to the pirates of the late 1700s and early 1800s the same zeal that they claim motivates twenty-first-century anti-American "holy warriors." In a direct comparison, one writer turned the Barbary pirates into modern-day terrorists: "Similar to the al Qaeda, Hezbollah, or the Palestinian Liberation Organization, some of the *Mohammeden* (Muslim) terrorists operated from sea-port fortresses throughout the Ottoman Empire."[11] Others who have examined the historical record of the Barbary Wars disagree.[12] Evidence abounds that neither the pirates nor the Americans considered religion central to their conflict. From his twelve-year imprisonment at Algiers, one American captive concluded in the 1790s that money was the Algerine god, that the pirates were far more interested in taking prizes than in waging holy war. And President John Adams and the U.S. Senate kept religion out of the negotiations. The Tripoli Treaty in 1797 explicitly declared that the United States was not a Christian state.

This book argues that the Barbary Wars were primarily about trade, not theology, and that rather than being holy wars, they were an extension of America's War of Independence. Americans expected their trading partners in 1783 to embrace the revolutionary principles of 1776 in governing commerce on the high seas. Having overthrown British imperial government and won the right of home rule, Americans based their case on such natural rights as liberty and equality. Claiming the freedom to be governed by representatives of their choosing, they took their place as an independent republic and insisted on equal standing within the community of nations. At home Americans embraced such revolutionary rights as that of freedom of religion, which came to mean liberty of conscience for all individuals and separation of church and state. In foreign trade, Americans hoped that the principles of equality and reciprocity would govern overseas commerce. Specifically, they wanted free access to all ports, and they expected no trading partner to impose duties higher than those the United States levied on the same goods. Further, they wished to enjoy most favored nation status, meaning that rates and regulations on U.S. goods would be the same as those placed on their commercial rivals. Such an arrangement would ensure that the Atlantic world afforded Americans the freedom and equality that they enjoyed at home.

Americans were quickly disabused of such notions. While 1783 marked the official recognition of its political independence, the United States in that year was beset on all sides by barriers to free trade. Spain blocked access to the Mississippi, and Britain prohibited trade in the British West Indies. Moreover, the British Parliament, hoping to reduce America's threat as a commercial rival, sought to keep the United States subject to the same onerous trade regulations that had vexed American merchants before the revolution. The most overt and bellicose attacks on U.S. trade came from the Barbary pirates, who in 1784 and 1785 captured American vessels and enslaved U.S. citizens. Those raids by Moroccan and Algerine corsairs were powerful signals that if the United States were to enjoy the principles of independence beyond its borders, it would have to fight for them just as it had fought for home rule.

To understand the Barbary Wars, one must pay close attention to the context in which they took place. That necessitates, first, understanding the Atlantic world, both its origins and its geographic, political, and commercial boundaries in the late eighteenth and early nineteenth centuries.[13] The Atlantic world emerged during Europe's age of exploration, beginning in the late fifteenth century, and by the time of the Barbary Wars, its physical dimensions were extensive. On the eastern side of the Atlantic, the region included western Europe and West Africa, and on its western side, the eastern seaboards of North and South America. It also encompassed two major seas, the Mediterranean and the Caribbean. The Barbary States were situated along North Africa's Mediterranean coast, with the Kingdom of Morocco as the westernmost, located along the Strait of Gibraltar. The three remaining Barbary States were the republics of Algiers, Tripoli, and Tunis, moving eastward from Morocco. The United States in 1783 consisted of thirteen states, from New Hampshire in the north to Georgia in the south, with settlement reaching from the Atlantic to the Appalachian Mountains.

The architects of the Atlantic world were Europe's maritime powers; Spain and Portugal had taken the lead in the fifteenth century, followed by France, Holland, and England. All were motivated primarily by the quest for riches, the desire to expand the Christian faith, and the hope for advantage over their political rivals. In 1492 Spain launched the first transatlantic expedition by sponsoring Christopher Columbus's voyage seeking a western trade route to the lucrative East Indies, the source of foods, spices, and fabrics that Europeans demanded in greater and greater quantities. While failing to find the desired shortcut, Columbus and the explorers who followed discovered a new world in the Western Hemisphere where they planted European colonies, including New Spain, New England, New France, and New Amsterdam. Each sought wealth by extracting valuable commodities from America's land, forests, and seas, and each exploited Native Americans and African slaves for the hard labor required to gain those riches.

In the 1780s American goods were traded in an Atlantic world that was anything but free, as each of the great maritime powers hoped to gain sufficient wealth from the New World to dominate the Old. Locked in fierce commercial and political competition, the Europeans followed the dictates of mercantilism, a set of perspectives and strategies aimed at amassing the greatest wealth, which, they believed, translated into dominating power. Using American riches, each hoped to build an army and navy powerful enough to defeat its rivals. Mercantilists faced a twofold challenge: to extract more wealth from America than did their competitors, and to keep that wealth within their respective empires. In the early stages of exploiting newly discovered America, each of the European powers sought wealth by discovering, extracting, and exporting gold and silver bullion from native deposits. Spain was the clear winner, striking it rich at the Potosí mines and shipping tons of silver back home. English explorers failed to find similar veins in North America and relied instead upon piracy to confiscate bullion from Spanish galleons. For their exploits, sea robbers such as Francis Drake became England's mercantilist heroes.

Recognizing that gold and silver did not abound everywhere in the Americas, Europeans sought wealth through trade, and to that end Britain, Spain, and France built closed colonial trading systems. The idea was to plant colonies in America whose settlers would exploit the land, forests, and seas for exportable commodities to be shipped only to ports within the empire. Ideally, the colonies would produce sufficient quantities of food and fiber to make the empire self-sufficient, ending the need to import raw materials from the outside, which had to be paid for with gold or silver. In addition to supplying English industrialists with commodities, the colonies became important markets for the mother country's manufactured goods. Though the British found little gold and silver, their colonial system generated great wealth. On the other hand, the Spanish empire, while rich in precious metals, had difficulty holding on to its wealth. Lacking a manufacturing base to match its appetite for military hardware, Spain purchased goods from outsiders, and its wealth seeped into its rivals' coffers.

Beginning in the 1650s, England passed a series of Navigation Acts aimed at ensuring a tight seal around its closed colonial trading system. Competing with the Dutch, who had emerged as a powerful maritime rival, England enacted measures to deny the Dutch any benefits from trade with British North America. That meant, first, closing markets. England's American settlers were forbidden to import goods from Holland or to export commodities to Dutch ports. Moreover, the Navigation Acts disallowed all foreign vessels from playing any role in American commerce. The reality of overseas trade was such that oftentimes the carrier of goods reaped greater profits in a shipment than did the merchant whose goods were being transported. If the carrier in such a case were the Dutch and the merchant an Englishman, the bulk of the voyage's profits would be siphoned off to Holland. Under mercantilist doctrine, the Dutch would be the winner. Therefore Whitehall enacted laws governing the carrying trade as well as the merchandise carried, insisting that colonial commerce be restricted to shipping English goods in English bottoms to English ports.

By dissolving their ties with Britain in 1776, Americans hoped to chart their own course in the Atlantic world, trading in markets that offered them the greatest profits. But though independent in 1783, the United States, like the Barbary States, was a bit player on a mercantilist stage dominated by the great European powers and their violent contests of control. During the period 1783 to 1816 the Atlantic world was in upheaval. The wars between Great Britain and France following the French Revolution of 1789 put American commercial vessels at peril. Neither of the combatants recognized U.S. neutrality rights; both captured American ships, confiscated their cargoes, and impressed their crews. Both British and French interpreted American relations with the Barbary pirates in ways that fit their own diplomatic and military objectives and sought to influence events in the Mediterranean accordingly.

Situated within the Atlantic world, the Barbary Wars must be understood within the context of domestic politics in the early American republic as well. The first Barbary raids occurred under the Articles of Confederation, which left effective governing power in the hands of the individual states. The national Congress had no independent taxing authority and thus lacked funds for negotiating with or fighting the Barbary States. Further, sectional jealousies between the northern commercial states and the southern planting states undermined a united front. After ratification of the Constitution in 1789, conflicting interpretations of war-making powers ensured that America's response to continued corsair raids would take place within a highly partisan atmosphere.

Though political and economic questions are at the forefront of this study, cultural issues are also explored. Some historians have regarded the Barbary Wars as a cultural window through which Americans viewed their opponents with an emphasis on their non-Christian, non-Western, nonmodern perspectives. Without question, some U.S. newspapers, dramas, speeches, and sermons focused on such Islamic beliefs as "jihad," expressed curiosity about the pasha's "seraglio," and denounced the Barbary enslavement of Christians. As often as not, however, Americans considered Barbary beliefs and practices in a cultural mirror that reflected on the United States. When, for example, Americans commented on Islam, they were likely to turn the discussion to a scrutiny of religious intolerance among certain sects in the United States. And when Americans denounced the Algerine captivity of U.S. citizens, they also decried the barbaric, un-Christian slaveholding in the South.

ONE

THE AMERICAN REVOLUTION CHECKED

In August 1785, shortly after the Algerine attacks on the *Maria* and *Dauphin*, John Adams reflected on the state of American independence from his diplomatic post in London. In a letter to John Jay, he confided, "I find the spirit of the times very different from that which you and I saw . . . in the months of November and December, 1783"—that is, just after Britain recognized the United States as a sovereign state. Then expectations were high that the two nations would prosper under reciprocal trade agreements. But alas, a very different climate prevailed just two years after the Treaty of Paris. "Now," Adams continued, "the utmost contempt of our commerce is freely expressed in pamphlets, gazettes, coffee-houses, and in common street talk."[1] Rather than becoming America's main trading partner, Britain had reinstated and even reinforced trade regulations through navigation acts that blocked the United States from lucrative markets and extorted high tariffs in others. At the same time, Algiers declared war on American shipping. After independence, instead of becoming an equal partner in the Atlantic world, the United States was again a dependent—subjugated by British trade restrictions and defenseless against the Barbary pirates.

Americans viewed the pirates as vestiges of an unenlightened and vanishing time when depredations of the powerful, not the rule of law, dictated the rhythms of trade. American independence promised to usher in a *novus ordo seclorum*, a new age that would transform the "tribute-demanding" Atlantic into a free-trade zone.[2] Thomas Jefferson spoke for many of his countrymen when he envisioned an end to the old mercantilist system. "I would say then to every nation on earth," Jefferson declared just a week before the Algerines captured the Boston schooner *Maria*, "your people shall trade freely with us, and ours with you, paying no more than the most favoured nation, in order to put an end to the right of individual states acting by fits and starts to interrupt our commerce or to embroil us with any nation."[3] Free trade would help everyone, Americans argued, expanding the overall volume of commerce so greatly that an individual country would benefit from even a modest share. Such reasoning made no sense to the Barbary pirates. They too subscribed to the notion of a zero-sum game: there was a fixed amount of trade available, and thus what one country gained was always at the expense of another.

While American merchants and Barbary pirates confronted each other from very different orientations, neither controlled the arena in which they clashed. In the 1780s both parties were on the margins of an Atlantic world dominated by the great European maritime powers. To understand the Barbary Wars, therefore, it is necessary to consider American-Barbary relations within the larger context of the Atlantic world and the aims of those who wished to keep the renegades from North Africa and the upstarts from North America on its fringes. Events need to be viewed from London as well as from Algiers and Philadelphia. One example will suffice. In late 1784 and early 1785, while deploying a naval squadron to patrol the Mediterranean and thereby protect His Majesty's shipping, the British circulated reports that the Algerines had captured an American ship and planned to seize others. Though the reports proved groundless, the damage to American shipping was real and immediate. One Henry Martin explained to Jefferson, "In consequence of these reports, the underwriters at Lloyds will not insure an American Ship to Cadiz or Lisbon for less than 25 percent whereas the customary insurance for English vessels is no more than 1¼ or 1½ percent and therefore no American Ship has any chance of getting freight either to Spain or Portugal."[4] America and the Barbary States confronted each other in the shadows of the Union Jack.

While they were still under British rule, American merchants had been expected to operate within a closed colonial system of trade that funneled imperial wealth and profits into the City of London, thereby enhancing the crown's geopolitical power. But during the tumultuous decades leading to England's civil war in the 1640s, colonial commerce received very little attention from Whitehall. Colonial traders took advantage of the upheaval, selling their produce in non-English markets, including those of England's chief Atlantic rivals, Spain and France. With the downfall of the British monarchy in 1649 and the dismantling of the House of Lords, domestic politics, not colonial trade, predominated in Commonwealth England. Scores of factions tried to shape England's future course, from royalists who wished to restore the Stuarts to the throne to radicals who wanted to abolish ancient privileges, thus leveling English society. The Navigation Acts of 1650–51 represented the sole attempt during the Commonwealth period to ensure that the colonies remained "subordinate to Parliament" and that "all colonial trade . . . [was] carried in English ships," but inadequate enforcement allowed the colonists to evade the measures. Then, when the royalists triumphed and brought Charles II back from exile in 1660, the cash-strapped monarch was determined to collect all royal revenues, including colonial duties imposed by the Navigation Acts.

Committed to mercantilist doctrines, the Restoration court at Whitehall refocused attention on international trade, including that of the American colonies. While earlier monarchs had granted monopolies to individual companies for the purpose of exploiting trade in a given region of the world, Charles II sought a "total integration of the country's trade based on national monopoly, with the state playing a leading role."[5] While in practice the British mercantilist system was never as integrated as Charles II wished, it nonetheless circumscribed the markets open to colonial merchants.

That American merchants wished to be freed from imperial trade restraints well before the revolution is evident in their repeated attempts to develop illicit commerce with non-British ports and to smuggle goods past British customs officials. New England traders in particular were notorious violators of the Navigation Acts. After the Restoration, Charles II and his Privy Council observed that Massachusetts Bay officials regarded the colony as a "free State" subject only to laws of their own making. To bring New England into compliance, the Privy Council dispatched agents to gather intelligence on trade violations and to warn perpetrators that His Majesty was determined to enforce commercial regulations. They had their work cut out for them. In his 1676 report to Secretary of State Sir Joseph Williamson, agent Captain John Wynbourne noted that in Boston Harbor ships "dayly arrived from Spain ffrance Holland & Canareys" loaded with goods that were to have been imported only from England. And outgoing American ships carried enumerated commodities to Europe, ignoring provisions in the Navigation Acts to transport colonial crops only to England.[6]

Agent Edward Randolph's similar dispatch of June 17, 1676, described a colony pursuing independence in religion, governance, and trade. Like Wynbourne, he found Boston Harbor teeming with European ships, "contrary to the late Acts of Parliament for encouraging Navigation and trade." And as they had with Wynbourne, Boston officials struck an independent, if not defiant, tone in explaining their actions. Randolph reported that Governor John Leverett "freely declared to me that the Laws made by Our King and Parlmt obligeth them in nothing but what consists with the Interest of New England."[7]

For all of their evasion of the Navigation Acts, colonial merchantmen depended on the British for protection against pirates and privateers. Algerine pirates routinely preyed on British and colonial vessels, capturing ships and their cargoes while enslaving their crews. They then demanded tribute for cessation of future depredations and ransom for release of the captives. English monarchs had long concluded that it was less costly to pay tribute than to fight. Besides, they found the Barbary States useful tools in English commercial policy, as pirates became willing raiders on Britain's trading rivals who did not pay tribute. It meant a constant state of negotiation and threat, with the Barbary powers hoping always to increase tribute payments and the British hoping to strike a balance of economic and diplomatic cost-effectiveness. It was under this largely reliable umbrella that colonial American merchantmen passed safely through the Strait of Gibraltar and into the Mediterranean, sometimes escorted by British warships and always carrying the prescribed passes.

By the 1760s, however, even loyal colonial merchants were reappraising their position within British mercantilism. Following the expensive French and Indian War, the British Parliament imposed a round of new taxes designed to raise revenue from the colonists and strengthened provisions for enforcing trade regulations. Parliament hoped that the Revenue Act of 1764, often referred to as the Sugar Act, would generate an additional forty thousand pounds sterling by placing duties on a number of foreign goods much demanded by the colonists, including coffee, sugar, and wine. It also contained new regulations concerning the loading and unloading of ships in American ports designed to assist customs collectors in detecting smuggling. Its most controversial feature was the duty on foreign molasses. Under the existing schedule of duties, the rate was six pence per gallon, but colonists routinely evaded its payment by smuggling molasses into the colonies from the French West Indies. By reducing the new rate to three pence per gallon, George Grenville, the king's chief minister and architect of the new tax, hoped the lower rate would make the tax more palatable to colonists and that their greater compliance would result in increased royal revenue. Colonists, however, protested the measure, viewing the lower duty as a bribe aimed at enticing them to pay the tax and thereby acknowledge Parliament's taxing authority.

Convinced that the act would cripple colonial trade, especially that with the West Indies, the Loyalist merchant and planter James Habersham of Georgia chose to lecture British lawmakers. In a letter to Georgia's agent William Knox, Habersham urged him to work "in concert with any Agent or Agents of the northern provinces" to protest the act, "as particularly affects the Trade of this province." He acknowledged that the act did not harm Georgia "in so great a degree as some of the Northern Colonys," yet he explained that Georgians had long exported lumber, horses, and cattle to the West Indies, a trade that had "principally been the Means, whereby most of the Inhabitants have acquired the little property they possess." Because Georgia planters and merchants owned few vessels, the majority of the exports had been carried on sailing vessels of northern registries that in return brought "a few Negroes and sometimes Cash." Although the Georgia produce often constituted a small portion of the ship's cargo, according to Habersham this "growing commerce promised the greatest advantage to us."[8]

The following year Parliament proposed the Stamp Act; the new taxes and regulations could not have come at a worse time. Still suffering from the recession that followed the French and Indian War, merchants throughout the colonies protested the measure and all other acts restricting American trade. A group of four hundred Philadelphia merchants complained in a November broadside "that the many difficulties [we] now labour under as a Trading People, are owing to the Restrictions, Prohibitions, and ill advised Regulations, made in the several Acts of Parliament of Great-Britain, lately passed to regulate the Colonies; which have limited the Exportation of some Part of our Country Produce, increased the Cost and Expence of many Articles of our Importation, and cut off from us all Means of supplying ourselves with Specie." This in turn left them unable to pay down their enormous debts to British merchants. Free access to world markets, the protesters argued, would benefit Anglo-American merchants on both sides of the Atlantic.[9]

But far from granting the colonists more commercial freedom, Parliament in 1767 imposed the Townshend duties on a wide range of colonial imports, further tightening Britain's noose around colonial trade. The incensed Americans responded by waging commercial warfare. Reasoning that Britain was a country whose economic lifeblood was trade and recognizing that the American colonies were Britain's largest single market, the increasingly rebellious colonists decided to deny that market through nonimportation agreements. Beginning in Boston and spreading elsewhere, Americans entered into solemn associations, pledging to import no goods from Britain except a few essentials until Parliament repealed the offending duties.

Propagandists whipped up support by depicting the boycott as consistent with the loftiest republican principles. Borrowed from British political history, republicanism was a set of ideas formulated by opponents of arbitrary power. First expressed in the Commonwealth period following England's civil war, it was revived in the 1720s when England's first prime minister, Robert Walpole, consolidated Parliament's power. Republicans feared centralized power in the hands of placemen, officeholders who did the bidding of others. Such vicious men put private gain above the public good; in consolidating their grip on power, the argument went, they raised taxes to support a swollen court and, the republicans' bête noire, a standing army. Republicans opposed such measures in the name of freedom. Taxes, they argued, threatened property, and property represented the foundation of political independence. If a person owned land or if he operated a profitable mercantile house, his economic independence allowed him to vote his conscience. To protect that sacred status, republicans advocated vigilance and virtue: vigilance to detect any ministerial grab for additional power and virtue to resist the temptation to sacrifice civic good for private gain.[10]

Nonimportation went against merchants' instincts. They were in business to make profits by importing and exporting goods, and the idea of letting their ships rot alongside quays lined with empty warehouses was difficult to embrace. For those who obeyed the Continental Association, as the boycott was called, forgoing personal gain was an act of patriotism. No one was a greater champion of American overseas commerce than Alexander Hamilton, yet he supported the measure as a means of freeing the colonists from imperial slavery. "We can live without trade of any kind," he wrote, adding, "Food and clothing we have within ourselves."[11] Traders unwilling to make the sacrifice found themselves beset by angry republicans who tarred and feathered them for ignoring the boycott of English manufactures.

For many New England merchants, the Tea Act of 1773 represented the culmination of a long chain of trade abuses they suffered at the hands of the mother country. While the three-pence-per-pound tax sparked new popular protests of "taxation without representation," the law's provisions represented to American merchants commercial slavery. Aimed at bailing out the East India Company, the bill authorized that company to sell its tea directly to American consumers through agents of its choosing. Moreover, by granting the company drawbacks or refunds of British duties on tea imported from the East Indies, Parliament enabled it to undersell colonial merchants who had purchased tea from high-priced middlemen or had smuggled it from Dutch suppliers.[12] With the Tea Act, British restriction of markets reached the colonies themselves; Parliament would determine who could sell the colonists their tea and at what terms. How, asked patriot merchants locked out of a key market at home, could continued dependence on Parliament be termed anything other than slavery?

When the First Continental Congress convened in Philadelphia in 1774, the delegates identified trade restrictions as the first chains that enslaved the colonists. Addressing Parliament on behalf of the Congress, John Jay cited the new imperial measures enacted since the end of the French and Indian War as the final step in a "plan for enslaving your fellow subjects in America." But even before those odious acts, Jay wrote, Parliament through the Navigation Acts had systematically drawn "from us the wealth produced by our commerce." "You restrained our trade in every way that could conduce to your emolument," he charged Parliament, and "you exercised unbounded sovereignty over the sea. You named the ports and nations to which alone our merchandise should be carried, and with whom alone we should trade."[13]

Parliament's new imperial measures complicated the colonists' cost-benefit analysis. On the one hand, taxes, imposed at will by a legislature that did not represent the colonists' interests, were rising, even as tighter enforcement mechanisms made smuggling more difficult. On the other hand, the British connection continued to provide protection in a dangerous world. With the passage of the Stamp Act in 1765, Americans began to think that British oppression of their rights outweighed the advantages that His Majesty's Navy afforded. In early 1766 the *Pennsylvania Gazette* reported that "a Bond for a Mediterranean Pass, with an American Stamp to it, was burned at the Coffee-House" in Philadelphia.[14] Clearly the oppressive stamp set too high a price for safe passage in the Mediterranean.

In his bestselling *Common Sense* (1776), the radical revolutionary Thomas Paine made a compelling case for the connection between independence and free trade. Aimed at fence-sitters, the widely read pamphlet argued that if the colonies severed their ties with Britain, American overseas trade would flourish. To those who feared that the loss of British military protection would encourage European powers to attack American shipping that crossed the Atlantic unescorted, Paine answered, "Our plan is commerce, and that, well attended to, will secure us the peace and friendship of all Europe; because it is the interest of all Europe to have America a *free port*." To those who maintained that American trade would suffer if the colonies left the British Empire and its guaranteed markets, Paine replied, "Our corn will fetch its price in any market in Europe, and our imported goods must be paid for, buy them where we will." An independent America would have all of Europe as its proper market for trade, a far larger field of opportunity than the highly restricted markets to which dependent America was confined under British rule.[15]

In drafting the Declaration of Independence six months later, Thomas Jefferson recast the free-trade argument in the language of natural rights. All persons, he argued in the rhetoric of political economist John Locke, had certain rights that no government could take from them, including the right to own property and to dispose of it at will. By restricting the colonists' ability to sell their goods under terms of their choosing, Parliament had violated those rights; Americans, by dissolving all connections with Britain, could reclaim them.[16]

With the Declaration of Independence and the outbreak of war, Americans lost all protection against piratical predations in the Mediterranean. Worse, the British navy shifted its role from defending colonial trade to interdicting it and blockading American ports. Recognizing that the fledgling United States lacked an adequate navy, Congress sought help from abroad. In a letter dated December 21, 1776, the Committee of Secret Correspondence instructed Benjamin Franklin, Silas Deane, and Arthur Lee, commissioners representing the revolutionary states in Paris, to draw France into the conflict by whatever means necessary. Not only was it "all-important" for America's military operations "that France should enter the war as soon as may be," there was also an economic motive. With its war debts mounting, the United States needed revenue from overseas trade, and as the committee noted, "the British recall of their Mediterranean passes is an object of great consequence." Without a naval escort, U.S. ships were vulnerable to the Barbary pirates; consequently the commissioners were instructed to intercede with the court of France "to prevent the mischiefs that may be derived to American commerce therefrom."[17] In the resulting Treaty of Amity and Commerce (1778), France pledged to provide for the "Safety of the said United States

... against all ... Depredations on the Part of the ... States of Barbary."[18]

With the military assistance of the French, in 1781 the United States defeated the British at Yorktown in what proved to be the last major conflict in the war. As optimism rose that independence would become a reality, Americans began to think about their place in the postwar world. Some, most notably New England merchants, believed that the United States must recognize world trade as it was, which meant that America had to protect its commercial interests with laws of navigation and import duties as did every other nation. Rejecting this status quo, other commercial and political leaders envisioned a world of free trade.

John Adams and Benjamin Franklin represented the two views in an exchange of letters in 1781. Adams suggested that duties on American exports were necessary for generating revenues to pay the interest on war debts. Franklin reminded him that "England raised indeed a great revenue by duties on tobacco, but it was by virtue of a prohibition of foreign tobaccos, and thereby obliging the internal consumer to pay those duties." He feared that the imposition of duties would only lead to trade wars. Franklin asked, "If America were to lay a duty of 5 pence sterling p. lb. on the exportation of her tobacco, would any European nation buy it?" He thought not, suggesting that the colonies of Spain and Portugal as well as Ukraine would "furnish it much cheaper." Besides, Franklin believed that the costs of levying and collecting duties outweighed the benefits, particularly those expenses necessary to "guard our long coast against the smuggling of tobacco."[19] "I find myself rather inclined to adopt that modern [opinion]," Franklin concluded, "which supposes it best for every country to leave its trade entirely free from all incumbrances."[20]

American merchants sided with Franklin. In their view, the War of Independence was as much about guaranteeing commercial freedom as it was about securing natural rights. And indeed, they pointed out that without a vigorous overseas trade, American liberty at home would be an empty shell. One 1781 article, signed by "Leonidas," summarized the arguments for the importance of overseas commerce to the republic. First appearing in the *Pennsylvania Gazette* and reprinted in Boston's *Independent Chronicle and Universal Advertiser*, the piece noted that 1776 had brought a declaration of commercial as well as political independence.

> The whole world (Britain excepted) is open to the productions and demands of his country. Commerce has become therefore not only inoffensive, but useful; nay more, It has become absolutely necessary to the happiness of America.[21]

In contrast to Britain's antiquated and unenlightened mercantilism, which promoted jealousy, competition, and war, free commerce among nations would one day usher in "universal peace and benevolence."[22] Through trade, the author exulted, the United States will receive "all the improvements in arts and sciences of countries, where men are maintained by societies for the sole purpose of adding by their discoveries to the pleasures and conveniences of life." Commerce, he wrote, would bind the globe together in one common system of interests and benevolence."[23] George Washington echoed Leonidas's sentiments in a letter to the Marquis de Lafayette: "I cannot avoid reflecting with pleasure on the probable influence that commerce may hereafter have on human manners and society in general." He dreamed of a time when "the benefits of a liberal and free commerce will . . . succeed to the devastations and horrors of war."[24]

But America's place in the world after 1783 was a far cry from the one Americans had hoped would follow independence. Disunited and weak at home and beset by foreign predators abroad, the United States was hardly the vanguard of a new world order. While recognizing American sovereignty on the one hand, Britain continued to treat the new republic as a commercial colony on the other. Instead of entering into a reciprocal trade agreement between two independent states, Britain continued to subject U.S.

commerce to the restrictions of the old Navigation Acts without extending the benefits of free access to British markets. And rather than restraining the Barbary pirates, the British let them loose to prey upon American merchantmen.

At home, the postwar Confederation showed little national unity. Writing from Paris in late 1783, John Jay lamented what he called the lack of "a national spirit in America."[25] He declared that "the spirit of enterprise and adventure runs high in our young country," but there was an absence of a "vigorous and wise government" to support enterprising citizens. Contrary to terms of the Treaty of Paris, Britain continued to maintain garrisons at frontier posts they had promised to abandon, and the Barbary States, Jay wrote, have "alarmed us" by regarding American vessels as fair game.[26] Lacking a strong central government to devise and direct a coherent foreign trade policy, the states pursued separate courses. More interested in commerce than navigation, southern states opposed trade restrictions on foreign imports because they feared retaliation against their exports, and they were content to ship their produce in foreign bottoms. Concerned primarily with protecting their shipping interests, northern states insisted on the right to ship American goods in American vessels and advocated navigation acts that would retaliate in kind against foreign powers that restricted American trade.

By demanding the full measure of independence at home, the American states undermined the independence of America in the Atlantic world. Under the Confederation, only the individual states had taxing authority, making Congress dependent on them for the means to advance and protect American interests abroad. Merchants engaged in overseas shipping knew that without national resolve and power, commercial independence would elude them. Leonidas stated the case simply: "With vain do we amuse ourselves with these prospects of the blessings of commerce to the world, while Britain maintains the sovereignty of the ocean."[27]

The means of checking British naval power was an American navy. Knowing that his readers would be skeptical that a new country could mount an effective opposition to the world's greatest maritime power, Leonidas noted that the British could deploy only a small number of ships along the American coast. He called on Congress to require each state to build one or two armed vessels as the nucleus of a naval fleet. A modest land tax would defray the cost. Americans would gladly pay such a levy, Leonidas hopefully predicted, if officials could "assure the farmer, that the only design of it was to create a demand for, and to increase the price of his grain. The merchant could not object to this tax when he reflected that the first advantages arriving from it would center in his compting-house."[28]

While Leonidas was correct about the need for a navy to protect commerce, he was wrong about the immediate threat to American shipping: it wasn't the British Royal Navy but rather the Barbary pirates. When the Sallee Rovers captured the *Betsey* barely a year after the Treaty of Paris recognized the United States as an independent state, the dreams of free trade faded. Then when the Algerine corsairs enslaved the crews of the *Maria* and the *Dauphin* in 1785, it became clear that any power, including the "petty tyrants" of Barbary, could intercept American shipping at will. And the new national government provided no remedy. Fearful of replacing British despotism with a tyrannical state of their own, the revolutionaries in the Continental Congress had insisted that power reside within the individual states. Thus under the Articles of Confederation, ratified in 1781, the central government consisted of a single body—a congress with representatives from each state—with limited powers. It had no power to tax, and it could not regulate commerce. Moreover, the federal government had no executive branch to enforce its laws; nor did it possess a judicial branch to interpret them. And while it did have the authority to establish and maintain a Continental army and a Continental navy, Congress depended on the individual states to staff, provision, and pay for both.

During the War of Independence, the states had been willing to underwrite the enormous cost of the Continental Navy. The limited fleet authorized by Congress on October 13, 1775, played an important, though hardly decisive, role in winning the war. Its primary mission was to disrupt British supply vessels supporting His Majesty's troops and to protect merchant ships transporting much-needed war matériel. With the exception of John Paul Jones's operations in the North Sea and his raids on the British coasts, this "cruiser navy"—consisting of "small ships—frigates, brigs, sloops, and schooners," assembled through new construction, purchase, and conversion of merchantmen—rarely challenged the superior Royal Navy.[29] It was the French fleet that proved to be decisive in the Battle of Yorktown, driving off the Royal Navy and thereby preventing the Redcoats' escape to the sea. Nonetheless, the Continental Navy succeeded in capturing hundreds of British merchant vessels during the war while managing to maintain a transatlantic supply lane of its own.

The Continental Congress began dismantling the navy even as the fighting wound down and peace negotiations began. The navy represented perhaps the most expensive single item in the national budget, and to republicans a standing navy, as well as a standing army, represented a threat to liberty. Thus while some ships under construction were completed as a precaution against renewed hostilities, progress toward a treaty rendered them superfluous. The *Bourbon* was launched at Middletown, Connecticut, on July 31, 1783, and was advertised for sale in September, about a year before the Moroccan pirates boarded the *Betsey*.[30] Within two years Congress had sold the *Alliance*, and the Continental Navy ceased to exist.

After the War of Independence, Thomas Jefferson charted the course of American trade in the Mediterranean. He reported that before the war "about one-sixth of the wheat and flour exported from the United States, and about one-fourth in value of their dried and pickled fish, and some rice, found their best markets in the Mediterranean ports." He estimated that the commerce "loaded outwards [totaled] from eighty to one hundred ships annually, of twenty thousand tons, navigated by about twelve hundred seamen." But, Jefferson noted, the Mediterranean trade "was abandoned early in the war," and "after the peace which ensued, it was obvious to our merchants, that their adventures into that sea would be exposed to the depredations of the piratical States on the coast of Barbary."[31] The American dream of free trade faded when small bands of pirates brought commerce to a standstill. And the meaning of American independence was brought into question.

Like the Americans, the Barbary pirates had fought for their independence and knew it to be tenuous. The Barbary States had been founded in the sixteenth century as regencies of the Ottoman Empire, and like the British American colonies, they operated under imperial policies that emanated from a distant metropolitan center. Just as Americans had once heeded instructions from Whitehall in London, the Barbary pirates took their orders from the grand seigneur or emperor of the Ottoman Empire in Constantinople. Similarities in their origins, however, cannot mask significant differences in their development over time. While the United States flourished under the prosperity and protection of a powerful, expanding imperial center, the Barbary States languished under an empire that had already reached its zenith and was in decline.

Arabs had conquered North Africa in the seventh century when Muslims from the Arabian Peninsula embarked on a period of expansion to the east and west. They raced across North Africa and moved into Europe through the Iberian Peninsula. But while they managed to plant Islamic institutions deep into Spain, their North African possessions were fragmented, small, and weak and thus vulnerable to the machinations of more powerful states in the region.[32] For eight hundred years, traders along the Barbary Coast plied their goods on the fringes of the Mediterranean world.

Events in the second half of the fifteenth century transformed Algiers and the other Barbary powers, squeezed by aggressive powers from the eastern and western Mediterranean, from commercial to pirate states. In 1453 the Ottomans captured Constantinople and sought to make the Barbary States their tributaries in the fight against the Holy Roman Empire. Then in 1492 Spain expelled the last Moors from Granada and pursued them into North Africa in search of land and power. These two events "altered beyond redemption" the "trading equilibrium of Muslim and Christian in the western Mediterranean." More specifically, though they were tributaries of Constantinople, the Barbary powers enjoyed little protection or benefit from their alliance with the Muslim power. The Ottoman Turks were too far removed and preoccupied with consolidating their continental territories. Thus the Barbary States faced Spanish power alone. Unable to match Spain's military might, Algiers became a tributary of Ferdinand the Catholic under terms of a 1510 treaty. The following year Ferdinand imposed a 50 percent surtax on Algiers's woolen imports in order to generate revenue to pay for Spain's North African expeditions.[33] Relegated to tributary status under a harsh commercial regime, Algiers sought to bolster its economy through piracy. If Spain insisted on extorting Algiers's profits through exorbitant taxation, the Algerines reasoned, then they could recoup their losses by any means.

The Barbary States did not set out to make piracy the centerpiece of their economies. Their preference was to profit from trade with the rich Mediterranean markets, and indeed by the fourteenth century they had established a lucrative niche. Because of North Africa's shortage of native timber, their leading import was European raw and finished wood. Other commodities in high demand included copper, precious metals, fine silks, woolens, and cotton cloth. In turn Algiers and the other Barbary States exported to Europe black slaves, Barbary horses, salted fish, leather hides, salt, wax, grain, olive oil, and dates. Commerce between Algiers and Europe's Mediterranean powers grew so extensive that Venetian and Florentine merchant ships made regular calls at the Maghrebi port. During the later 1400s the Barbary powers secured a place in the Mediterranean commercial network, adhering to a strictly enforced set of trade regulations and customs payments.[34] The clash of the Holy Roman and Ottoman Empires resulting in Spain's harsh treaty of 1510 brought this situation to an end.

Spain effectively controlled the Maghreb from Morocco in the west to Tripoli in the east. In the early sixteenth century the Ottomans launched their offensive to bring North Africa under their control and thereby secure its ports as bases for protecting Turkish shipping routes in the Mediterranean. Leading the expedition to reclaim the Mahgreb were two brothers, the best known of whom was Khayr ad-Din, or Barbarossa, who seized Algiers in 1516 and by 1529 had brought the entire region, except for Tunis, under Turkish lordship. In recognition of Barbarossa's great service to the empire, the grand seigneur named Khayr ad-Din high admiral of the sultan's navy, and in 1534 Barbarossa captured Tunis and annexed it to the Ottoman Empire. He had reversed the retreat and secured Barbary for the Turks, thereby reclaiming important ports from which Turkish sea power could be extended throughout the southern Mediterranean.[35]

The Ottomans' reconquest did not go unchallenged. Fearing Turkish dominance of the Mediterranean, Holy Roman emperor Charles V called for a "virtual crusade" to check Ottoman aspirations. A coalition of nearly all the European powers with ports on the Mediterranean drove Barbarossa from Barbary in 1536, thereby returning Tunis and Tripoli to Spanish rule. The French, however, pursued an independent and contrary course and concluded a treaty with the Turks, providing Barbarossa with safe haven in Nice. This crack in European unanimity offered the pirates a strategic option they would prove adept at exercising on numerous future occasions: exploiting one European power's desire to seek advantage over another by making separate deals. In this instance, France's Francis I enlisted Barbarossa's assistance in defeating the Duke of Savoy and annexing his lands. In exchange, the French permitted the Turks to use Toulon to winter in, turning the port into "a sort of second Istanbul."[36]

The Barbary States were caught in the middle of the struggle between the Turks and the Europeans for control of the Mediterranean, but their status remained the same: tributaries, first to the Spanish and then to the Ottomans. In 1571 the Ottoman and Holy Roman Empires fought a climactic naval battle that left the Barbary regencies with a great deal of autonomy but also little protection. In the Battle of Lepanto, with about two hundred ships arrayed against one another in the Gulf of Patras off the Ionian Sea, the two powers clashed: the "Christian fleet," under the command of Don John of Austria, defeated the Turks. The battle redefined the Mediterranean. The Ottomans and the Spanish recognized each other's spheres of power, the former relegated to the eastern Mediterranean and the latter to the western.

Located in the Spanish sphere but locked out of European markets and operating without major naval support from Constantinople, the Barbary powers turned to piracy in earnest. At the center were Algiers, the base that Barbarossa had established in 1529, and Tripoli, a corsair port modeled after Algiers by Barbarossa's successor, Dragut. A prolonged war of piracy ensued throughout the sixteenth century, as Barbary pirates raided Christian shipping, and Christian pirates, most notably from Malta, attacked Muslim trade. Pirates on both sides captured prizes, confiscated cargoes, and enslaved crews. From the First Crusade in the late eleventh century, Christians and Muslims alike justified their marauding on religious grounds while accusing the other of piracy and depredations. It is fairer to say that both parties were engaged in similar activity, sending out privateers under their respective flags to raid each other's shipping.[37] For the Barbary regencies, piracy, however, soon became more than forays against the "infidels"; it became the center of their economic and political life.

The apogee of Barbary power came in the first half of the seventeenth century. By 1640 an estimated 150 corsair vessels operated from the North African ports, two-thirds of them from Algerine ports. Moreover the pirates no longer relied upon oar-powered galleys, having developed swift, maneuverable sailing ships well adapted to the shallow waters around their well-protected ports and equally suited for raids on passing commercial vessels. In part fueled by piratical successes, Algiers grew into one of the largest cities in the Mediterranean with a population of around a hundred thousand, bigger than Genoa, Marseilles, Barcelona, or Leghorn. Ever opportunistic, the pirates took advantage of renewed conflicts among the Christian states, such as the resumption of the Spanish war against the Dutch in 1621 and Spain's war with France that began in 1635.[38] One belligerent was always all too willing for the Barbary pirates to raid its enemy's shipping.

In the second half of the seventeenth century, the Barbary regencies suffered a reversal of fortune. The English and the Dutch sent powerful fleets into the Mediterranean to reduce the pirates' threat to commercial vessels. British admiral Robert Blake's squadron subdued the corsairs in an attack from which the Barbary forces never recovered.[39] By the end of the century the Algerine naval force had been reduced by 75 percent. By the time they raided American shipping in the late eighteenth century, the Barbary powers had been diminished to petty states, none of them able to launch more than a dozen corsairs.

Before the 1784 capture of the *Betsey*, most Americans knew little of the Barbary pirates beyond what they read in fictionalized accounts of bloodthirsty marauders. Daniel Defoe's *Robinson Crusoe*, first published in 1719, introduced Anglo-American readers to the Sallee Rovers. Sailing on a trader to the Canary Islands, Crusoe's ship is "surprised" by pirates in a fast-moving corsair, who overtake the English vessel and fasten the two ships together with a grappling iron. Scores of fierce-looking Moors swarm aboard. The survivors are taken into the port of Salé, where they become "miserable slaves." By including both "American" and "Pyrates" in its full title (which was an impressive sixty-five words long), *Robinson Crusoe* attracted the attention of American colonists, especially New Englanders, for whom shipping was prominent. Though they had access to the many editions printed in London, American readers demanded more, and colonial printers accommodated them. At least as early as 1774 an American edition appeared, and thereafter at least a dozen more before the Algiers Treaty was signed in 1795. New England presses in particular, including those in Portland, Maine, Windham, Connecticut, and Worcester, Massachusetts, published the hair-raising tale of imperiled seamen, whose real-life counterparts faced all-too-real dangers in Barbary.[40]

Periodic newspaper reports of actual pirate captures reinforced Crusoe's tale. For example, a 1759 *Pennsylvania Gazette* report told of the Sallee Rovers in "some piratical Vessels" sweeping down on the British warship *Litchfield* and boarding with a "croud of men." They then "stript them," took them into the port of Salé, and forced them to work as slaves.[41] For Americans, the enduring image of the Barbary pirates was that of lawless sea robbers who sought ill-gotten gains with no regard for their victims.

After the captures of the 1780s, some Americans attempted to render a more accurate and balanced portrayal of the Barbary pirates. One such effort was Mathew Carey's *Short Account of Algiers* (1794). Drawing primarily on descriptions penned by Western consuls and captives, the republican newspaper publisher wrote a historical sketch that attempted to explain rather than condemn cultural differences, especially religious beliefs and practices. He was, however, less charitable in his assessment of the government of Algiers. While Algiers bore the "title of a kingdom," Carey observed, "it is however a military republic." At the head of the state was the dey, who was elected by a divan or council made up of senior army officers. These elections, in Carey's telling, were hardly republican affairs; rather, the dey "seldom secure[d] his office, without tumult and bloodshed." And violence was commonplace. Carey quotes one British consul who reported that the dey enjoyed having "the heads of his subjects to be struck off in his presence."[42] Algerine deys gained and kept power by means that struck Europeans and Americans as barbaric and brutal.

Europeans and Americans learned about Barbary politics primarily through the prism of Western diplomats, who no doubt emphasized its violent nature as a means of justifying military action against the regimes. Despite the bias, the reports provide a reliable account of the structure of power and the prominence of the Barbary ruler. The dey stood atop a military regime filled with aspirants to the throne. Accordingly, the ruler took steps to ensure the structure's stability and to check the ambitions of potential challengers. Just beneath the dey in dignity and power was the aga of the janissaries, a position of so much potential threat that, Carey wrote, the aga "enjoys his post but two months, and then retires upon a pension." Other important officers included a secretary of state, twenty colonels, eight hundred captains, and four hundred lieutenants. "Among these officers," Carey wrote, "the right of seniority is strictly observed. A breach of this point would be expected to produce a revolt among the soldiers, and might perhaps cost the dey his life." Even so, private soldiers sometimes attempted to assassinate the leader, "as any private soldier who has the courage to murder him, stands an equal chance of becoming his successor."[43]

While the dey protected himself from those beneath him, he paid tribute to his overlord, the grand seigneur at Constantinople, as did the heads of the other Barbary States. Tribute was the coin of piracy. Just as the dey paid off Constantinople, he, and the other heads of Barbary States, sought tribute from the European capitals. By demanding presents such as precious metals, Spanish dollars, and military equipment, the dey could meet his obligations to his nominal overlord while strengthening his own power base. In a strategy that added insult to injury, the dey also exacted tribute in the form of armaments that could be used to extort yet more tribute.[44] In 1785, for example, the Spanish agreed to provide the Algerines 25 brass artillery pieces, 25 iron cannons, 4 mortars, 4,000 bombs, 10,000 balls, 2,000 quintals (a quintal equals 100 kilograms) of gunpowder, and 5,000 quintals of musketballs. All of that was in addition to a payment of 1 million pieces of eight.[45]

Algiers was no Islamic republic; religious leaders did not run the state. Indeed, Muslim clerics occupied a separate and subordinate role to that of the dey and his janissaries. At the top of the religious hierarchy was the mufti or high priest, followed by the cadi, the "supreme judge in ecclesiastical causes, and in such civil matters as the civil power does not interpose in," and the grand marabout, the chief of an order of hermits. Distinguished by the "largeness of their turbans," these officials occupied a place in the divan, occupying seats "below the dey, on his right hand." About two thousand Turkish officers and soldiers dominated the council.[46]

The Algerine rulers governed through fear, reinforced by swift, brutal, and public punishment of offenses against society. While some European and American observers emphasized the dey's harsh treatment of Christian slaves, he was equally ruthless toward his own Islamic subjects. Christians were sometimes "roasted alive" or hung from walls by hooks; sufferers were known to "hang thus for several days, alive, and in the most exquisite torture." But Muslims fared no better. "A Moor convicted of house-breaking," Carey reported, "hath his right hand cut off and fastened to his neck." Those convicted of treason were "placed between two boards, and sawed asunder." And adulterous women were "fixed by their necks to a pole, and held under water till they are suffocated."[47]

Carey reminded his readers, however, that the pirates were not the only slave masters who treated humans as commodities. He noted,

> For this practice of buying and selling slaves, we are not entitled to charge the Algerines with any exclusive degree of barbarity. The Christians of Europe and America carry on this commerce an hundred times more extensively than the Algerines.[48]

Pirating in the Barbary States was a capitalist enterprise. Entrepreneurs invested in building and furnishing a raiding ship, sometimes selling shares to *armadores*, usually small shopkeepers.[49]

The principal investor hired a *reis* or captain to command the vessel, who then put together a crew and enlisted the services of soldiers. Completing the complement of men was a scrivener, a government official whose task was to record the booty to ensure that the dey as well as the investors received their agreed-upon portions. It was a high-risk, high-reward business.

A reis's success depended on leadership, courage, and knowledge as opposed to ethnic and religious identity. One of Algiers's richest captains of the seventeenth century was Ali Bitchnin, an Italian named Piccinio who arrived in Algiers as the commander of a pirate ship that had operated in the Adriatic. Seeing an opportunity to capture more lucrative prizes by raiding European vessels from Algiers, he converted to Islam and soon rose to prominence as a daring, courageous raider who amassed a fortune. With his own flotilla of cruisers, Bitchnin rivaled the dey in power and prestige. Sometimes a great reis rose to power through the ranks. Such was the eighteenth century's most notable Algerine captain, Hamidou Reis. While most successful corsairs were either European renegades or Turks, Hamidou was the son of a Moorish tailor who began life aboard pirate cruisers as a cabin boy and by initiative and courage worked his way up to being a captain. By the 1790s he was named admiral of the Algerine fleet and became America's nemesis.[50]

The pirate fleets were small, built for raiding commerce rather than trading it. One of the American captives in Algiers, Richard O'Brien, provided in 1786 an eyewitness account of the Algerine force, noting that Algiers possessed no merchant ships except for a few coasting vessels that transported wheat from port to port. The French were the principal carriers of the modest trade that Algiers carried on with other Mediterranean powers. Piracy, not trade, was the primary occupation of the Algerine fleet, which numbered nine vessels with a total of 188 guns of various calibers. Of the corsairs, O'Brien wrote, "the vessels are small to the metal they carry."[51] The marine forces of Tunis and Tripoli were of comparable size. Rarely were the pirate cruisers of Barbary manufacture. For the most part, they were refitted prizes captured from Europeans and, after 1785, Americans, or they were new ships built by their tributaries as part of the price of peace. In addition, European merchants competed for the privilege of supplying the Barbary States with naval supplies and ordnance.

The pirates who manned the cruisers were a cosmopolitan lot. Many if not most were Christian captives who provided the hard labor, rowing the galliots that were continued in use throughout the eighteenth century and managing the rigging and sails of the fast, sleek caravelles, xebecs, and frigates.[52] Crews numbered between 300 and 450 men, depending upon the size of the ship and the number of guns, and comprised both sailors and marines. It was the responsibility of the sailors to close with the enemy. Then the marines, who constituted a majority of the crew, would spring into action.[53]

A pirate raid usually began with deception and ended with fury. The Barbary vessel would fly a foreign flag in order to "lure the unsuspecting victim within striking distance." Then gunners perched on the rigging would "ply the shot with unabated rapidity," raking the victim's deck. Meanwhile "the fighting men stand ready, their arms bared, muskets primed, and scimitars flashing, waiting for the order to board." When the reis gave the signal, the pirates leaped aboard the prize. According to one description, "their war-cry was appalling; and the fury of the onslaught was such as to strike panic into the stoutest heart." After overcoming the crew, the pirates chained survivors, who would become hostages for ransom or slaves for sale, manned the captured ship, and proceeded to their home port.[54]

The arrival of a successful corsair was the occasion for celebration in Algiers or any of the other ports along the Barbary Coast. The dey received from one-eighth to one-fifth of the cargo plus the captured vessel. The owners and reis received half the remaining cargo as their share, with the other half going to the crew and soldiers.[55] A particularly rich prize resulted in liberal spending by the direct benefactors, which had a multiplier effect as shopkeepers and vendors of all kinds participated in the bounty. Moreover, for the dey the prize was the means of exacting tribute from the nation whose ship was taken as well as ransom for the enslaved crew.

Algerine attitudes toward slaves reflected similarities to and differences from those of American slaveholders. Like southern planters, pirates considered slaves to be an invaluable source of labor, especially hard manual labor. Barbary slaves provided much of the manpower for the pirate fleet and supplied intellect, skill, and leadership in designing and building new vessels. So valuable were slaves that at times of peak demand for labor, the dey refused to redeem some of them at any price. There were, however, major dissimilarities between slavery in Barbary and in the American South. First, American slavery existed on a much larger scale: in 1790 there were 697,624 slaves in America as compared to about 3,000 in Algiers.[56] Second, while manumission was rare in the United States, it was not only possible for most slaves in Algiers but likely. Indeed, one of the primary purposes for taking slaves was to seek ransom money for their release. Some slaves even rose to the command of corsairs. A third difference was ethnicity and religion of slaves. In the United States, slavery was defined by race: all slaves were either Africans or Native Americans. In Barbary, slaves were a mixed lot: European Christians, North African Moors, and sub-Saharan Negroes.

While the dey relied on privateers and their slave crews to raid ships and bring in prizes, he assumed responsibility for defending Algiers from enemy attacks. On numerous occasions from the sixteenth to the eighteenth century, a European power or alliance would attempt to reduce or eliminate the pirate threat by waging war against the Algerines. Most often the strategy was simple: position a massive fleet at the entrance to the harbor at Algiers, bombard the city's defenses, sink the small navy guarding the walls, and land soldiers to occupy the dey's capital. It never worked. Europeans tended to underestimate the Algerines' resources and resolve. The English consul at Algiers in 1785, having seen the Algerines repulse an assault by a Spanish-led coalition in 1784, watched the pirates prepare for what promised to be a more massive attack the following year. He doubted that a force three times the one then sailing for Algiers could prevail. He noted the "formidable" artillery of the castle, to which the Algerines had recently added a new battery that they called the "Devil's Battery." If the invaders managed to take out the artillery, they then faced a "most numerous and warlike enemy," whose army was battle hardened and better disciplined. The consul advised Europeans to pay the demanded tribute. Only gold, "that seducing metal," would succeed "against a place so well fortified."[57]

Organized, ensconced, and opportunistic, the Barbary pirates played foe against foe, power against power. Britain, fearing the loss of the carrying trade to the Americans, turned to the Barbary States for assistance. Rather than ordering the Royal Navy to attack American shipping, Carey explained, England "adopted the miserable expedient of turning loose the Algerines, that these execrable ruffians might plunder our property, and plunge our fellow-citizens into slavery."[58]

In May 1784 the U.S. Congress instructed its commissioners in Paris—Adams, Franklin, and Jefferson—to negotiate bilateral "treaties of amity and commerce with the Commercial powers of Europe." The resolution enumerated the cities and countries that it would be "advantageous" to have as trading partners, including Russia, Vienna, Prussia, Denmark, Saxony, Hamburg, Great Britain, Spain, Portugal, Genoa, Tuscany, Rome, Naples, Venice, Sardinia, and the Ottoman Porte. Additionally, Congress resolved that "treaties of amity, or of amity and commerce, be entered into with Morocco, and the regencies of Algiers, Tunis and Tripoli, to continue for the same term of ten years, or for a term as much longer as can be procured." The terms of the treaties to be negotiated embraced the American principles of equality and reciprocity. The proposed wording called for commercial exchanges consistent with "the most perfect reciprocity." Parties would be allowed to transport their goods in their own ships to each other's ports freely, paying only those duties required of the most favored nation.[59] If the United States could obtain those terms with the European and Barbary powers, then American merchants could enjoy the profitable trade they had long anticipated.

But alas, the Barbary pirates' capture of American vessels and enslavement of their crews underscored the gap between American rhetoric on free trade and the realities of Atlantic commerce. Though small, weak, and relatively insignificant, the Barbary States were part of a tribute-demanding system endorsed by Europe's major powers and designed to restrict trade competition. Colonial American merchants, operating under British protection, had once been part of that mercantilist structure, sailing freely to British ports and enjoying a monopoly in certain enumerated commodities. Now flying the U.S. flag, merchant vessels were unwelcome newcomers who threatened to take market share from the established maritime powers. British merchants were particularly concerned about American ships reducing His Majesty's dominance in the carrying trade. Thus, while signing the treaty recognizing American independence in 1783, Parliament refused to enter into a treaty of amity and commerce.

While Americans viewed free trade as a natural outgrowth of their revolution, Europeans had a different perspective. One letter from Europe, reprinted in American newspapers, noted America's desire "to trade with all the world upon the most liberal and extensive plan." As colonial dependencies subject to British trade regulations, they had been part of the mercantilist scheme; as independent states embracing the free-trade doctrine, they "must necessarily create a new influence [in the Atlantic world], and occasion new points to be discussed, respecting the general system of commerce."[60] In short, the new republic and its insistence on new ways of international trade threatened Europe's delicate balance of power that had been worked out over the centuries, often with much bloodshed.[61]

Britain's goal was to continue to regulate American trade by restricting its access to markets. Fearing the United States as a commercial competitor, Parliament refused to negotiate a commercial treaty that was favorable to the new republic and instead excluded Americans from the lucrative West Indian trade. Britain was not alone among the maritime powers in restricting American commerce by imposing navigation restrictions and expensive duties that reduced the competitiveness of American goods in the Atlantic market. Spain also refused to enter into a commercial treaty and, perhaps more devastating to the struggling postwar American economy, denied Americans free navigation of the Mississippi River. By blocking the means of shipping produce downriver to New Orleans, Spain rendered farmers' produce noncompetitive in the Atlantic market because of high transportation costs. In a letter to James Madison, Thomas Jefferson summed up the sentiments of many Americans when he bemoaned "our vital agonies by our exclusion from the West Indies, by late embarrassments in Spain and Portugal, and by the dangers of the Mediterranean trade."[62] Jefferson knew that commerce was the lifeblood of independent citizens in the new republic. Indeed, the young nation's political survival depended on its commercial success. If farmers and planters could not export their produce, they would lose their economic independence, and the loss of economic independence could mean the loss of political independence.

To Adams, Britain had little reason to behave differently. First, the British were confident that they would, under any circumstances, continue to dominate the American trade. "Even in the case of war," Adams noted, British manufacturers expected to feed America's insatiable appetite for British goods. Second, Britain was confident that "the American States are not, and cannot be united. The landed interest will never join with the commercial interest, nor the southern States with the northern in any measure of retaliation, or expressions of resentment." Based on those two assumptions, the British had already begun what Adams termed "commercial hostilities," so called "because their direct object is not so much the increase of their own wealth, ships, or sailors, as the diminution of ours." Adams called on Congress to "enter into this commercial war," despite the risk it might escalate into a "military war."[63]

While Americans likely found British attitudes toward American trade predictable, many were taken aback by French reactions. An American in Paris reported with disappointment that "a nation that has so essentially supported our independence" was now expressing "the difficulties attending a free trade with America." The merchants of France, the writer noted, readily grasped that American free trade would not only injure their own private interests but greatly diminish France's current high level of importation from her American dependencies. "Besides," the commentator added in his characterization of French concerns, "if France granted free trade to America, her other trading partners would demand the same."[64] In short, American merchants increasingly confronted the sobering reality of world markets that were closed to them, even by their allies.

Europe's great maritime powers viewed the Barbary pirates as nettlesome yet useful. On the one hand, they saw them as outlaws who raided legitimate commerce and extorted tribute. That perspective fueled the impulse to subdue the pirates by force. On the other hand, Britain, France, and Spain considered the Barbary pirates useful allies in their mercantilist struggles for commercial supremacy. Regardless, Europeans found the pirates to be independent opportunists who pursued their own objectives. Sometimes the Barbary States would make a treaty and then threaten to violate the terms unless the tributary agreed to even more generous "presents." At other times they would fight instead of treating with a particular power. And though no match for European navies in the Atlantic, the pirates were worthy adversaries inside the Strait of Gibraltar.

On occasion the European powers, acting either singly or in concert, attempted to subdue the pirates by making a direct assault on their homelands. One such initiative occurred on the eve of the Algerine attacks on the two American vessels. While rumors swirled in London of pirate attacks, official pronouncements from Madrid in July 1784 gave Americans hope. The Spanish and French announced that they were combining forces to eliminate the Algerine scourge from the Mediterranean. While Britain refused to join the alliance, the Royal Navy ordered a "Squadron of five Line of Battle Ships, and four Frigates . . . on a Cruise of Observation into the Mediterranean." On the other side of the Atlantic, Americans were delighted to learn that the Europeans were "going in Conjunction, with a very great naval Force against Algiers."[65]

With no navy of their own, Americans could only hope that the French and Spanish coalition would subdue the Barbary pirates and clear the Mediterranean for legitimate trade. American newspaper readers followed the action from the sidelines, dependent on more powerful nations to rid them of a dreaded enemy. Previously, they had read of the growing pirate menace. Reports indicated that the Algerines had sent out on raids more ships and more men than they had in years, and that they carried with them "very heavy metal." Americans were consequently heartened by reports from Spain detailing the allies' preparations and resolve. The commander of the fleet, Don Antonio Barcelo, had developed new, deadly weapons armed with gunpowder that had twice the explosive power of that currently used. Perhaps of more interest to Americans than the new technology was the bold war aim. Unlike the half measures of the past, this attack on Algiers promised "not only . . . to bombard the place, but to land, and be at once in good earnest revenged of the Algerines for their insults to the European nations."[66]

In October intelligence arrived of the "compleat destruction of the city of Algiers, which was set on fire in six or seven different places, . . . and all the public buildings burnt to the ground." The newspaper account claimed that "a prodigious number of people are slain." Don Barcelo, it was claimed, had kept his forces in the bay facing Algiers "to compleat the total destruction of the city, that if possible, no vestige might remain to cause any trouble in future to any of the European powers."[67] The Mediterranean, Americans surmised, was now secure for commerce.

Initial reports proved overly optimistic. What the Algerines lacked in firepower, they made up in surprise tactics. When the allies began the engagement on September 21 with a ten-hour bombardment of Algiers, they expected the Algerine gunboats to come out and fight. Instead, the crafty pirates kept their maneuverable boats deep inside the harbor, forcing the heavy warships to come after them. The strategy worked. While the bombardment destroyed a few gunboats and damaged the city's fortifications, the pirates withstood the assault and repulsed the European force inside the harbor, where the corsairs had the advantage.[68]

The hoped-for demise of the Algerines proved premature. To Americans, the implications were disturbing. A letter from a merchant in Cádiz to a gentleman at Beverly, Massachusetts, dated August 25, 1785, gave a chilling account of renewed pirate activity that would have a profound impact on American shipping in the Mediterranean. Instead of defeating the Algerines, the Spanish negotiated a treaty with them. "This high and mighty nation," the merchant said of Spain, "who threatened to annihilate Algiers and all thereto belonging, now are to pay an immense sum of money, for what? Why, to have the honour of letting the pirates pursue their old business unmolested."[69]

Ships' captains arriving in American ports brought a steady stream of ominous correspondence. European countries had begun providing naval escorts for their merchant fleets in the Mediterranean; the United States having no navy, American merchantmen entered the region unescorted. Moreover, Europeans expressed a new respect for the pirates, noting that any attack on the corsairs would likely result in a "very smart engagement." Just months earlier Americans had believed that the scourge of Barbary was about to be removed. Now the mood had turned to dread and fear. Playing on that fear, the commodore of the Algerine pirates began sailing under an ensign that boldly displayed a death's-head and a battle-ax.[70]

After independence, American merchant ships faced hostilities from the pirates and their European co-conspirators, especially the British. The British Parliament was divided over trade policy with the United States. Some members, like William Pitt, were sympathetic to America's desire for free trade, arguing that it was in Britain's best interest to cultivate commerce with a growing nation that represented an expanding market for British goods. Opposing such leniency toward a potential trade rival, Lord Sheffield urged members of Parliament to consider the threat America posed to Britain if the United States were allowed the freedom to trade that it wished. Great Britain, he wrote, "has not found itself in a more interested and critical situation than it is at present. It is now to be decided whether we are to be ruined by the independence of America, or not." By comparison, "the peace . . . was a trifling object." A mercantilist to the core, he argued that American trade must be thwarted at every point, because the new republic's gains would result in Britain's loss.[71] For Sheffield, the Barbary pirates were the key to keeping the United States out of the Mediterranean: "It is not probable the American states will have a very free trade in the Mediterranean; it will not be the interest of any of the great maritime powers to protect them there from the Barbary States."[72] Lord Sheffield merely echoed the sentiments attributed to France's Louis XIV: "if there was no Algiers he would build one."[73] Like the Sun King, George III and Parliament determined to deny the upstart Americans free navigation in the Mediterranean by encouraging Algerine depredations on their shipping.

In spring 1785 Americans grew ever more suspicious that the British were behind Barbary threats on U.S. shipping. Amid warnings from Americans in southern Europe that the Algerines were targeting vessels sailing under "American colours" came increased evidence of British involvement. British underwriters of maritime insurance refused to write policies for any American vessel sailing to the Mediterranean "without a pass and British colors," and one writer observed that the British gave Algerine corsairs the run of the English coast in order to capture American merchantmen departing from British ports.[74]

One of the most damaging reports of British assistance to the pirates arrived in the United States just three months before the Algerines captured the *Dauphin* and the *Maria* in July. An American writing from London indicated that the Algerine fleet was being fitted out at Gibraltar, a British possession. To the reporter, and no doubt to all Americans who believed in a British conspiracy against U.S. commerce, the message was clear: "those Barbarians are countenanced in their Depredations upon our Commerce by the British Court." Americans should heed the warning and prepare for war. While the pirates were on cruise to take prizes, the British had bigger aims: "Above all, it seems utterly to extirpate the Commerce of their States in their own Vessels in the European Seas, and of course to establish the favourite System of Lord Sheffield, of the British becoming Carriers of all the Property imported and exported between Britain and America."[75] For Americans already aroused by Parliament's refusal to sign a treaty of commerce with the United States, the reference to Lord Sheffield was proof enough that Britain and the Barbary pirates were allies in forcing Americans to pay tribute for the right to trade and to consign the carrying trade to the British.

TWO

TRIBUTE OR ARMS?

Responsibility for dealing with the hostage crisis in Algiers fell on the only body that represented all Americans under the Articles of Confederation, the Congress of the United States. The framers of the Articles wanted a body that would be powerful enough to win independence and meet external threats but not so powerful as to interfere with states' rights. Its structure was spare, consisting only of a Congress; there was no executive or judicial authority. Lacking any coercive power over the states, Congress could only request funds, depending upon the goodwill of the individual states to meet the requisition. When they established the Confederation during the War of Independence, the framers specifically hoped that it would be adequate to defend the fragile republic. Jonathan Dickinson of Pennsylvania had specifically voiced concern about "protection against the piratical states," citing the need as a point of the "utmost moment."[1] Knowing that independence meant losing British protection against pirate raids, he wondered how America was going to safeguard its valuable Mediterranean trade.

By any reading, the Articles of Confederation were inadequate to answer the threat posed by the Barbary pirates. First, the individual states retained sovereignty—indeed, the first national constitution was styled a "league of friendship" between the member states.[2] Second, Congress lacked the powers necessary to protect the Mediterranean trade. Answering the Barbary pirates through diplomacy required having the power to negotiate treaties of commerce, but the Articles forbade Congress to make any treaty that restrained the states from imposing their own duties and regulations. Making good on any threat of war depended on possessing a naval force, which could be funded only through tax revenues, but the Articles granted Congress no independent taxing authority. America, then, was unprepared to protect its ships against the piratical attacks that most thought were sure to come, and in 1785 the Algerines demonstrated just how defenseless unescorted American merchant ships were.

Thomas Jefferson, for one, viewed the United States as more vulnerable to pirate depredations in the Mediterranean than were the European countries that traded in the region. As he explained in a report to Congress, while European commerce was "spread all over the face of the Mediterranean, . . . ours must all enter at a strait only five leagues wide." At the narrow western entrance to the sea, pirate cruisers could "very effectually inspect whatever enters it."[3] Without diplomatic treaty or naval escort, American ships approaching the Strait of Gibraltar would present to the Barbary pirates a temptation too easily gratified.

Thus it was totally unexpected when the pirates situated closest to the strait recognized American independence and invited the United States to enter into a peace treaty and trade agreement. In April 1778 the emperor of Morocco contacted Benjamin Franklin through an emissary, Stephen d'Audibert Caille, and expressed his desire for a trade agreement with the United States. Caille, a French merchant residing at Salé, represented himself as the emperor's consul for nations who had none in Morocco. Worried by French officials' warnings that "it was not safe to have any correspondence" with Caille, Franklin nevertheless forwarded the Frenchman's letter to Congress without comment, and it was referred to the Committee for Foreign Affairs on September 1, 1780, where plans to negotiate a series of bilateral trade agreements with all the maritime states of Europe as well as with each of the Barbary States were already under way. President of the Congress Samuel

Huntington responded to the emperor's overtures for peace in a December 1780 letter. He assured the sultan of America's "earnest desire to cultivate a sincere and firm peace and friendship" with Morocco. Asking the emperor to extend protection to any American vessel that should come within any Moroccan port, he pledged that the United States would reciprocate wherever it could.[4]

From these promising beginnings, little would come quickly. The United States was preoccupied, first, with fighting for its independence and, second, with diplomatic efforts to gain postwar recognition from France, Spain, the Netherlands, and, after peace was won, Britain. For his part, the Moroccan emperor faced drought and famine at home, and his diplomatic attention was focused primarily on the question of Gibraltar and relations with European powers, especially Spain and Britain. Contact between the United States and Morocco was only renewed in early 1783 and then outside official channels. An American merchant at the Spanish port of Alicante, Robert Montgomery, met a Moroccan emissary at the Hapsburg court and assured the diplomat that Congress had authorized him to begin negotiations for a treaty of commerce. Emperor Sidi Muhammad was delighted but skeptical: his new foreign minister, the Genoese painter Giacomo Francisco Crocco, warned Franklin that American failure to follow through with treaty negotiations might "forever indispose [the sultan] against the United Provinces [of North America]."[5]

In a May 7, 1784, resolution, Congress instructed its European commissioners Adams, Franklin, and Jefferson to begin negotiations with Morocco as part of a larger plan to secure American trading rights in the Atlantic world. The Moroccan emperor, the first head of state to recognize American independence and the first to offer a treaty of peace and commerce, was to be thanked and the ministers were to apologize for the lack of congressional response to the emperor's repeated attempts to open direct negotiations between the two countries. "The occupations of the war and distance of our situation have prevented our meeting his friendship so early as we wished," the instructions read. But with the war over, the

American ministers now had powers "delegated to them for entering into treaty with him, in the execution of which they are ready to
proceed."[6] The Moroccan treaty, it was hoped, would set the pattern for agreements with the other Barbary powers.

Regrettably, communication channels were slow and Sidi
Muhammad had grown tired of waiting. It had been six years since
he had recognized the United States; the emissaries he had sent to
Paris to meet with Franklin had returned empty-handed; and the
letters he had forwarded to Congress were answered only after long
delays and then with words instead of action. He decided to force
the Americans to move more quickly by capturing a U.S. merchantman and then demanding that Congress negotiate a treaty with
him. The emperor had at his disposal four squadrons of privateers
that he could call upon for the mission, two on the Mediterranean
(one at Tangier and the other at Tétouan) and two on the Atlantic,
one at Rabat and one at Salé. He gave the assignment to the latter:
the much-feared Sallee Rovers, whose very name represented terror in the imagination of many Americans.

Salé was ideally suited as a pirate haven. Located about
150 miles south of Tangier on the Atlantic coast, the walled city
was situated on the estuary Bou Regreg, which provided easy entrance to the Atlantic while at the same time offering protection to
the fleet. A canal off the Bou Regreg gave the corsairs direct access
through a gate in the city walls to a harbor completely enclosed
within the ramparts. Sometime in the fall of 1784 the Sallee Rovers
left their base at Salé in quest of an American prize. They desired a
protected cove near shipping lanes where they could hide while
awaiting an eligible target. On this occasion they sailed to Cape St.
Vincent, an imposing headland at Portugal's southwestern tip by
which merchant vessels sailed on their way to and from the busy
Spanish port of Cádiz. In addition to being located on a busy shipping route, the two-hundred-foot-high promontory provided the
pirates cover against detection. On October 11, 1784, the Sallee
Rovers spotted the merchant vessel *Betsey* on its return trip to the
United States from Cádiz. They quickly ran down the slower brig-

antine, overpowered its crew, and took the ship captive. Upon the emperor's orders, the pirates brought the ship and crew to Tangier, where they were held hostage. Sidi Muhammad announced that his intention was not to confiscate the cargo or to enslave the men but to secure a peace treaty with America. Indeed, release of the ship, crew, and cargo would occur as soon as a treaty was concluded.[7]

News of the attack caused American merchants to reassess the Mediterranean market. They knew that the capture meant, at minimum, higher insurance rates on cargoes shipped to the region. More likely Americans would have to ship their goods in foreign bottoms, a blow to the new republic's aspirations of becoming a leader in the carrying trade. Some enterprising merchants, however, sought to open new markets in the East Indies, far from the threat of the Barbary pirates. Upon the completion of the successful voyage of the *Empress of China* a year later, John Jay applauded the pioneering merchants' and sailors' "spirit of enterprise and adventure" and hoped for lucrative trade in the future.[8]

While the capture spurred merchants to seek alternative markets, it also had the effect on American lawmakers that Sidi Muhammad sought. Determined to do all within its power to prevent "further progress of the war, as well as to procure the liberty of our Countrymen who are made prisoners," Congress moved quickly.[9] It instructed the commissioners to seek assistance from any nation kindly disposed toward America. Specifically, the commissioners were to gather intelligence about treating with the Barbary pirates and determine the terms of European treaties with the Barbary States, particularly payments in presents, ransom, and tribute. Accordingly, the commissioners wrote the French foreign minister, the Comte de Vergennes, requesting help, reminding him that France had an obligation to provide it "according to the tenor of the eighth article of the treaty of commerce" ratified in 1778.[10]

The commissioners also enlisted the services of their friend the Marquis de Lafayette. Within a short time he reported back with "every intelligence I could obtain" concerning treaty costs, including information from Holland, Sweden, Denmark, Venice, Spain,

Portugal, England, and France. He noted that France was "upon a much more decent footing with those pirates than Any other Nation" and therefore was not "obliged to pay Certain tributes." Upon concluding its current treaty, France had paid the Moroccans 367,021 livres (about $1.5 million today) but agreed to no annual tribute. Sweden, on the other hand, paid about the same amount in presents plus 100,000 livres ($500,000 today) each year.[11] In mid-1785 Thomas Jefferson replaced Benjamin Franklin as American minister to France and conducted his own investigation into how much "the nations of Europe give to the Barbary states to purchase their peace." Though most courts were not forthcoming with the information, he concluded from "some glimmerings" that the Barbary pirates collectively would "tax us at one, two, or perhaps three hundred thousand dollars a year."[12]

The heavy costs of negotiating peace divided the American ministers over the wisdom of seeking a treaty. Adams, "engaged earnestly in the Business of Treating with the Barbary Powers" since 1778, thought that the best way to secure the Mediterranean trade was to enter into treaties, even if it meant paying tribute. Franklin disagreed, questioning if the volume of trade justified the payment of presents to the pirates.[13] Jefferson was the most bellicose, preferring war to tribute. The United States, he thought, ought to offer Morocco a commercial agreement on the basis of equality and reciprocity. If the emperor seriously sought peace, he would accept such a pact. If, on the other hand, he demanded tribute, then, Jefferson asked, "why not go to war with them?"[14] The author of the Declaration of Independence could not fathom the notion of winning the war against Britain and then losing the peace by becoming a tributary to a bunch of pirates.[15]

All three, however, appreciated that relations with the Barbary States occurred within a larger European context. Even Jefferson did not view the Sallee Rovers' capture of the *Betsey* as an act of war. "The Emperor of Morocco who had taken one of our vessels," he reported to Nathanael Greene, "immediately consented to suspend hostilities, and ultimately gave up the vessel, cargo and crew."[16] John Adams flatly observed that "he did it merely to induce us to treat."[17] Adams was more inclined to blame Europeans for enabling Morocco to outfit pirates than he was to accuse the emperor. The maritime powers, Adams believed, were all too eager to encourage Barbary raids on American shipping in the Mediterranean, and he cited what he considered to be damning evidence. When in 1783 the emperor of Morocco's ambassador to Holland demanded "materials for some frigates," the emissary succeeded in part because "none of the great maritime powers have the courage or the will to refuse such requisitions." But cowardice seemed married to opportunism: those materials were now "employed in corsairs against American trade," with the consequence that one "vessel appears to have been taken and carried to Tangier."[18] It was clear to Adams that America's challenge in the Mediterranean had sinister ties to European courts.

At the same time that the Moroccans captured the *Betsey*, rumors (as it happened, unfounded ones) circulated in London that Algerine corsairs had also taken some American vessels. Provoked, some Americans called for war against the Barbary States, a response that Adams thought a mistake. The war hawks, he claimed, had "more spirit than prudence." For one thing, he pointed out, the Barbary problem was enmeshed in European politics and called for diplomacy, not war. He believed that as long as France, England, Holland, and other maritime powers were willing to pay tribute to "these robbers" and even encourage the pirates to raid American shipping, an American declaration of war against the North African states would be in vain. For one, "the contest would be unequal":

> They can injure us very sensibly, but we cannot hurt them in the smallest degree. We have, or shall have, a rich trade at sea exposed to their depredations; they have none at all upon which we can make reprisals. If we take a vessel of theirs, we get nothing but a bad vessel fit only to burn, a few guns and a few barbarians, whom we may hang or enslave if we will, and the unfeeling tyrants, whose subjects they are,

will think no more of it than if we had killed so many cater-
pillars upon an apple-tree. When they take a vessel of ours,
they not only get a rich prize, but they enslave the men, and,
if there are among them men of any rank or note, they demand most exorbitant ransoms for them. If we could even
send a force sufficient to burn a town, their unfeeling governors would only insult and deride.[19]

Though opposing a declaration of war, Adams acknowledged
the gravity of the situation. The capture of just one American vessel
had brought U.S. commerce in the Mediterranean to a virtual
standstill; alarmed insurance brokers in London were unwilling to
underwrite maritime policies for American ships at anything other
than exorbitant rates. While declaring that "something should be
soon done," Adams feared an American overreaction and warned
Congress against making a mistake that would make matters worse.
He feared two prevailing miscalculations. One, best articulated by
Franklin, claimed that the value of U.S. trade in the Mediterranean
did not justify the payment of tribute to the pirates. The United
States should simply write off trade in the region, leaving European
carriers to transport American produce to Mediterranean ports
while the United States operated in the Atlantic beyond the pirates'
reach. The other side of the debate took the Jeffersonian view that
it would be an act of national humiliation "to treat with such enemies of the human race, and that it would be more manly to fight
them." Nothing less than American independence demanded it.

Adams opposed both arguments as rash, emotional responses
to a matter that required cooler reasoning. The first group, he argued, failed to appreciate the value and extent of the Mediterranean
trade, "in which every one of our States is deeply interested." They
also underestimated the pirates' ability to undermine U.S. interests
all over the Atlantic. The second group overestimated America's
ability to combat the pirates and underestimated the pirates' ability
to defend themselves.[20]

Congress agreed with Adams, and on March 11, 1785, decided

to treat with the Moroccans, appropriating the modest sum of $80,000 to conclude treaties with all four Barbary States. Shortly after the instructions reached Paris, Jefferson replaced Franklin as minister to France; negotiations with the Barbary pirates would rest with Adams and Jefferson. Working from notes left by Franklin, Jefferson drafted a proposed treaty for the Barbary States and forwarded it to Adams in London for review and revision. In an accompanying letter, Jefferson expressed "extreme" anxiety regarding the treaty. He continued to prefer fighting to paying tribute, and he told Adams that naval war hero John Paul Jones would be an excellent choice as emissary to Algiers, the most bellicose of the Barbary States. In the "very probable event of war with those pirates," he wrote, Jones would then be well acquainted with the pirates' ports, force, and tactics.[21]

Jefferson's proposed treaty was a commercial agreement between equal partners. No mention was made of one party's being tributary to the other. Expressing the principle that "free vessels [make] free goods," it would outlaw such actions as that taken by Morocco against the *Betsey*. The proposal called for "most favored nation" status, arguing that neither of the signatories should pay greater duties than the lowest rates offered citizens of any country. In addition, the treaty forbade either party to enslave subjects of the other. And to protect the interests of their citizens, both sides would have the right to a resident consul.[22] After making a few minor alterations, Adams approved the document.

Recognizing that neither Adams nor Jefferson had time to conduct negotiations with the Barbary States, Congress authorized them to appoint an agent to act on their behalf. Accordingly, the commissioners named Thomas Barclay to negotiate with Morocco. Barclay had served during the American Revolution on the Navy Board and had helped secure provisions for the Continental Army. In 1782 Congress appointed him consul general to France, and no doubt it was his diplomatic experience at European courts that prompted his selection to negotiate with the Algerines. The commissioners instructed him to first "procure an immediate suspension of hostilities" if the Sallee Rovers were still pursuing American vessels. Second, Barclay should negotiate a treaty of amity and commerce conforming to Jefferson's draft. Third, he was to keep the total expenses, including his travel, for the treaty to no more than $20,000. Recognizing that they had only $80,000 to spread among all four Barbary treaties, the commissioners urged Barclay to use his best efforts to bring the costs "as much below that sum as you possibly can." He was to suggest that the United States, emerging from a "long and distressing war with one of the most powerful nations of Europe," should not be expected to offer presents "so splendid as those of older and abler nations."[23]

Before Barclay arrived in Tangier, two developments lent added weight to his mission. First, on July 9 Sidi Muhammad returned the *Betsey* and its cargo to the United States and released the crew. The emperor's action signaled his interest in concluding a peace treaty with the United States and thus brightened the prospects for Barclay's success. But within weeks of that goodwill gesture, another Barbary power declared war on the United States. Acting under the authority of the dey of Algiers, corsairs captured two American vessels and took their crews captive. For months, rumors of Algerine attacks had slowed American commerce in the Mediterranean; now rumor had become reality. The treaty with Morocco took on additional importance as the United States wished to capitalize on the emperor's friendly disposition and secure a treaty with a Barbary State that could serve as a model for future negotiations with Algiers.[24]

Arriving in Marrakesh on June 19, 1786, Barclay found the emperor eager to reach an agreement. In addition to wanting to open trade with the United States, Sidi Muhammad had been encouraged by French and Spanish diplomats to enjoy the fruits of Mediterranean commerce rather than fear reprisals for piracy. Barclay seized the initiative, introducing Jefferson's draft as the basis of discussion. It presented only one sticking point: the question of tribute. Following instructions, Barclay told the emperor that he "had to Offer to His Majesty the Friendship of the United States and to receive his in Return, to form a Treaty with him on liberal and equal Terms. But if any engagements for future presents or Tributes were necessary, I must return without any Treaty." The emperor's desire for a trade agreement outweighed his hope for tribute, and he signed the treaty as drafted. With an exchange of favors—Barclay gave presents to the emperor, who agreed to send letters to the other Barbary States recommending that they conclude treaties with the United States—the negotiations concluded.[25]

After the emperor signed the treaty on June 23, Barclay was exultant. Secured for a cost under his $20,000 cap, the treaty meant that American vessels could now pass through the Strait of Gibraltar with friendly forces on either side, and in case of an American war, naval vessels would be able to refit in safety at Moroccan ports. The carrying trade of the Mediterranean was now available to American merchants, as were the profits that came with it.[26]

Congress agreed. After ratifying the treaty on July 18, 1787, it pronounced itself "well pleased."[27] In their first negotiations with a Barbary State, the Americans had gotten exactly what they sought: a trade agreement on the most liberal terms without following the European example of paying tribute. They now had a model that they could take to the three other Barbary powers.

American hopes that their success in Morocco would set a precedent were soon dashed, again off Portugal's Cape St. Vincent. On July 25, 1785, Algerine corsairs captured the *Maria* three miles southeast of the headland, and a week later they captured the *Dauphin* of Philadelphia about two hundred miles west of Lisbon. Algiers was a much more formidable power than Morocco. The Algerine corsairs that captured the *Maria* and the *Dauphin* were crewed by battle-hardened warriors who had successfully defended Algiers against the Spanish-led coalition that had bombarded the fortified city for days without taking it. Indeed, rather than subduing Algiers, Spain had agreed to pay an estimated

$2.5 million in presents, tribute, and ransom money. Further, unlike Sidi Muhammad, Muhammad V, the dey of Algiers, was well pleased with his piracy-based economy. With no desire to replace raiding with trading, the dey viewed the capture of the American vessels as an expansion of Algerine revenues. Another significant difference between the emperor of Morocco and the dey of Algiers was their treatment of American captives. The former had refused to allow the Sallee Rovers to sell the *Betsey*'s crew into slavery, whereas the latter enslaved the twenty-one American sailors taken in the summer of 1785. Along with negotiating a peace treaty, the U.S. government had to purchase their enslaved countrymen's freedom.

The Algerine declaration of war on America exposed the inadequacies of the American Confederation as the Moroccan capture had not. While $20,000 was sufficient for the Moroccan agreement, it fell far short of what the dey demanded, demands that escalated until they ultimately reached about $1 million (more than $18 million in today's money). With no taxing authority of its own and with public credit in disarray, America could fund neither an expensive treaty with Algiers nor a navy to fight the pirates.

America's negotiator, John Lamb, and his assistant, P. R. Randall, received a very different reception in Algiers from that enjoyed by Thomas Barclay in Morocco. Arriving in Algiers on March 25, 1786, the Americans stayed at the home of the French consul, through whom they requested to see the dey. The reply was hardly encouraging. In Randall's words, the dey said "that if we came on the Subject of Peace he would not see us, but if we wished to visit him and talk to him on other Matters he would be glad to see us." It would be the dey, not the Americans, who would set the terms of any discussion. All the relevant options were his alone. He could treat with the Americans, selling them their enslaved compatriots. Or he could capture more American vessels and send the price of peace even higher. Third, he could do nothing for the time being, make a separate peace with Portugal, America's principal naval protector in the region, and then dictate the terms of allowing Americans into the Mediterranean.

Randall depicted the Algerine dey as a worthy foe. Though eighty years old, he was in firm control of the regency, beloved by his people and respected by his officers. A self-made man, he had risen to his position from that of a shoemaker through great industry and frugality. After becoming dey, he continued to live by those virtues. Rather than laying out great wealth for his own enjoyment, he "increased the publick heap to a great Pinnacle of Riches." Randall noted that the "principal Production" of the state's revenue came from a tithe on all prizes taken by his pirates as well as tribute from European states. As best as Randall could ascertain, the Algerines held about fifteen hundred captives, including the twenty-one Americans taken after declaring war on American shipping in the summer of 1785. Unwilling to negotiate peace, the dey indicated that he was willing to release the Americans for a total ransom payment of $59,496. Unwilling to part with such a sum and yet having no treaty, the American negotiators returned to Paris empty-handed.[28]

The dey's intransigence renewed the debate among Americans over U.S. policy toward the Barbary States in general and Algiers in particular. The opposing views of the two men responsible for negotiating with the piratical states—Thomas Jefferson and John Adams—set the parameters for the broader debate that occurred in Congress and throughout America. Adams took the position that, given the long-standing policy of European maritime powers to pay tribute to the pirates, the United States had little choice but to do the same. Summarizing his argument for immediate negotiations, Adams claimed that "our friends cannot procure us a peace, without paying its price; that they cannot materially lessen that price; . . . that paying it, we can have the peace in spite of the intrigues of our enemies; [and] . . . that the longer the negotiation is delayed, the larger will be the demand."[29]

Jefferson contended that war was the better option. In taking that stance, he persisted in a firmly held opinion. Long an advocate of a military response to piracy, he wrote in a November 1784 letter to James Monroe, "We ought to begin a naval power, if we mean to carry on our own commerce." No warmonger (indeed, his political opponents made much of his lack of military experience and his flight before a 1780 British invasion of Virginia while governor), Jefferson nevertheless thought that war was justified in this instance.

Making his case to Adams, Jefferson repeated his conviction that fighting the pirates was preferable to paying tribute. He listed six reasons for advocating war. First, he argued, justice demanded punishing the captors of American citizens. Second, America's honor as a free, independent nation had to be defended against piratical depredations. Third, by fighting and defeating the Algerines, the United States would earn respect in Europe, and that respect would redound to America's interest in future dealings with the great maritime powers. Fourth, going to war would have benefits at home by arming the federal government with "the instruments of coercion over its delinquent members." Military power, that is, would serve to bring the states in line as well as the Barbary pirates. Fifth, a military response would cost less than paying tribute. And sixth, he concluded, war was at least "equally effectual" as negotiations in the short term and far more durable in the long term.[30]

To Adams, the question of whether to negotiate or fight boiled down to the practical versus the desirable, or the possible versus the preferable. Taking a realistic view, he calculated the comparative costs of diplomacy and war. He began by estimating the cost of making peace with the Barbary States. "Set it if you will at five hundred Thousand Pounds Sterling," he told Jefferson, "tho I doubt not it might be done for Three or perhaps for two." Adams then turned to the question of "what Damage shall we suffer, if we do not treat." The costs ranged from higher maritime insurance premiums, which would likely increase if U.S. vessels sailed without proper passes, to "the total Loss of all the Mediterranean and Levant Trade." At risk, he concluded, was "more than half a Million sterling a year." Adams next considered the cost of fighting, which he estimated to be "at least half a Million sterling a year without protecting your Trade." He reminded Jefferson that unless the United States were willing to engage in constant war with the Barbary States, ultimately a peace would have to be negotiated regardless. In short, he argued, "when you leave off fighting you must pay as much Money as it would cost you now for Peace." Thus Adams thought a negotiated peace was the better and cheaper option. Put bluntly, he calculated that "For an Annual Interest of 30,000 pounds sterling then and perhaps for 15,000 or 10,000, we can have Peace, when a War would sink us annually ten times as much."[31]

Jefferson countered with calculations of his own that gave the advantage to fighting instead of negotiating. He envisioned a "fleet of 150 guns, the one half of which shall be in constant cruise." The cost: 450,000 pounds sterling and an annual expense of "300 pounds sterling a gun," resulting in a total cost of "45,000 pounds sterling a year." He reasoned, "Were we to charge all this to the Algerine war it would amount to little more than we must pay if we buy peace." But, he added, in reality the cost of fighting the Barbary pirates would be less than the total cost of the navy: "as it is proper and necessary that we should establish a small marine force (even were we to buy a peace from the Algerines), and as that force laid up in our dockyards would cost us half as much annually as if kept in order for service, we have a right to say that only 22,500 pounds sterling per annum should be charged to the Algerine war."[32]

Adams was unconvinced. He believed that the United States would spend "a great sum" to fight Algiers and would still have to lay out more money to pay for the presents the dey would surely demand at the end of the conflict. Adams contended that the cost of peace, even if it ran into hundreds of thousands of dollars, was a small price to pay for reopening America's Mediterranean trade. "At present we are sacrificing a million annually, to save one gift of

£200,000," he pointed out to Jefferson. "This is not good economy." The United States might have two hundred ships in the Mediterranean at this moment with a combined freight that would vastly exceed the cost of peace if Congress would only buy it.[33]

Adams and Jefferson were of one mind, however, regarding the importance of Congress finding the will and the resources to act decisively. Given congressional inaction to date, Adams was less than optimistic. "My indignation is roused beyond all patience," he wrote, "to see the people in all the United States in a torpor, and see them a prey, to every robber, pirate, and cheat in Europe."[34] He thought it time that "laws at home . . . be made in conformity to the state of affairs abroad."[35]

A war might be just the thing needed: so wrote Revolutionary War naval hero John Paul Jones in a letter Jefferson forwarded to secretary of foreign affairs John Jay. Jones opined that the Algerines' war declaration was not altogether bad. He had been appalled by the petty jealousies that lawmakers evidenced in putting local concerns ahead of national interests; the war, he wrote, "will produce a good effect, if it unites the People of America in measures consistent with their national honor and interest, and rouses them from that illjudged security which the intoxication of Success has produced since the Revolution."[36] Jay echoed Jones's sentiments in a message to Congress urging a military response to the Algerine declaration of war:

> This War does not strike me as a great Evil, the more we are treated ill abroad, the more we shall unite and consolidate at Home. Besides, as it may become a Nursery for Seamen, and lay the Foundation for a respectable Navy, it may eventually prove more beneficial than otherwise. Portugal will doubtless unite with us in it, and that circumstance may dispose that Kingdom to extend commercial Favors to us farther than they might consent to do, if uninfluenced by such Inducements. For my Part, I think it may be demonstrated, that while we bend our Attention to the Sea, every naval War

which does not do us essential Injury will do us essential Good.[37]

Jay proposed a series of measures aimed at putting the United States on a war footing and protecting its commerce. In a paper delivered to Congress on October 20, 1785, he stated that the time for a negotiated peace had passed. "That this Declaration of War being unprovoked, and made solely with Design to acquire Plunder," he wrote, "it would not in the Opinion of your Secretary, become the United States to answer it by Overtures for Peace, or Offers of Tribute." America's emissaries to the other Barbary States should continue to pursue treaties, but they should "take no Notice of Algiers."[38]

Of course, Algiers could not simply be ignored. "Both the Honor and Interest of the United States demand that decided and vigorous Measures be taken to protect the American Trade and meet these predatory Enemies in a proper Manner." Jay laid out several specific recommendations. First, Congress should require all merchants trading with Spain, Portugal, the Madeiras, the Canaries, and all other ports in the Mediterranean to arm their vessels and man them with crewmen trained to defend against pirate attacks. Recognizing that such measures would be expensive, Jay thought Congress should bear some of the cost. Accordingly, he offered a resolution whereby Congress would supply all American-built ships carrying twenty or more guns with military stores and with "Money to pay the Men necessary to man her." Second, Jay proposed a national navy for the purpose of cruising the Mediterranean. Specifically, he recommended that Congress authorize the building of five warships, each with forty guns, and the appointment of a "brave experienced Commodore" as well as a "Board of Admiralty" under the direction of "one good Commissioner."[39]

While confident that his proposals would protect American commerce, Jay was less confident that Congress could actually put them into practice. The problem was constitutional. To carry out Jay's plan, Congress needed the authority to regulate commerce and the power to levy taxes. It had neither. Under the Articles of Confederation, the funds necessary to build a navy must come from the states. Even if the United States could borrow funds from another country, the states would have to appropriate amounts sufficient to service the debt. Yet the young nation was uniquely hobbled in its ability to secure loans. Put simply, America's public credit was deplorable. Congress had insufficient funds "for paying even the interest of our former loans, either foreign or domestic." Though pressed to remit overdue payments to France, the United States remained in arrears to its most faithful ally in the War of Independence. No European government or bank would look favorably upon an American loan request, Jay argued, because of "the reluctance of the States to pay taxes, or to comply with the economical requisitions of Congress." Worse, the states' refusal to "give efficacy to their Federal Government" was a topic of "common conversation in Europe."[40] In refusing to enter into a trade agreement with the United States, British officials had argued that such a pact would be meaningless because any one state could refuse to comply with congressional trade regulations. Indeed, it was Congress's inability to regulate interstate commerce that led to a series of attempts to enlarge congressional powers. One attempt occurred in 1785, when George Washington hosted a conference at Mount Vernon between commissioners from Virginia and Maryland to discuss trade regulations between the two states. That meeting ended with a call for a second and expanded conference at Annapolis, where delegates from every state would discuss commercial issues.

Attendance at the Annapolis Convention, which convened on September 11, 1786, disappointed its organizers. Only nine states agreed to send delegates, and only five delegates arrived on time. Doomed before it began, the convention's most significant action was a call for yet another convention, to be held in Philadelphia, for the purpose of discussing not only commerce but also all measures for strengthening the federal government. After protracted debate, on February 21, 1787, Congress endorsed the plan to revise the

Articles of Confederation, and the delegates convened in Philadelphia in May 1787.

Future secretary of the treasury Alexander Hamilton had long been of the opinion that independence backed by inadequate power was an empty promise. Immediately after the War of Independence, even while he exulted in the conclusion of the "great work of independence," he warned John Jay that much must be done to "reap the fruits of it." He declared that "every day" brought new proofs of the inefficacy of the Confederation, and he saw little evidence that the states were willing to amend its defects. Hamilton blamed state politicians who fomented suspicion of a distant, powerful national government. This was dangerously wrongheaded. Want of resources during the fight for independence had caused the country to suffer through a prolonged war; now the country faced bankruptcy and ruined credit, which jeopardized independence itself.[41]

Jay concurred with Hamilton's views, elaborating on how the nation's poor credit complicated foreign relations. From his post in Paris, he noted that "our reputation also suffers from the apparent reluctance to taxes, and the ease with which we incur debts without providing for their payment." Further, it was frustrating, he said, to see so little of a "national spirit" pervading among Americans that would unite and invigorate the union. The consequence was that in European courts, the United States suffered a "diminution of our respectability, power, and felicity."[42]

In 1787, two years after the Algerines captured the two American ships, Jay's predictions had become reality. Now secretary of foreign affairs, Jay wrote derisively that "it has come to pass that almost every national object of every kind is at this day unprovided for; and other nations, taking the advantage of its imbecility, are daily multiplying commercial restraints upon us." Indeed, he asked, "is there an English, or a French, or a Spanish island or port in the West Indies to which an American vessel can carry a cargo of flour for sale?" His answer: "Not one." In addition, Jay noted, "the Algerines exclude us from the Mediterranean and adjacent countries; and we are neither able to purchase nor to command the free use of those seas."[43] To John Jay, the message was clear: weak, ineffective government was squandering American independence.

Rufus King, a Massachusetts delegate, agreed. In a letter outlining his assessment of the state of the union, he declared that the country was bankrupt. The federal government had insufficient authority to generate revenue for the common treasury; the credit of the individual states was little better; collectively, such a condition could only lead to "a Violation of national engagements, & a loss of national Character." Second, King considered the "embarrassments of commerce" resulting from the weak Confederation. American merchants could not compete with their commercial rivals, who were delighting in "our disjointed condition." King concluded with the dismal assertion that "it is not possible that the public Affairs can be in a much worse situation," adding that the only consolation lay in the knowledge that the country could not long remain as it was presently constituted.[44]

While Americans at home grew more frustrated with the inadequacies of the Confederation, Adams and Jefferson began to lose patience in Europe, first with Congress, then with each other. A strong advocate of treating with the Barbary States, Adams raised the fundamental question, "But how?"

> Where is the money? France calls upon us to fulfil our engagements with her, both for interest and principal, and our creditors in Holland, who are very numerous, will soon be uneasy, unless something is done for their security. Holland is the only place where we can borrow money, and there it will be impracticable, unless our European debt at least be consolidated.[45]

Jefferson voiced similar sentiments. Congress had commissioned him, Adams, and Franklin to treat with the Barbary States but had appropriated no funds with which to do so.

Further undermining American interests in the Atlantic world was the fact that the individual states, not Congress, were in charge of setting commercial policy. While Massachusetts and New Hampshire had passed commercial measures designed to retaliate against Britain's Navigation Acts, each state had also imposed double duties on imported goods arriving in vessels owned by persons other than citizens of the state. Frustrated, Europeans threatened a trade war if the individual states continued to impose their own regulations and tariffs. Compounding the problem, Jefferson had to admit that he and the other American ministers were as much in the dark about the various states' intentions as were the Europeans.[46]

The Algerine capture of twenty-one Americans gave a sense of urgency to the call for a stronger national government. Rufus King cited Congress's efforts to deal with the Barbary pirates as an example of the government's dependence on the states. Congress had requested that the states levy an impost to raise money for negotiating with the Barbary States, but the measure had failed because of what King called the "deranged condition of the confederacy." Excessive state control over the collection of the imposts, King argued, would mean that "no money will come into the federal Treasury." As a result, he lamented, "our Barbary Negotiations will issue in a fruitless attempt for peace." While Congress pleaded with the states to send money for negotiations, the Barbary States' demands escalated. Instead of the original estimate of $80,000, King noted, "it turns out that 200,000 Guineas will be the least sum necessary to accomplish this object in a proper mode—will you tell me where the money can be had?"[47]

Pierse Long of New Hampshire joined a growing number of legislators at the convention who believed that only a navy could protect American shipping. And time was running out. Spain had concluded a treaty with Algiers, and Portugal was close to concluding a truce. That meant "the United States will be [the pirates'] single object." Long went a step further: "what is to hinder their destroying our Trade in the proper season, even on our own coast." He asked, "Is there no way that can be found out, to begin a navy?"

The nation required a navy, but a navy required "a great deal of what we have none of—*Vizt. Cash.*"[48] Timothy Bloodworth, a congressman from North Carolina, put the case bluntly: "we cannot Negociate [with the Barbary powers] for want of money."[49]

The Rhode Island delegation, too, linked pirate depredations on American shipping with the "exhausted state of the federal treasury." The delegates were outraged that while states, including their own, refused to fund the confederation, the "despicable" Barbary pirates were "embarrassing our most beneficial commerce" and enslaving fellow citizens. The delegation thought that unless the most "vigorous exertions" were made to secure American liberty against piratical depredations, the consequence would be "our total ruin as a Nation."[50]

Though he favored fighting the Algerines, Thomas Jefferson stated flatly from his post in Paris, "We are not at this moment in a condition to do it." What rankled was the realization that the United States was not truly independent. Indeed, if England were to declare war on America, he knew, the United States would have to rely upon other countries to transport American produce. What was particularly frustrating was his belief that the republic could defend its interests with even a small navy. Ironically, it would have to be employed in a way similar to that of the Barbary pirates. With a "small naval force" and a few privateers patrolling the waters around the British West Indies, the United States could threaten British interests in the Caribbean just as the small squadrons of corsairs stymied American commerce in the Mediterranean.[51]

With Jefferson continuing to advocate war against the Barbary States, Adams grew ever testier in opposition. His opposition rested on financial and political considerations. Fighting a war cost money the republic did not possess and offered no guarantee of victory. Furthermore, Adams reminded his colleague of their own deep-seated political jealousies. There was a growing rift between southern and northern interests: the former favored free trade policies that supported their large-scale production of cash crops while the latter desired measures strengthening commerce and the carrying trade. Throwing down a political challenge, Adams declared that if Jefferson could persuade the southern states to support a navy and a war against the Barbary States, then he, Adams, would answer for the states from Pennsylvania northward. Knowing the deep republican sentiment among southerners against big, expensive government, Adams was confident that Jefferson could not garner sufficient support below Pennsylvania, particularly when fighting the Algerines would cost perhaps a "million annually" and peace could be had for perhaps $200,000. Adams granted that it would be "heroic" to fight the pirates and restore honor to "Christendom," and that America would be victorious "if we should set about it in earnest." However, he warned, "the difficulty of bringing our people to agree upon it, has ever discouraged me."[52]

Given Adams's confidence that the southern states would not agree to a costly war, it is ironic that no one better understood the need for a new constitution that would give the national government coercive power over the states than did James Madison, a Virginia planter. Even during the War of Independence, Madison recalled, the states only "imperfectly" fulfilled their obligations to the union. To him, the reason was clear: state politicians were "courtiers of popularity," and the best way for them to win popular support was by advocating local interests. Madison wondered what would happen if a state's authority over its counties rested on the same basis as Congress's over the states: that is, if it were merely voluntary instead of coercive. "If the laws of the States were merely recommendatory to their citizens," Madison asked, "what security, what probability would exist, that they would be carried into execution?"[53] To him, the country needed a new constitution that gave the national government coercive powers over the states. Only then would America's ministers abroad have the resources and confidence to negotiate with foreign powers, or threaten the use of force against those attacking American interests.

The new U.S. Constitution that Madison was so instrumental in drafting in the summer of 1787 created a national government with sufficient power to deal with the Barbary pirates. First, it stripped states of their powers to enact navigation acts governing overseas trade; it gave Congress full power over commerce. Second, it granted Congress the authority to levy taxes, giving the central government an independent source of revenue. Third, it gave Congress the power and means to build and maintain a navy. No longer would foreign policy be determined by the trade policies of the individual states or their willingness to comply with congressional requests for funds. Further, the new taxing authority was necessary for sound public credit, allowing the United States to raise funds abroad. And with a navy, if the United States would but build it, resisting the Barbary pirates by force was, for the first time, a viable option.

While the new Constitution provided America's commissioners with the power they had long sought in their efforts to negotiate a peace treaty with Algiers and secure the release of the captives, another nine years would pass before either goal was attained. Domestic politics and foreign affairs explain the long delay. It took two years for the states to ratify the Constitution and another six months to convene the first Congress and inaugurate George Washington as president. In addition, John Adams and Thomas Jefferson, the commissioners who had spent almost five years struggling with the Algiers problem, left their respective posts in London and Paris and joined the administration in New York, Adams as vice president and Jefferson as secretary of state. When Washington convened his cabinet, the priority was fiscal policy, not Algiers. Indeed much of the period from 1789 through 1791 involved heated debates over Secretary of the Treasury Alexander Hamilton's proposals for funding national and state debts. Disputes over fiscal policy created political factions within the administration, and in 1794 resistance to the new excise tax culminated in the so-called Whiskey Rebellion. Though the administration launched new diplomatic initiatives in 1791 to negotiate a peace treaty with Algiers, domestic considerations overshadowed them.

Developments in other parts of the Atlantic world also diverted the Washington administration's attention from the Algerine question. First, the French Revolution of 1789 widened the divide between America's emerging political factions, the pro-British Federalists led by Alexander Hamilton and the pro-French Democratic-Republicans led by Thomas Jefferson. Second, when the French declared war on Great Britain, Spain, and Holland in 1793, the Atlantic became as dangerous for American merchantmen as the Mediterranean. Despite Washington's proclamation of neutrality, English and French warships and privateers raided American vessels, confiscated their cargoes, and imprisoned their crews. Washington dispatched John Jay to London to negotiate a commercial treaty with Britain that he hoped would, among other things, respect American rights as neutrals on the high seas. His return in 1794 with an agreement that was silent on those rights touched off a bitter fight between Federalists and Democratic-Republicans, making cooperation on the Algiers question more difficult.

Despite these lengthy delays, the Algerine problem demanded attention. American prisoners would not let Congress forget them, writing numerous letters pleading with the lawmakers to meet the dey's ransom demands. On February 22, 1792, almost seven years after Algiers imprisoned the Americans, Congress appointed John Paul Jones to treat with the dey. As secretary of state, Jefferson authorized Jones to pay up to $100,000 for the peace, $13,500 in annual tribute, and $27,000 in ransom. In addition to negotiating, Jones was also to gather intelligence on the Algerine military capabilities; Jefferson feared that the duration of any peace that might be bought was uncertain and that force might yet be necessary.[54]

But fortune conspired against the American cause. Before he could depart for Algiers, John Paul Jones died. Congress then appointed Thomas Barclay, who had successfully negotiated the Morocco Treaty, but he too died before undertaking the assignment. The deaths caused further delays, and while the circumstances called for understanding and patience, the Algerine dey had run out of both. Dey Ali Hassan had succeeded Muhammad V, who died on July 12, 1791. Formerly minister of marine, Ali Hassan was eager to prove himself, and in Algiers that meant capturing prizes and exacting tribute. When he became chief, he followed the custom of demanding presents from signatories to treaties. But recognizing the British as possessing the strongest navy and a power "that would not admit of any Gross insult," the dey renewed the pact with Britain without any alterations. From Spain, however, which had signed its costly treaty with Algiers while Hassan was minister of marine, the dey demanded "immence presents" and the surrender of Oran, a Spanish-held port on the Algerine coast. Similarly, Hassan required "extra presents" from the Dutch, Swedes, and Venetians. As he extracted funds through negotiation, Hassan was eager to capture prizes from those countries with whom he had no peace treaty.[55]

Without the protection of a treaty or navy, American shipping was a potential source of new prizes for Hassan's pirates. Since 1787, however, Portugal, strategically located near the entrance to the Mediterranean, had defended American vessels against Barbary depredations. Importing large quantities of American corn and flour, Queen Maria I of Portugal had promised protection by her men-of-war.[56] For the next six years the Algerines did not pursue American merchantmen for fear of entanglements with Portugal's navy. But as Americans in the region warned repeatedly, if Algiers and Portugal ever settled on a peace, Algerine corsairs would be free to sail westward through the Strait and prey on American targets. In October 1793 warning became reality. David Humphreys, U.S. minister to Lisbon, dispatched the bad news: "Authentic advice is just Received that a truce for 12 months, is concluded between Portugal & Algiers—In consiquance of which eight Algeren Cruizers Viz Four frigates, one Brig & three Xebeques passed through the streights last night into the Atlantic."[57] For eight years Algiers–U.S. relations had been characterized by sporadic talks, rejected demands, and countless delays. They now entered a more militant and dangerous phase that would send the cost of peace soaring.

By the end of November the Algerine corsairs had captured eleven American vessels—five ships, four brigs, and two schooners. Their officers and crews, numbering 105 in all, joined the existing fifteen surviving American prisoners as Algerine slaves. As Americans gradually learned details of the raids, they understood how utterly powerless their fellow countrymen were against the corsairs. On one occasion the pirates boarded a captured merchantman and dumped part of its cargo of wheat into the Atlantic to improve its sailing capability, then armed her "on the spot" for further depredations against the United States.[58] The terror and humiliation continued when the captured crewmen arrived in Algiers. Stripped of their clothes, the naked Americans stumbled ashore, where they were placed in chains and marched off to the slave pen for auction.[59]

At least one American was not surprised by the Algerines' actions. Writing shortly after the 1793 captures, Philadelphia newspaper publisher and writer Mathew Carey bluntly conceded that American independence from Britain had brought with it the natural expectation that the United States "should, in some degree, suffer, by the ravages of the corsairs." Several circumstances, Carey wrote, made American ships "eligible targets of piratical rapine." The United States carried on "an extensive trade with Europe, which in the first place, presented a splendid temptation to plunder." Second, "America did not support, at her national expence, any maritime force whatever," and the absence of a navy to escort commercial vessels gave the Algerines an "irresistible motive to hostilities." Third, even if the United States had a navy, America "lies at the distance of more than three thousand miles, from the common range of the privateers of Barbary."[60] For 250 years the Barbary pirates had thrived as opportunists ever alert for valuable prizes; American merchantmen were merely their latest prey.

Carey's matter-of-fact explanation notwithstanding, other Americans called for an immediate and forceful response against Algiers and its British ally. One American merchant in Cádiz blasted Congress for failing to protect the country's shipping. Preoccupied with such domestic issues as funding systems and Indian wars, the lawmakers had neglected the needs of American merchants abroad. Not only did the government have to furnish "powers and means for a peace or a war with those pirates," but Congress had to recognize that Algiers did not act alone in capturing the eleven vessels. Any American plan to ensure commercial independence must include the pirates' "cursed abettors the English." The merchant was certain that the British were complicit in the new depredations and that they "used this dirty piratical, political tool" to undermine U.S. commerce.[61]

Congress soon received official intelligence implicating the British. Nathaniel Cutting, David Humphreys's assistant in negotiating with the Algerines, accused the British of inciting the pirates to capture American ships in order "to cramp our flourishing Commerce still further." He charged the British consul at Algiers, Charles Logie, with negotiating the "fatal Truce which has eventually wrested from a considerable number of our industrious Citizens their *Liberty*, from others their *property*—and from some, *both*." When Logie protested Britain's innocence, Cutting declared, "I do not believe him."[62] Neither did President Washington, who saw British involvement in the Algerine affair as part of a pattern of behavior aimed at hurting American interests. He cited British instigation of Indians on the American frontier and orders-in-council authorizing privateers and warships to interfere with American neutrality as evidence that Britain sought to keep America dependent in the Atlantic world.[63] More detached analysis indicates that the British involvement may not have been as sinister as Washington thought. While they had indeed arranged the Portuguese truce, their primary motivation had been to enable their Algerine allies to raid French shipping.[64] However, an unintended—or in the Americans' minds, an intended—consequence was that the Algerine corsairs were also free to prey upon American vessels outside the Strait of Gibraltar.

From Algiers the enslaved Richard O'Brien urged Congress to make peace. Exasperated by American delays and ineptitude, he reminded lawmakers that he and others had languished for more than eight years as prisoners and that he had repeatedly warned that the failure to negotiate a peace treaty would result in more captures and higher demands. He reported that the dey was also frustrated, charging Congress with having "treated his propositions with neglect and indifference." Having made treaties with the Dutch and the Portuguese, Hassan hinted that if the United States did not come to terms, he would continue to unleash his pirates on American ships. O'Brien once again urged Congress to obtain a peace with Algiers; otherwise the United States would remain the "dupe and buffoon of all Europe," with American vessels as the pirates' primary targets.[65]

The new captures mobilized Congress to resolve the Barbary problem as nothing else had. With uncharacteristic speed, the lawmakers took two steps, both backed by robust appropriations. First, Congress voted to assign a "sum of money to buy a cessation of hostilities from the regency of Algiers," eventually allocating a million dollars to purchase a peace and to ransom the American prisoners.[66] Second, on March 20, 1794, necessitated by the "depredations committed by the Algerine corsairs on the commerce of the United States," Congress authorized the establishment of a naval force consisting initially of six frigates at a cost of more than a million dollars.[67] Thus Washington, with congressional backing, decided to push for a peace while at the same time taking measures to protect future shipping in the Mediterranean. Four years later, faced with French insults during the XYZ Affair, Americans would be inspired by South Carolina congressman Robert Goodloe Harper, who vowed: "Millions for defense, but not one cent for tribute." But in 1794, weak and unprepared before the pirates of Algiers, America deemed it wise to pledge millions for defense *and* millions for tribute.

After Thomas Jefferson decided to leave public office at the end of Washington's first administration, the new secretary of state, Edmund Randolph, outlined the new American strategy for dealing with Algiers in a letter to David Humphreys, who was charged with carrying it out. He called for an alliance with friendly powers in the Mediterranean, especially Portugal, and for a U.S. navy. The American plan began to fall into place in March 1794. First, Portugal's Queen Maria I instructed her diplomats to begin negotiations with the United States. At the same time she declared war against Algerine corsairs and ordered her cruisers back on patrol; once again American vessels could sail to Portuguese and Spanish ports without fear of pirate attacks. That same month Congress authorized the establishment of a naval force for the express purpose of protecting American vessels against Algerine depredations.[68]

THREE

TRIBUTARY TO THE BARBARY STATES

In deciding to build a navy, American lawmakers reasoned that only the threat of attacks by overwhelming power would cause the Algerines to stop their raiding, negotiate a peace treaty, and release U.S. prisoners. While the navy bill was intended to cow the dey of Algiers, it had the unintended consequence of sparking a fierce partisan fight within Congress. Ironically, Thomas Jefferson, who had long advocated fighting the pirates rather than negotiating with them, opposed the measure, and his friend and political ally, James Madison, led the floor fight in the House against it. Debate over the navy bill occurred in a highly charged partisan environment. Regional differences, though not the only factor, continued to underlie the division, as southern planters generally opposed measures that increased the size and cost of the federal government while northern merchants favored a more vigorous defense of commerce.

Leading the opposition, Madison was concerned that a blue-water navy would require a huge outlay of capital to build and an enormous annual budget to maintain. Further, he questioned its potential effectiveness. It would be far better, he thought, to protect America's coastlines with relatively inexpensive gunboats. Representative Alexander Baldwin of Georgia agreed, arguing that an American attempt to "block up the Mediterranean" would be impracticable. Virginia congressman John Nicholas added that the American navy simply would not be a "match for the Algerines."

Madison kept Jefferson informed of the debate, and Jefferson, living as a Virginia squire at Monticello, replied with stinging political commentary. He called the Federalist proponents of an expensive navy "Monocrats," suggesting that they advocated only what was good for northern commercial interests, who he thought sounded like monarchists or at least aristocrats. The Federalists, rather than being interested in frigates to subdue the Algerine pirates, Jefferson charged, wanted a large military force and a high debt. With good republican logic, he complained that greater expense would mean more offices and jobs for congressmen to dispense as patronage. He feared that "some few will be debauched," putting their desire for private gain above the public good.[1]

Notwithstanding opposition from Madison and Jefferson, a majority in Congress favored the construction of warships. Fisher Ames of Massachusetts spoke for many when he argued that it would be "shameful" to buy peace from the pirates and that there was no guarantee that a treaty would end the depredations. He thought that Portugal would allow American warships to use its ports and that six frigates at the mouth of the Strait would "do the business." He ended his defense of the navy bill with a flourish on what was at stake: "Our commerce is on the point of being annihilated, and unless an armament is fitted out we may very soon expect the Algerines on the coast of America."[2] The House approved the bill by a vote of 50 to 39. On March 27, 1794, Washington signed the bill, and the United States would have a naval force of six frigates.

Dey Hassan was unimpressed by American threats, especially when America's navy existed only on paper. In October 1794, six months after Congress authorized the building of six frigates, the dey increased his demand for peace and ransom to more than $2 million. An astute political observer after almost ten years in Algiers, Richard O'Brien put the demand in context for the secretary of state and Congress. First, he said, no doubt "the political influence of the British" was working on Dey Hassan, as Whitehall sought a competitive advantage against commercial rivals. Second, the dey had no expectation of actually receiving that "exorbitant Sum" from a new nation three thousand miles away; he pointed out that in recent treaties negotiated with the Dutch and the Swedes, the dey had asked for three times more than what he eventually agreed to.[3] That was little consolation, however, to a fiscally strapped Congress.

Algiers and the United States approached negotiations with two different objectives. Hassan's primary interest was extracting the maximum amount of tribute, while Congress was most interested in securing protection for its citizens and commerce. While both sides made concessions, each could point to provisions in the final agreement that met their objectives. O'Brien's intelligence proved to be accurate: Hassan backed off his demand for $2 million and, on September 5, agreed to $600,000, about one-third of his original demands. The United States paid $60,000 at the signing and promised to deliver the remainder as soon as it could be raised. For Algiers, the tribute and ransom of $600,000 dwarfed the amount negotiator Joseph Donaldson had originally offered. Still, by any reckoning, the final sum was enormous.[4] In addition, Hassan would receive an annual tribute either in gold or in military goods.

For America, the treaty, though humiliating and a far cry from the Morocco agreement that they had hoped the Algerines would adopt, promised long-awaited commercial protection. The two countries agreed to reciprocal trade and granted each other most favored nation status. Moreover, Algiers pledged to grant the United States free navigation without "impediment or Molestations" and promised not to take anyone captive from an American vessel. Further, both sides agreed not to provide military aid to each other's enemies. And to maintain the peace, the United States agreed to have a resident consul at Algiers who would enjoy personal security and freedom and be able to worship according to his religious preference.[5]

The United States quickly learned, however, that Dey Hassan, not George Washington or the U.S. Congress, would dictate the terms. For the release of American prisoners, Hassan demanded lavish presents totaling more than $200,000. Further, he demanded that most of the tribute be paid up front and that the remainder be remitted annually. Much of the tribute came in the form of naval and military matériel, whose procurement, construction, and delivery costs escalated. In its final accounting, the Senate calculated the cost of the treaty to be almost $1 million ($992,463.25, to be exact), the largest single item in the U.S. budget. A decade earlier Congress had appropriated $20,000 for peace with Algiers, and now it was forced to appropriate fifty times that amount. Perhaps the dey's most insulting demand was that the United States build and deliver a thirty-six-gun frigate.[6] It was not lost on Americans that they were thereby providing the dey with the means of taking future Americans captive and exacting even more tribute.

Still, military and commercial circumstances led Congress to pay such an amount in tribute. First, in 1795 the six navy frigates would not be ready for deployment for another two years, eighteen months after the treaty with Algiers was signed. Second, Congress concluded that America stood to gain far more through trade in the Mediterranean than the peace treaty cost. Joel Barlow, who was in Algiers to assist Donaldson in the negotiations, estimated that, with peace, Americans would realize an annual profit of $600,000, matching the onetime cost of the treaty. Best known as a writer of political and literary works, Barlow was also a merchant, and he forecast a profit of another $450,000 each year from the business that had previously gone to European carriers. Subtracting the estimated annual tribute to Algiers of $40,000, Barlow reckoned America's annual profit from the peace treaty to be almost $1 million. Absent a treaty, however, America's marine insurance premiums would skyrocket, and the carrying trade would remain dominated by her competitors.[7]

For the American prisoners in Algiers, the signing of the Algiers Treaty on Saturday, September 5, 1795, was a glorious day. One of them, Samuel Calder, provided newspaper readers back home with an eyewitness account, spiced with the emotions of one who had long awaited such a day. He reported that when the dey "concluded a Peace" with the United States, the harbor at Algiers had literally exploded. The marine battery fired a twenty-one-gun salute to mark the occasion, and then, Calder observed, America's colors were hoisted on board a vessel in the harbor. Having entered the enemy's fortress on a captured ship, the seaman, one could imagine, thrilled at the sight of his native standard. His elation was tempered, however, by the realization that it would be two more months before the prisoners could expect to "get our irons off." The dey would set no one free until he received the promised tribute. Calder nevertheless ended on an optimistic note. Next spring, he thought, all payments would be made, and "the American flag will be free in these seas."[8]

Back in the United States, reaction to the Algiers Treaty was divided along partisan lines. During Washington's second term foreign policy assumed center stage, and political factions hardened into something approaching political parties. Indeed, by the time Washington submitted the Algiers Treaty to the Senate for ratification on February 15, 1796, partisanship had come to characterize congressional debate. First, Jay's Treaty with Britain sparked bitter invective between Federalists, who supported the pact, and Democratic-Republicans, who opposed it. Jay's Treaty was intended to resolve all outstanding issues between the two countries. In addition to addressing the question of attacks against U.S. merchantmen, Jay had hoped to conclude a trade agreement that would open British markets to American merchants. Jay's Treaty set off a political firestorm that eclipsed the Algerine Treaty, which had arrived in the United States at the same time. Both political parties welcomed the settlement with Algiers, but the Federalists and Democratic-Republicans bitterly debated the terms of Jay's Treaty.

Federalists, including President Washington, hailed Jay's Treaty as a major diplomatic victory for the young nation, noting that it settled such long-standing issues as the payment of pre–Revolutionary War debts and the removal of British forts on American soil. Led by Jefferson and Madison, Republicans denounced Jay's efforts as a humiliating sellout. Nonetheless, the Federalists won ratification, though not without deepening partisan divisions in the country and damaging relations between the United States and France. Each side enjoyed the support of major figures: Washington, Hamilton, and Adams for the Federalists; Jefferson and Madison for the Republicans. Dominating the Senate, Federalists succeeded in ratifying Jay's Treaty, but controlling the House, Republicans managed to wage a fierce battle over appropriating funds for enforcing the treaty's provisions. That battle raged anew when the Senate began deliberations on the treaty with Algiers.

Unlike the debate over Jay's Treaty, discussions of the Algerine Treaty occurred largely outside public scrutiny. Far more was at stake in the former treaty: besides persistent cultural ties between Americans and British, Britain's commercial potential for the United States dwarfed that of Algiers. But from the beginning of the negotiations with Algiers, Washington had urged Congress to maintain confidentiality, especially with respect to the amounts demanded for tribute and ransom, lest Tunis and Tripoli learn of them and demand equivalent amounts. Unfortunately, attempts at secrecy fueled partisan mistrust, and when the beys of Tunis and Tripoli inevitably learned of the settlement with Algiers, they not only demanded similar sums but threatened war. Despite the hardening of partisan lines and the saber-rattling beys, Washington greeted the ratification of the Algerine Treaty on March 6, 1796, with great relief. In his annual message to Congress, he applauded the "prudence and moderation" that had led to settlements with Great Britain, Spain, and Algiers, all being ratified in the span of a few months. They held, he declared, great promise for the "prosperity of our Country." Merchants from New York agreed, claiming that the agreements eliminated all the impediments that had plagued American shipping in the Atlantic world. The treaties, they claimed, were of the "greatest consequence to this young and rising country in affording a prospect of durable peace." The "uninterrupted progress" of the American Revolution, they declared, was now possible.[9]

One American in London agreed and interpreted the treaties as an important milestone in America's becoming "a really and completely independent people." Britain's encouragement of the Barbary pirates was, the writer argued, an attempt to perpetuate the "restrictive system" of commerce that had circumscribed American trade during the colonial period. Furthermore, he opined, Britain and Europe had attempted to continue America's commercial and political dependence "from the time of peace to this day."[10] But now the Barbary treaties represented a step, albeit small, in the completion of America's War of Independence.

Also writing from London, John Quincy Adams viewed the treaties as a vindication of his father's preference for negotiations over war. He was certain that had the United States heeded Jefferson's wishes, Americans would have gone to war and forgone all the advantages of a peaceful settlement. Nevertheless, he struck a cautionary note. Appointed minister to the Netherlands at age twenty-seven, Adams was an astute observer of political realities in the Atlantic world, which curbed his enthusiasm for the Algiers Treaty. "I suspect the Algerine peace is to be abused," he wrote. European officials had repeatedly warned him that pacts with the Algerines unraveled time and again. A coup, or the death of the dey, or the appointment of a new consul, or a real or fabricated violation of a treaty provision, could provide the pretext for new corsair raids on a tributary's shipping. Adams also thought that the United States had paid too high a price; peace, he was certain, could have been had "upon infinitely better terms."[11]

Confident that the Algiers Treaty meant peace, Congress moved quickly to disarm. Indeed, when it passed the act providing for a naval armament in 1794, it had appended a clause stating, "if a peace shall take place between the United States and the Regency of Algiers, that no further proceedings be had under this act." On March 15, 1796, Washington invoked that clause. Due only to fears of economic dislocation, including widespread unemployment among shipbuilders, Congress approved on April 20 a supplemental act authorizing the completion of two of the forty-four-gun frigates, the *United States* at Philadelphia and the *Constitution* at Boston, and one thirty-six-gun ship, the *Constellation* at Baltimore.[12] The result of pork-barrel politics, the projected three-ship navy would hardly be sufficient to force the Barbary States to honor American shipping in the Mediterranean.

Motivated by their aversion to debt, Republicans led the fight to reduce military expenditures. Expensive government, in their view, was the first link in a chain that eventuated in the loss of liberty: a big budget led to a national debt; mounting debt necessitated higher taxes; higher tax bills threatened individuals' property, in some cases causing landowners to sell parcels to pay their taxes; property was the basis of political independence; and the loss of independence meant the loss of liberty. Republicans had followed the same logic in resisting British tyranny before 1776, and now they were determined that the U.S. government would not burden its citizens with unnecessary debt, even in the name of national defense.

American confidence in the Algiers Treaty as a means of peace, however, proved misplaced. To Dey Hassan, the treaty was in force only when the presents and tribute arrived at Algiers. In spring of 1796, more than six months after the signing of the treaty in the fall of 1795, Hassan failed to receive the balance of the $600,000 promised at signing; he threatened to resume the war. On April 3 he announced that if the "money did not come, he never would be at peace with the Americans." Taking the threat seriously, U.S. diplomats warned American merchants that "the safety of American vessels entering the Mediterranean has become extremely precarious."[13]

While Dey Hassan threatened, the American prisoners remained in irons. The U.S. government was proving unable to assemble the cash and marine goods required by the terms of the treaty. To secure the prisoners' release and to win the right of free navigation, the Americans had agreed to pay what chief negotiator Joel Barlow called "extravagant sums of money."[14] According to the secretary of the treasury, Oliver Wolcott, the Algerine settlement totaled almost $1 million, or about 16 percent of the federal revenue for 1795.[15] Congress decided to borrow the money from the Bank of the United States and deposit the interest-bearing notes in London for remittance to Algiers. But because of America's shaky credit, the bonds depreciated, and the amount available fell short of what was needed. Further, much of the tribute was to be in the form of naval stores and military goods, which had to be procured or manufactured, assembled for transport, and shipped to Algiers. Without a naval escort, getting the gifts safely to the dey proved difficult. Eighteen months would pass from the time Samuel Calder viewed the thrilling celebration to the moment when he and the other captive Americans arrived in the United States. Indeed the wait proved fatal for three prisoners: Nicholas Hartford, Abraham Simmonds, and Joseph Keith succumbed to the plague that swept through Barbary in the summer of 1796.[16]

Ironically, Americans salvaged the peace treaty and won the release of the prisoners by agreeing to augment the dey's corsair fleet. Through an intermediary, a Jewish broker named Baccri who was trusted by Hassan, the American negotiators made one last attempt to salvage the peace. They offered him a new American-made ship with twenty-four guns on condition that he wait six months longer for his money. After insisting that the frigate be armed with thirty-six guns, Hassan agreed. The peace was saved, at least for the moment.[17]

The fact that the United States was building warships for the dey of Algiers repulsed George Washington. With the brig and two schooners, promised at the treaty's signing, and the new copper-bottomed thirty-six-gun frigate, the United States was now building and arming four warships for the Algerine pirates. In a 1796 letter to Secretary of War James McHenry, Washington said that he had found the provision "disagreeable" when he first read it and "more so in the compliance with it." Nevertheless, "there appeared no other alternative," he wrote, "but to comply, or submit to the depredations of the Barbary Corsairs on our Citizens, and Commerce." Paying tribute, even in the form of warships, was "preferred."[18] Having determined to carry out the terms of the Algiers Treaty, Washington brooked no delays by subordinates who disagreed with the policy. For the president, the debate was over, and the administration would fulfill the treaty provisions, no matter how distasteful.[19]

At the end of 1797, more than two years after the agreement was reached, the United States finally assembled the tribute and presents. Secretary of State Timothy Pickering instructed O'Brien, now U.S. consul to Algiers, to apologize to Dey Hassan for the long delay.

The causes of delay underscored the United States' weak position in the Atlantic world. As early as 1793 the naval stores and other forms of tribute had been ready to ship, but both France and Britain, at war with each other, had impeded American shipping. Further, the U.S. government, "loaded with heavy debts in the war for their Independence," was strapped for cash. It was hard pressed to procure the cannons and build the warships promised in the treaty. Even nature conspired against America's paying tribute. An outbreak of yellow fever in Philadelphia and elsewhere interrupted the building and outfitting of the frigate *Crescent*, the brig *Hassan Bashaw*, and the schooners *Hamdullah* and *Skjoldibrand*. O'Brien assured the dey that the quality of the ships would justify the wait.[20] When the *Crescent* and the *Hamdullah* arrived in Algiers in February 1798, O'Brien reported that the dey went from being "somewhat dissatisfied" with U.S. compliance to being "well pleased."[21] He was delighted with the workmanship of the American-made ships that would now join his raiding fleet.

Like Washington, Secretary of State Pickering found compliance with the Algiers Treaty distasteful. That a free and independent country would be forced to pay tribute to another country for the right to engage in trade was reprehensible. Further, he objected to tribute in the form of warships that the pirate fleet would simply deploy to intimidate future shipping. Pickering's more bellicose position found sympathy with the incoming administration of John Adams. The new president deemed paying tribute to the pirates an act of national humiliation and was determined to bring the practice to a halt.

As the Federalist candidate, John Adams was elected president in 1796 after a bitter campaign against the Republican Thomas Jefferson. Because of the constitutional provision that the two candidates receiving the greatest number of votes would become president and vice president, Jefferson became Adams's vice president. By 1796 the former friends who had worked together in Europe in the mid-1780s had become political antagonists. They and their respective parties had sharply different views of the world and the United States' place in it. Reflecting his New England heritage, Adams imagined America as a great commercial power, and he advocated a trade policy that would enable the country to compete under the prevailing mercantilist ideas of the Atlantic world. As a Virginian, Jefferson favored free trade that would enable planters to ship their goods to world markets on an equal basis with other countries. Despite their differences, Adams and Jefferson now agreed that the United States should no longer be a tributary to the Barbary States.

Adams's policy toward the Barbary powers resulted in no small part from intelligence provided by Joel Barlow. As U.S. agent to Algiers, he had become America's lead negotiator in February 1796, replacing Joseph Donaldson, whom Washington had appointed in June 1795 but who had fallen ill shortly thereafter. After Barlow signed the final Algerine accord, he sailed to Tripoli to negotiate another peace treaty. An astute political observer, he wrote dispatches that, even if infrequently heeded, proved to be America's most clear-eyed reports on Barbary affairs. In the midst of Senate deliberations on the Algiers Treaty, for example, he warned Congress that the Barbary pirates regarded treaties very differently than Americans did. He explained that the dey and his officers lived off the peace presents received from tributaries and that annual tribute payments went into the public treasury. Such an arrangement meant that it was in the pirates' interest to "break friendship with every nation as often as possible" in order to receive further rounds of presents. Permitting a nation to enjoy peace under a new treaty just "long enough to feel the advantage of a free navigation in these seas," they would then capture that nation's vessels and demand new peace offerings. Only France and Britain, "whose great Naval strength Over Awes" the pirates, were exempt from this treatment.[22]

In March 1796 Barlow advised Secretary of State Pickering that Algiers was in the process of launching raids against countries with which it had treaties. The corsairs were currently targeting Denmark, he reported, after which they would probably go after Venice or Sweden, most likely to be followed by attacks on Spain. After Algiers had thereby gained new presents and ransom money, "our turn will be the next." Unfortunately for the United States, the dey now considered the nation to be much richer than it had been in 1785, when the first two ships were captured. Initially regarded as being of "very little consequence," with a Mediterranean trade so light that it could not afford to pay much tribute, America was now perceived as a rapidly growing commercial nation and thus a more attractive target for piratical raids.[23]

To forestall the capture of American merchant ships, Richard O'Brien sought in 1796 to secure treaties with the remaining two Barbary States, Tunis and Tripoli. American hopes rose when Hassan offered to guarantee a peace with Tunis and Tripoli. After Algiers, the most difficult Barbary State to deal with was Tripoli. Led by the independent-minded Yusuf Karamanli, who in 1795 had toppled his predecessor in a bloody coup, Tripoli was determined to rebuild its navy into a force that would be feared in the Mediterranean. Yusuf, the bashaw of Tripoli, had no intention of bowing to pressures from Algiers or anywhere else.

Taking over a country whose economy was in shambles, Yusuf knew that his hold on power depended upon reversing the economic deterioration. To do that, he turned to the navy. European merchant ships taken as prizes represented far more wealth than the meager trade that the regency had been able to generate, and consequently Yusuf was committed to rebuilding the pirate fleet. Just like the dey of Algiers, Yusuf viewed treaties not as inviolate compacts between parties who honored their terms but as instruments for extracting ever-greater tribute. After demanding a lump sum for agreeing to a peace, he would insist on annual tribute to maintain amity. Then, upon any regime change in the treating nation, he would expect additional consular presents. At every real or contrived violation of the agreement, Yusuf would unleash his pirates to take the signatory's ships as new prizes, which became the occasion for a new round of negotiations, tribute, ransom, and presents.[24]

Preparing to raid Mediterranean commerce more aggressively, Yusuf rebuilt the Tripolitan navy and mended fortifications at the main base of Tripoli. Alarmed resident European consuls fully expected his fleet of eleven warships to begin raids against their countries' merchant vessels. Like the Algerine navy, the Tripolitan force consisted of a corsair squadron, each vessel of which was commanded by a reis, or captain, who reported to an admiral, who in turn reported to the marine commander, the highest naval office. The officers came from a variety of backgrounds. Most were Arabs or Berbers, some were Turkish mercenaries, and a few were European renegades.[25]

After rebuilding his navy, Yusuf wasted no time putting it to use. First, through the resident consuls, he called on the European powers to "re-establish proper treaty relationships with Tripoli by forwarding the traditional 'consular presents.' " Spain was first to pay, remitting $20,000 along with a navy vessel and eighteen artisans for the Tripolitan shipyards. Venice confirmed its existing treaty with a payment of $6,000. France gave $10,000 and, upon seeing Yusuf's displeasure, added two ships of twenty and sixteen guns respectively. Powers that resisted Yusuf's demands—including Sweden, Denmark, Holland, and Naples—were attacked by Tripoli's fleet. Captures of Swedish and Danish vessels yielded the bashaw a revenue of $12,000 and convinced the Scandinavian countries that they should negotiate. In the end, each paid the bashaw a sum of $100,000 for restoration of their captured vessels and for ransom of their sailors. To prevent future captures, the Swedes and Danes each paid an annual tribute of $5,000 to Tripoli.[26]

The first Tripolitan capture of American vessels occurred in 1796. With no treaty protecting ships against privateers and no navy to escort its merchantmen, the United States was an obvious target. Thus in August Admiral Murad Reis captured the *Sophia* and the *Betsy*. He released the *Sophia* because it carried treaty money that the United States owed the dey of Algiers, but he converted the *Betsy* into a corsair to be used in future raids. The crew was enslaved.

Like most of the European powers, the United States decided to negotiate a peace treaty to protect its commerce in the Mediterranean and to gain release of the American crewmen. The Americans gained the dey of Algiers's good offices in working out a similar pact with Yusuf, and at the opening round of talks in November 1796, Richard O'Brien offered $40,000 for peace and ransom. Insulted by a figure far below the nearly $1 million that the Americans had paid Algiers and the $180,000 they offered Tunis, the bashaw rejected the offer. But later in the month, under considerable pressure from the dey of Algiers, he agreed to a peace treaty for the "sum of $40,000, together with 'consular presents' of $12,000 cash and some naval stores—canvas, pitch, boards, etc."[27]

Tunis was the last of the four Barbary States to come to terms with the United States. On June 15, 1796, Joel Barlow received a copy of a six-month truce; sent by a French merchant in Tunis, Joseph Étienne Famin, the document declared the Tunisian bey's desire to conclude a peace treaty with the United States, stipulated the terms, and demanded an answer within six months, during which time Tunisian corsairs would not prey on American vessels. The implied threat was clear: if the United States did not meet his demands, the bey of Tunis, Pasha Hamouda, would withdraw that security and allow his privateers to take new prizes. Signing the truce as "commander . . . of the frontier post of the Holy War," Hamouda implied that Americans faced not only a tiny North African regency but the full might of the Islamic world.[28]

Desiring peace with all the Barbary powers, the United States accepted the bey's terms on August 28, 1797. While insisting on revising the text to guarantee reciprocity of trade relations between the two countries, the Senate ratified the treaty. The settlement cost the United States almost $180,000, far less than that with Algiers but no less humiliating a sum. Like the dey of Algiers, the bey of Tunis demanded that tribute be paid in naval stores and an American-built brig—again, instruments of war that threatened the peace and security of American merchantmen in the Mediterranean. The bill of particulars for items sent to Tunis included forty cannons, twelve thousand cannonballs, and three hundred quintals (more than three tons) of powder.[29]

In ratification hearings, senators were more concerned about trade reciprocity than about the details of tribute. Clearly the parties had different objectives in signing the agreement. The United States wished to secure trade in the Mediterranean while the Tunisians sought to strengthen their ability to raid future shipping.

With the Tunisian treaty, U.S. vessels finally sailed in peace throughout the Mediterranean, from the Strait of Gibraltar to the Bosporus. Thirteen years after Congress had instructed Franklin, Adams, and Jefferson to negotiate peace treaties with the four Barbary powers, the mission was accomplished. The cost was high. In monetary terms, the treaties totaled about $1.25 million, or a little over 20 percent of the federal government's annual budget. In human costs, the enslavement of Americans—some for more than ten years—had been difficult to endure. Mocking the freedom and independence that Americans had expected following victory over the British, the prisoners had languished in Algiers as slaves.

Americans put the best face possible on the peace accords. Rufus King pronounced American affairs in the Mediterranean "settled or nearly so" after the Tripoli Treaty. He was particularly pleased to point out that the United States stood "well with Algiers," though the fact that the man who had taken a dozen American ships and enslaved a hundred American citizens was now advancing the nation's pursuit of peace with two other Barbary States struck King as a "strange event."[30] President John Adams also found the dey's attitude toward the United States odd. After the Algerine Treaty went into effect, the dey ordered yet two more American-built frigates, "constructed and equipped . . . with guns and all other requirements complete." Adams knew that some congressmen would balk at providing the most aggressive of the Barbary States with arms that would make it even deadlier, but the president argued that compliance was actually in America's interest. To Adams, Algiers had become the guarantor of peace in the Mediterranean and, in securing treaties with Tunis and Tripoli, America's advocate. He reasoned that if the United States accommodated the dey, American merchantmen could trade freely in the region. Long an advocate of buying peace rather than fighting the pirates, Adams believed that a robust American Mediterranean trade would more than justify the price of peace. Therefore, he concluded, the United States was under a "peculiar obligation" to fill the dey's orders for the frigates.[31]

To help maintain the peace, the United States appointed consuls to reside in the capitals of the Barbary States. Richard O'Brien continued as America's consul general at Algiers, with "superintending power" over the consulates at Tunis and Tripoli. James Leander Cathcart, many years prisoner at Algiers and for a time the dey's head Christian clerk, became the consul at Tripoli, while William Eaton, a U.S. Army captain, headed the consulate at Tunis. With resident consuls, Americans would oversee their own affairs in Barbary, no longer dependent on European diplomats whose interests often conflicted with those of the United States.

But instead of ushering in a period of peace and prosperity, the five years after making peace with Algiers marked the nadir of American relations with the Barbary pirates. Not only did Algiers make further demands, upon threat of capturing additional American vessels, but Tripoli and Tunis looked for any excuse to raid American ships. Not coincidentally, the Barbary threats occurred in the late 1790s, when the modest U.S. naval program was unavailable for missions against the Barbary States. Because of growing British and French hostilities against American shipping, the administration was forced to deploy its new navy, not against the Barbary pirates for which it was built, but against the French in what has become known as the Quasi-War. The new republic did not have the resources to fight two wars simultaneously, and thus the pirates could subject the American flag to the basest treatment with impunity.

The French Revolution had set in motion a chain of events that once again led to war between the French and the British, including a naval war waged in both the Atlantic and the Mediterranean. John Adams continued George Washington's policy of neutrality. For the United States, the conflict, which commenced during Washington's second administration, put commercial shipping at risk. When Washington proclaimed American neutrality in 1793, he hoped to continue shipping nonmilitary goods to both parties. Neither of the two European powers, however, recognized American neutrality, and both issued orders to their respective navies to intercept all commercial vessels sailing to enemy ports. Consequently, American ships in the Atlantic faced attacks from British and French privateers and warships in much the same way that they confronted attacks from Barbary corsairs in the Mediterranean. The difference was magnitude: the French captured more than three hundred American vessels, while the Barbary States took fewer than thirty.

From the perspective of revolutionary France, Jay's Treaty was a betrayal. Not only had America concluded a treaty with France's enemy without consultation, but it had also failed in its obligations under a 1778 treaty to fight alongside the French. Further, the United States violated the 1778 treaty when it reached an agreement with Algiers without consulting France.

As a result of these real and perceived offenses, revolutionary France increased its seizures of American ships. When in December 1796 the United States sent Charles Cotesworth Pinckney to Paris as the new American minister, the French refused to receive him. As tensions mounted between the two countries, the United States turned once again to the question of protecting American commerce with a naval force. In December 1796, as President Washington drafted his final annual address to Congress, he turned to the question of diplomacy and naval power in a letter to Alexander Hamilton. He thought that commerce in the Mediterranean "will always be a precarious establishment unless a protecting force is given to it." He conceded the Republican point that a navy was costly, especially given the "present uncertain state of our Fiscal concerns." Nonetheless, he strongly advocated the commencement of a navy. Hamilton concurred, and Washington repeated his views in his message to Congress. He cited the treaties with Britain, Spain, and Algiers as the basis of a lasting peace, but seeing war clouds on the horizon, he urged Congress to safeguard America's trade interests with the "gradual creation" of a "moderate Naval force."[32] When Congress began debating the question, the old divisions surfaced. A Federalist-led Congress and pork-barrel politics managed to authorize the president to deploy three frigates. Consequently, on May 10, 1797, the frigate *United States* was launched at Philadelphia, followed on September 7 by the *Constellation* at Baltimore and on October 21 by the *Constitution* at Boston.

In his annual message to Congress at the close of 1797, incoming president and Federalist John Adams reported on France's refusal to negotiate and spoke of the need "to place our country in a suitable posture of defense." In February 1798 Adams provided Congress with details of French depredations in U.S. waters. He had learned of "several captures and outrages" committed within the territory of the United States. On one occasion, the crew of a French privateer called the *Vertitude* "first plundered and then burned, with the rest of her cargo, [a ship] of great value, within the territory of the United States, in the harbor of Charleston, on the

17th day of October last." In April President Adams informed
Congress of the infamous XYZ Affair, in which French agents
demanded a large bribe for the restoration of relations with the
United States. Then, in words that echoed those voiced in 1794 by
advocates of a naval force to subdue the Barbary powers, Adams
wrote, "The naval establishment must occur to every man who
considers the injuries committed on our commerce, the insults offered to our citizens, and the description of vessels by which these
abuses have been practiced."[33]

The XYZ Affair outraged Congress as an affront to national
honor. France and the United States had been allies during the
American War of Independence and were signatories to a treaty
that pledged mutual respect and assistance. Now the French were
demanding tribute, treating Americans no better than the Barbary
pirates did. Congress reacted to the insult by passing two retalia-
tory measures. The first was economic: they suspended all trade
between the United States and France, including the French West
Indies. Later, Adams lifted the prohibition of trade to St. Domingo,
where a slave revolt was in the process of removing French rule.
The second was an act of war: Congress authorized the defense of
merchant vessels against "French Depredations." Specifically,
armed merchant ships could repel by force any assault by a French
ship, and the American privateers could pursue, subdue, and capture the attacker.[34]

On April 27 Congress passed an appropriations bill authorizing the purchase or construction of up to twelve warships, each
with no more than twenty-two guns. To expedite the building
of a viable naval force, several merchant vessels were purchased
and converted into fighting ships, and one of these, the *Ganges*, a
Philadelphia-built merchantman, was fitted out and put to sea less
than thirty days later. By the end of 1798 the United States could
boast of having twelve ships in service: six built, including the three
frigates begun in 1794 to combat the Algerines, and six merchant
vessels purchased and retrofitted. Another fourteen warships were
in various stages of construction. In addition, Congress authorized

the construction of America's first ships of the line, seventy-four-gun ships that would match the firepower of the most powerful European warships. Sailors and officers numbered about four thousand, and that number grew rapidly as new vessels came into service.[35]

To manage naval affairs, on April 30 Congress created a Department of Navy, and Benjamin Stoddert, a Maryland merchant who had served during the Revolution as secretary of the Board of War, was named secretary. Congress set the navy's annual budget at $950,000, almost the exact amount of tribute and ransom that the United States had paid to Algiers in 1795. While the United States spent "millions for defense but not a cent for tribute" in the Atlantic, it spent not a cent for defense but millions for tribute in the Mediterranean.

On July 7, 1798, Congress all but declared war on France: the lawmakers passed "An Act to Declare the Treaties Heretofore Concluded with France, no Longer Obligatory on the United States."[36] With that measure, Congress declared that America's ten-year alliance with France was over.

In the winter of 1798, America's naval might paid off. A fleet of fourteen warships supplemented by about two hundred armed merchant vessels captured more than eighty French ships and drove France's warships from American waters. The young navy had proven itself, a development followed with great interest by Americans on the Barbary Coast. As the United States flexed its naval muscle in the Atlantic, American consuls in the Barbary States pleaded for a show of force against the pirates who continued to raid ships and extort tribute.

On July 18, 1799, William Eaton, the U.S. consul to Tunis, asked William Smith, the American minister at Lisbon, for assistance in obtaining a naval force in the Mediterranean. Eaton believed that the ever-increasing demands of the bey of Tunis considerably weakened America financially. He calculated expenditures to Tunis at more than $100,000 and estimated that they would reach $200,000 if the United States met the bey's "stipulated regalia and extraordinary demands." He added that American interests were equally vulnerable to ongoing threats from Algiers, whose emissaries intimated that the dey wanted the United States to give him one of the seventy-four-gun ships of the line authorized by Congress in 1798 as restitution for American violations of the peace treaty.[37]

But the only warships sailing to the Barbary Coast from the United States in the late 1790s were the corsairs built for the pirates as part of America's tribute. The brig *Hassan Bashaw* sailed through the Strait of Gibraltar in early 1799, not to attack the Barbary pirates but to satisfy their appetite for American-built ships of war. Further, the vessel was laden with cargo, most of which consisted of naval stores and armaments that the pirates would put to use against American merchantmen.

Indeed, the Barbary pirates were exacting ever-greater sums of tribute from the new republic. On February 23, 1799, Secretary of State Timothy Pickering sent the chairman of the Ways and Means Committee an estimate of amounts needed to satisfy Barbary demands for the year. The United States owed Algiers more than $140,000 in tribute, and that was after the cost of the three warships had been deducted. In addition, Congress needed to appropriate $150,000 to satisfy the demands of Tunis and Tripoli.[38] Americans who had hoped that negotiating with the Barbary pirates was less costly than fighting them were beginning to have second thoughts.

By 1800 John Quincy Adams questioned the wisdom of his father's preference for treating with Algiers. First, the younger Adams repeated his skepticism of a lasting negotiated settlement with the Algerine pirates. "All the security which our navigation can enjoy in the Mediterranean by virtue of any treaty with the Barbary Powers," he wrote, "must be precarious." Second, the cost of the treaty, high to begin with, had escalated. Adams claimed that America had "submitted to an expense so much more considerable than had ever before been applied to that purpose by any European power."[39] Such a costly treaty not only made the United States vulnerable to new, more exorbitant demands by the Barbary pirates, but also exposed the new republic to the ridicule of Europeans who viewed American diplomacy as naïve and incompetent.

Adams's prediction that the Barbary pirates would extort additional sums from the United States soon came true. In 1800, at about the time Adams expressed his fears, Captain William Bainbridge of the United States sailed the frigate *George Washington* into Algiers laden with American presents. After receiving the gifts, the dey then ordered Bainbridge to reload his vessel with tribute goods that Algiers owed the Ottoman sultan at the Grand Porte and transport them to Constantinople under the Algerine flag. Bainbridge found it humiliating that an American warship was ordered to do the dey's bidding and briefly considered refusing. He bristled at the thought of being ordered by a foreign power to carry out a mission very likely at odds with American interests. But as Richard O'Brien informed the captain, the United States was hardly in a position to defy the dey. America was after all at least one and a half years in arrears to Algiers. In addition, a recent peace treaty between Algiers and Portugal meant that the United States could no longer expect protection from the Portuguese against pirate attacks. America faced Algiers alone.[40] Recognizing that he was outgunned in the Algerine port, Bainbridge agreed to the dey's demand after lodging a strongly worded protest. He described the degrading flag-changing ceremony: "the Minister of Marine, came on board with his admiral, and several Algerine captains, who went into the main-top, and hauled down the American pennant, and hoisted the Algerine mission flag."[41]

Once again Americans read newspaper accounts of the Barbary pirates making a mockery of U.S. sovereignty and independence. Bainbridge's account of the transfer of the *George Washington* to Algerine service appeared in American newspapers within months of the incident. Readers followed the painful transformation of Bainbridge from the proud commander of an American warship to the humiliated agent of the dey of Algiers. Bainbridge tried to explain to his fellow countrymen the dilemma he faced. "Bound by the orders of my government on one hand," he explained, and "viewing the loss of property & slavery of our Citizens on the other" left him with a "delemma, that none can express but those who feels it." He then gave his reply: "I cannot accede to this demand voluntarily." Implying that he would reluctantly obey an official request, he closed by stating his view of the matter: "Sir I cannot help observing that the event of this day makes me ponder on the words INDEPENDENT UNITED STATES."[42]

Outgunned by the Algerine navy and under the shadows of the harbor's shore emplacements, Bainbridge had watched his ship fall under control of persons he considered barbarians and pirates. Summing up America's servile stance in Algiers, he wrote, "The light that this Regency looks on the United States is exactly this: you pay me tribute, by that you become my slaves, and then I have a right to order as I please." As he viewed the matter, and as he wrote the secretary of the navy, the United States had "no alternative but compliance or war." He opted for the latter, arguing, "had we 10 or 12 frigates and sloops in those seas, I am well convinced in my own mind that we should not experience those mortifying degradations that must be cutting to every American who possesses an independent spirit."[43]

Six months after Bainbridge stood by as the American flag was replaced by the Algerine banner, James Cathcart, consul to Tripoli, witnessed another humiliation to the Stars and Stripes. When the United States rejected the bashaw of Tripoli's demands for additional tribute, Yusuf Karamanli ordered that the flagstaff outside the American consulate be chopped down and Cathcart expelled.[44] Cathcart explained the American position and the bashaw's response in a "VERY IMPORTANT CIRCULAR" that appeared first as a letter to his fellow consuls in the region and then as a reprint in American newspapers. In it, Cathcart informed his fellow consuls that he had repelled "certain unjust demands" made by the bashaw of Tripoli, but in consequence the bashaw had publicly announced "that he would declare War against the United States of America in six months to commence from the 22d day of October

1800, if his demands were not complied with." Cathcart noted that the bashaw's recent treaty with Sweden exacted $250,000 "for peace and the ransom of their captives" plus $20,000 in annual tribute, adding that the Tripolitans expected a similar agreement with the United States, notwithstanding the treaty already in force.[45]

American newspaper readers learned from Richard O'Brien, consul at Algiers, that the problem was grave and went beyond Tripoli. Through a letter to the American consul at Málaga, Spain, he informed American merchants that "the Tripolitans have demanded a large sum of money of the Swedes, as the price of peace, and it was expected they would demand the same of the United States." He feared that the problem went beyond Tripoli, indicating "there will be a rupture very shortly with Tunis." O'Brien closed by asking all consuls in the Mediterranean "to give the alarm to the Americans" sailing in the region and suggesting that "some ships of war would be of service" in combating the threats.[46]

From Tunis, William Eaton tried to explain to the Adams administration what was at stake. Under protection of the treaties with the Barbary powers, American trade had flourished. Indeed, Eaton claimed, "the commerce of the United States in the Mediterranean . . . is nearly equal to that of all other carrying nations." Now that profitable trade was threatened by a "predatory war from these licensed pirates." The United States, he hoped, would use all means necessary to stop the piratical depredations. He could not refrain from noting that the Americans' first display of naval power in the Mediterranean hardly awed the Barbary pirates. Referring to the Algerines' transforming *George Washington* into a cargo vessel for the purpose of transporting tribute to Constantinople, Eaton saw both irony and humiliation in the fact that the "first United States ship of war which ever entered the Mediterranean should be pressed into the service of a pirate."[47]

In early spring 1801 the Barbary pirates stepped up their provocation, and Americans began reading ever more ominous reports from the Mediterranean. Although the United States had negotiated a peace treaty with each of the Barbary powers, the Barbary pirates and their political overlords were growing bellicose. All of them demanded that America make immediate and full payment of all tribute due, including that in arrears. In Algiers's case, the United States was eighteen months behind in meeting treaty terms, and the dey now demanded full payment. Complicating the situation in Barbary, interstate jealousy prompted demands for even greater tribute. In particular, Tripoli disliked the fact that it received less than Algiers, and the bashaw was determined to win equity, by force, if necessary.

It took the humiliation of the *George Washington*, treaty violations from Algiers, Tunis, and Tripoli, and a formal declaration of war from Tripoli to finally stir America to action. Newly elected president Thomas Jefferson and his secretary of state, James Madison, had long agreed with Bainbridge and the consuls that force was necessary for American independence in the Mediterranean. But constrained by their own republican sensibilities regarding a standing army and navy and restricted by their desire to reduce federal expenditures, they had maintained a wait-and-see attitude. After Tripoli declared war, their tone changed.

FOUR

THE CULTURAL CONSTRUCTION OF
THE BARBARY PIRATES

Throughout the lengthy negotiations with the Barbary States, Americans tried to make sense of the enemy by exploring the cultural divide separating the United States and the Barbary powers. In what was hardly a fair, detached analysis of a distant people, they depicted a fierce enemy whose history and culture stood in sharp contrast to that of irenic Americans. In the background of this chauvinistic portrait were European stereotypes of Arabs, Moors, and Muslims: Barbarian descendants of sword-wielding marauders who emerged from the Arabian Desert in the seventh century, raced across North Africa, and invaded Europe. In the foreground were American perceptions of Barbary pirates formed from recent events: corsairs raiding legitimate shipping and enslaving innocent people. Such a portrayal stood out in bold relief against a self-image of virtuous republicans who fully embraced the ideals of the Declaration of Independence.

Artists, journalists, historians, playwrights, and poets developed several dyads in painting the Barbarians in dark and Americans in bright hues. The first was piracy and trade. To American audiences, the enemy was a band of lawless pirates who took what they wished from passing ships in ruthless attacks. Americans needed little prompting to understand these sinister characters because they knew about similar villains closer to home, namely fierce Caribbean buccaneers who showed no regard for human and property rights. By contrast, Americans saw themselves as champions of free trade, not just for themselves but for people everywhere. No person or nation, from a pirate to the British Empire, had the right to interfere with the free exchange of goods. A second contrasting pair was tyranny and freedom. In depicting Barbarians, American writers characterized the ruling beys and deys as absolute rulers who gained power through bloody coups and wielded it through intimidation. Similar to European monarchs who oppressed their people, Barbary strongmen brooked no dissent, and their subjects submitted to tyranny with a fatalistic resignation. On the other hand, as they had repeatedly said to themselves and the world before 1776, Americans were a people who would rather die as free men and women than live under slavery and tyranny. After winning independence from Britain, Americans devised a constitution that placed sovereignty in the hands of the people, a bold claim that ultimate power lay with the governed, not the government. A third coupling was Islam and Christianity. The focus was less on theological differences than on the kind of society that each fostered. To Americans, Muslim submissiveness allowed tyrants to flourish while Christian, especially Protestant, dissent challenged every infringement of the individual's freedom of conscience.

To put these contrasts in their sharpest relief, the plays, paintings, poems, and narratives dealing with the Barbary States singled out the most despicable pirate behavior and compared it with the loftiest American ideals. For American readers and audiences, little was left to the imagination: the United States was locked in a struggle of liberty versus tyranny and good versus evil.

Fundamental to all historical and cultural analyses was the condemnation of the Barbarians as pirates. From there Americans tried to explain these "outlaws," puzzling over why the Barbary States in the first place chose piracy over legitimate trade. The answer that confronted Americans was dark and sinister: Barbarians simply operated outside the cultural norms of civilized society. Further, Americans regarded states that supported pirates and provided them safe haven, including Algiers, Tunis, and Tripoli, as "piratical states," thereby rejecting the British view that the corsairs were privateers operating under commissions issued by legitimate states during time of war. In cultural terms, they viewed those states as rogue entities that sponsored sea robbery. Third, Americans came to see that piratical states were anything but democratic republics; rather, from the perspective of U.S. citizens, the deys and beys of Barbary were tyrants. Not only did they sanction violence against foreign subjects; they subjected their people to unimaginable cruelties. Struggling to understand why people would live under oppressive regimes, Americans pointed to Islam and deduced that submissiveness to Allah resulted in a willingness to follow tyrants.

Americans defined pirates as felons who committed "robbery or other acts of violence on the seas . . . without having any authority from, and independently of, any organized government."[1] They were renegades who refused to submit to international conventions and acted on their own authority for private gain. The laws of nations, however, recognized pirates as privateers if they met certain conditions. Their government had to commission them to arm their vessels; and they only attacked ships against whom their government had declared war. During its War of Independence, for example, the United States relied heavily upon privateers to disrupt British supply ships. But the state withdrew its sanction of privateering as soon as the war ended.

In reality, each nation defined for itself who it considered a pirate. Though they condemned piracy against English shipping, Sir Walter Raleigh and Queen Elizabeth I regarded Francis Drake as an enterprising patriot when the daring mariner stole millions from Spanish galleons in the late sixteenth century. Raleigh said that the immense magnitude of Drake's theft elevated him to a status beyond that of pirate. He asked, "Did you ever knowe of any that were pyratts for millions? Only they that risk for small things are pyratts."[2] Two hundred years later, however, the English rejected the claims of rebellious American colonists who insisted that Captain John Paul Jones's daring raids against British warships in English waters made him a naval hero and not a pirate. Furthermore, the British and the Americans disagreed on the question of whether the Barbary corsairs were pirates. The English Parliament considered them privateers and even afforded them the same protection as British privateers who augmented His Majesty's Navy. Having suffered unprovoked attacks by the corsairs, Americans of course found this preposterous.

Indeed, it was particularly galling to Americans that European powers legitimized the piratical states and paid them tribute when they could have easily destroyed them. After Portugal, the U.S. ally, signed a truce with Algiers in 1793, Nathaniel Cutting reported his "mortification" upon seeing the "Pyratical Flag display'd in the Bay of Gibraltar." By its actions, Portugal had extended the range of Algiers and set its corsairs loose to "ravage the Commerce of America in the Atlantic."[3] To Americans, European states that harbored pirates were responsible for much of the spilled blood. It did not help that those same Europeans were enjoying lucrative trading relationships with the Barbary States that Americans could only envy.

The Morocco Treaty had given some Americans hope of converting the Barbary States into thriving commercial centers. Such optimism had emerged in the late 1780s, when American ships arrived at Moroccan ports and traded iron and specie for mules. Encouraged by that beginning, Americans longed to trade with Algiers and the other "piratical states." Moreover, they considered the $20,000 or $30,000 rendered to the dey of Algiers a small price to pay for gaining a new trading partner.[4]

Robert Montgomery, a merchant and U.S. agent at Alicante, tried to convince Algiers to convert from piracy to trade. In mid-1791 he wrote to Jefferson and asked for the opportunity to negotiate a peace agreement with Algiers. He intended to "make a tryal of peace" with Algiers and convince the dey to swap the pirate's tribute for the merchant's profit. But alas, the dey would have none of it and instead demanded immediate payment of tribute and ransom and threatened new corsair attacks if the United States did not immediately meet his demands. The rebuff not only revealed Montgomery's naïveté but also suggested that Americans in general misjudged the degree to which the Barbary States favored piracy as a legitimate, even justifiable, basis for their economies and cultures.

North Africans insisted that piracy be understood within its historical context. Americans and Europeans viewed the Spanish Reconquest as a legitimate reclamation of territory and sovereignty; the Moors saw it differently. They pointed out that a longer view of the struggle between the Moors and Spain reveals that the real pirates and kidnappers were Europeans. When Spain expelled Muslims from Iberia, that Christian power confiscated their property, denied the Barbary powers favorable trading terms, raided their territory, and enslaved their people. In a report to the American commissioners, Thomas Barclay, having heard the Moroccan version of the Reconquest, explained that Moroccans raided Spanish ships because of Spain's atrocities during the expulsion of Iberian Moors. On one occasion during the Reconquest, the Spanish had banished seven hundred thousand families and on another Ferdinand and Isabella had expelled seventeen thousand more. These acts, in the Moroccan telling, were piratical and justified any similar measures the Moors might take against the Spanish.[5]

American negotiators realized that each side brought to the bargaining table competing historical interpretations that complicated negotiations. How could merchants and pirates find common ground when they proceeded from different, even contrary, historical and cultural assumptions? Moreover, what confidence could American merchants have that pirates would even honor a peace accord? Europeans had long known that pirate treaties were observed mainly in the breach. While there might have been honor among thieves, there was none between thieves and their prey.

One common assumption that Americans and Barbarians brought to the table was the belief that political stability rested on economic prosperity. At the same time that the Washington administration was negotiating with Algiers, it put down a taxpayer revolt by struggling farmers on the American frontier. In 1794 Washington discovered how difficult it was to collect taxes from enterprising farmers who had turned their grain into whiskey to lower their shipping costs. That same year the dey of Algiers refused the American plea that he forgo piracy. He knew that if he did not adequately remunerate the captains and crews of the pirate ships and the janissaries who manned the fortifications, he faced the threat of a coup attempt. A lucrative pirating season, then, was a political necessity.

To Americans, piracy was more than a legal or economic issue; it also had cultural implications. They regarded the Barbary pirates as "barbarians." That ancient term had a double meaning in the late eighteenth century. In its customary usage, it referred to marauding bands of uncivilized Germanic hordes: the Vandals, Goths, Alemanni, and Visigoths who had destroyed the glorious Roman Empire. In its modern meaning, *barbarian* referred to the inhabitants of Barbary, whose very name conjured images of lawless men. John Adams referred to the Barbary States as a "nest of banditti," a metaphor that George Washington employed as well.[6]

In viewing the pirates as barbarians, Americans evoked dark images from antiquity that they reserved for their worst enemies. The term *barbarian* applied to anyone whose behavior was deemed unenlightened and was neither geographically specific nor entirely racially driven. Native Americans with their "savage" customs and "benighted" views were categorized as barbarians. Even western Europeans such as British general Charles Cornwallis, whose conduct Congress concluded was "disgraceful to the arms of any enlightened people," was considered a barbarian.[7] Ultimately those who behaved according to the principles of enlightened republicanism—a set of values best expressed, Americans believed, in the United States—were civilized, and those who continued to act under the tyranny of ruthless force were barbarian.

Americans regarded Ali Hassan as the supreme embodiment of Barbary tyranny. What they knew of him came primarily through the observations of prisoners like Richard O'Brien. O'Brien knew Hassan to be a volatile man, who displayed "Blustering Convulsions of Passions" in threatening consuls who did not accede to his wishes. He characterized Hassan as a hungry lion who, determined not to starve, would eat his friends if he could not catch his enemies. Hassan considered the Christian nations the primary source of his riches and vowed to extract all he could from them either through piracy or through extortion. O'Brien described Hassan in some detail because he knew that dealing with Algiers meant dealing with an individual, a strongman whose personality and whims were central to the outcome of negotiations.

While condemning Hassan as a tyrant, Mathew Carey, newspaper editor and author of a popular history of Algiers, also judged the Barbary States' European allies by their own standards and found that in many ways the Europeans, too, fell short. Carey compared the tyranny of the "founders of the piratical states" with that of the "conquerors of Mexico and Peru" and found no Barbary leader as tyrannical as the Holy Roman Emperor Charles V (1519–56), the "butcher of two or three millions of innocent people." Further, Carey said, "this tyrant consigned to the executioner, fifty or an hundred thousand of his protestant subjects in the Netherlands." Carey was eager that Americans should denounce tyrants equally, European Christians as well as North African Muslims. He objected to European histories that denounced the Barbary pirates for their "infamous trade" and "perfidious murther" but praised Charles V as an "illustrious" figure.[8] The United States, Carey reminded his American readers, must wage war against tyranny in all its manifestations.

The American view of the Barbary pirates changed over time. During the course of the 1790s, American officials both in the Mediterranean and in Philadelphia shifted their perspective from regarding the pirates as fierce, fearless predators who had defied European powers for centuries, to regarding them as undisciplined, insolent, and vulnerable defenders of a bankrupt way of life. European intelligence initially led U.S. emissaries to overestimate Barbary might, in large part because European powers wanted Americans to stay away from the Mediterranean trade. In addition,

Americans observed the repeated failures of European bombardments of Algiers and other Barbary ports and concluded that the
pirates possessed a military genius and an indomitable will to defend their homelands.

As they gained more firsthand knowledge, however, Americans
came to hold a different view. Reports from captives—and after
1795, consuls—portrayed the Barbary pirates as weak. In 1799
Joseph Ingraham, chargé d'affaires to Tripoli, provided a report on
Barbary defenses and the people who manned them. Algerines,
whom Europeans had long regarded as the most ferocious, were, in
Ingraham's view, an "undisciplined, half-starved" lot who had allowed the batteries at Algiers to degrade into a "ruined condition."
Ingraham saw little to fear from Algerine generals and leaders who
spent "day after day" smoking tobacco and playing chess while
their soldiers and citizens walked around in rags. He concluded,
"Such is the military, and such the industry of Barbary—Yet to the
shame of humanity they dictate terms to powerful nations!!!"[9]

In explaining the Algerines' torpor, Ingraham suggested a link
between religion and politics in Algiers. What struck him most
about the Muslims who acquiesced to the tyranny of the Barbary
rulers was their resignation to a mean existence. Rather than demand an equitable government that safeguarded individual rights
and promoted opportunity, Barbary citizens prayed "away their
lives under the shrines of departed saints."[10] Ingraham was far from
alone in seeing religion at the root of Barbary tyranny and vulnerability.

Although Americans did not believe that the Barbary Wars
were wars of religion, they did recognize that religion played an important role in how each side viewed the other. Americans organized their sharp distinctions between American Protestantism and
Barbary Islamism under three headings: first, individual religious
liberty; second, religion as an instrument of the state; and, third, religious posturing in negotiations between the United and Barbary
States. Rather than engaging in disputes over theology, these critics
judged the two religions by their fruits, especially the kind of soci-

ety each engendered. The contrast was not simply Christianity versus Islam; rather, Americans made religious freedom the fulcrum of comparison. Their starting point was the recent religious settlement reached in the U.S. Constitution: the prohibition of a state church and the guarantee of free religious exercise to all. Using that model of unfettered religious freedom, Americans condemned all religious coercion, whether practiced by Britain and the Church of England or by Spain and the Roman Catholic Church or by the Barbary States and Islam.

No two men were more deeply involved in the Barbary Wars than John Adams and Thomas Jefferson, and both had also been instrumental in the fight for religious freedom in the United States. Adams had drawn a sharp distinction between church-state relations in the Old and New Worlds. In Old World Europe, he contended, both church and state enjoyed unchecked power, "encroaching, grasping, restless, and ungovernable power."[11] The United States, once freed from Britain's ecclesiastical as well as civil oppression in 1783, determined that no similar church-state tyranny would take root in the new republic. In America, the rule of law would prevail. The result, Adams would argue, was American Protestantism, characterized by toleration, compared to Spanish Catholicism or Algerine Islam, marked by tyranny. Indeed, in their struggle against Britain, Americans had denounced ecclesiastical as well as civil oppression.

Regarding religion as a natural right, Thomas Jefferson had led the fight in Virginia for complete religious freedom. The individual, not the state, he argued, should decide religious matters. Further, he advocated a free marketplace of religion wherein all sects were free to make their competing claims, and he believed that, if given free play, reason would winnow truth from superstition and speciousness.[12]

Adams's and Jefferson's views prevailed primarily because the United States was a pluralistic society comprising scores of voluntary sects jealously defending their own rights. Each defined its own beliefs and practices, and none was willing to submit to a

state-mandated religion, even if it were characterized as "Christian." While Americans disagreed among themselves over religious
teachings and practices, they were united in their desire for the free
exercise of religion. Invoking what some would later call America's
"civil religion," Americans viewed religious liberty and toleration
as one of the hallmarks of the *novus ordo seclorum* that they hoped
to spread throughout the world. In that new order, the United
States represented, not a Christian state, but an open society that
safeguarded the natural right of everyone to worship according to
his or her own lights. Thus, when Americans compared their religious culture with that of other countries, including the Barbary
States, they emphasized religious freedom over all else.

Two cultural productions contrasted religious freedom in Algiers with that in the United States. The first was a poem published
in New York in 1797 entitled *An American in Algiers*, dramatizing
a religious standoff between the dey and an American prisoner.
The poem ends with the brave and faithful American rejecting an
offer to denounce Christianity, stating that he would rather be sold
as a slave than deny the "Saviour of this world."[13] The message was
clear: it was better to maintain one's freedom of conscience than
compromise one's faith in the face of tyranny. By contrast, a second
cultural production portrayed an Algerine Muslim's journey to
America. Peter Markoe's *The Algerine Spy in Pennsylvania* was a
fictional work that told the story of Mehemet, an Algerine spy who
eventually embraces American freedom and converts to Christianity.[14]

Markoe's work linked religion with a particular political regime:
Islam was the religion of a tyrannical state, while Christianity was
the religion of a free republic. His message was not to depict the
Barbary conflict as a holy war between the followers of Christ and
the followers of Allah but, like America's War of Independence, as
a war against a tyrant who trampled on American freedom.

Beyond the question of freedom of conscience for individuals,
American criticism of religion examined the role of religion in di-
recting public policy. In particular, it explored how Islam and the

Koran justified piracy and the piratical states that sponsored it. To explain the link between religion and tyranny in Barbary, American commentators turned to the history of Islam and its rise and spread as a religion of the sword. In judging the relative merits of American Christianity and Barbarian Islam, Americans considered both to be religious and political systems, giving greater weight to their political nature. Far more important than theological distinctions was the political atmosphere that each engendered, and to Americans that difference became a stark contrast between freedom and tyranny. Americans' views of Islam, like those of Catholicism, flowed from Anglo-American presses of the seventeenth and eighteenth centuries. One book, originally published in the late seventeenth century in London and reprinted a hundred years later in the United States, was the English clergyman Humphrey Prideaux's *The Life of Mahomet; or, the History of that Imposture which was begun, carried on, and firmly established by him in Arabia: and which has Subjugated a Larger Portion of the Globe, than the Religion of Jesus has yet set at Liberty*. The lengthy title contrasted Christianity as a religion of liberty and Islam as a religion of subjugation. Subscribing to a providential view of history, many Americans, therefore, had no difficulty at all accepting Prideaux's interpretation that Islam was God's punishment. Prideaux's work circulated widely in England and Europe from its publication in 1697 through at least eight more editions by 1730. While its readership in America is unknown, Jefferson and other devotees of the Enlightenment owned copies.

While Prideaux's polemical history convinced some Americans that Islam fostered tyranny, it was the French philosophe Abbé Constantin-François Chasseboeuf de Volney who offered an explanation as to why Muslims were willing to live under that tyranny. In his *Travels Through Egypt and Syria*, reprinted in New York in 1798, Volney argued that tyranny existed in Islamic countries because the religion promoted a submissive citizenry, resigned to accept whatever occurred as the will of Allah. Like Calvinism, Abbé Volney argued, Islam taught predestination, the idea that one's life was foreordained by an omniscient deity and that faithful individuals must accept their fate. In his travels through Muslim countries, Volney was amazed at how readily men and women accepted economic hardship and political despotism, all the while being quick to explain their plights with the statement, "It is written."[15]

Cultural portrayals of submissive Muslims were echoed in the dispatches of American diplomats directly involved with the Barbary pirates. Before assuming his post as U.S. consul to Tunis, William Eaton read Volney. After living among the Tunisians and seeing their unquestioning acceptance of the bey's commands, he concluded that Volney's observations of Muslims "exactly fit them here." He depicted the Tunisians as cowering in "solemn fear of the frowns of a bigot," Muhammad, who had been dead a thousand years. Eaton concluded that, "humbled by the double oppression of civil and religious tyranny," the Tunisians have "little enterprise and are grossly ignorant."[16]

No doubt some Americans sought to understand Muslim resignation by reading the Koran itself. Thomas Jefferson had a copy of George Sale's 1734 translation in his library, and James Cathcart quoted from it. Sale, an English lawyer and student of Middle Eastern history and culture, prefaced his translation with a lengthy introduction commenting on what he regarded as the salient beliefs of Islam. Like Volney and Eaton, he portrayed Muslims as submissive. Explaining that Muslims accepted the Koran as God's "absolute decree" and believed that Allah predestined all things "both of good and evil," Sale concluded that the faithful had, as the very word *Islam* implies, to submit.[17]

Barbary officials themselves attested to a close tie between religious duty and political obedience. Shortly after the first pirate attacks on Americans, Thomas Jefferson and John Adams met in London with Ambassador Abdrahaman of Tripoli and asked why his government sanctioned the enslavement of Christians. He replied that the Koran regarded non-Muslims as "sinners" and that Muslims had a "right and duty to make war upon them wherever they could be found, and to make slaves of all they could take as

On June 28, 1815, Commodore Stephen Decatur arrived off Algiers with a formidable American squadron and demanded the dey sign a treaty with the United States that ended U.S. tribute to Algiers.

On October 31, 1803, the United States frigate *Philadelphia* ran aground near Tripoli and was captured by the Tripolitans, who imprisoned the crew of more than three hundred, including the ship's commander, William Bainbridge. With a modern warship in its possession and hundreds of captives, Tripoli sharply increased its demands for tribute and ransom.

In a daring nighttime raid on February 16, 1804, led by Lieutenant Stephen Decatur, American sailors blew up the *Philadelphia* under the harbor castle.

Under orders of Commodore Edward Preble, the American squadron launched an all-out naval attack on Tripoli on August 3, 1804.

Returning from the August 3, 1804, attack on Tripoli, Captain Stephen Decatur avenged his brother's death in hand-to-hand combat against a Turk in the Tripoli harbor.

Although sickened at building warships for the Barbary States as part of America's tribute payment, President Washington thought it prudent to negotiate rather than commit the new, weak republic to war.

Fearing the loss of trade, John Adams, first as commissioner to London and then as second president of the United States, advocated negotiating commercial treaties with the Barbary States.

A consistent advocate of fighting the Barbary pirates rather than paying tribute, Jefferson as president took the United States to war against Tripoli in 1801.

As secretary of state under Jefferson, Madison supported the Tripolitan War, and as president he dispatched two powerful naval squadrons to the Mediterranean in 1815 to defeat the Algerines.

Former consul to Tunis William Eaton convinced Jefferson to authorize a ground assault against the Tripolitan stronghold of Derne. After crossing the Libyan Desert with a handful of sailors and marines and hundreds of Arabs loyal to Hamet Karamanli, brother and enemy of Yusef, the bashaw, Eaton, under cover of a naval bombardment, took Derne on April 27, 1805.

Commander of the first squadron that Jefferson dispatched to the Mediterranean, Commodore Richard Dale established a blockade of Tripoli in fall 1801 but soon discovered that without maneuverable gunboats to patrol the harbor, the large frigates were ineffective in keeping the corsairs bottled up.

Under the command of Lieutenant Andrew Sterrett, the schooner *Enterprise* defeated the Tripolitan corsair *Tripoli* on August 1, 1801, in the first naval battle of the Tripolitan War.

As commander of the third squadron sent to the Mediterranean during the Tripolitan War, Preble went beyond maintaining a blockade of the Tripoli harbor, launching assaults and bombardments against the city's defenses.

Prisoners." The ambassador vowed that Tripoli based its actions on the "Laws of the Prophet," which suggested that one's civic and religious duties were the same.[18] Further, he added, Islam gave great incentive to Barbary pirates to fight infidels to the death. It was written in the Koran that making war against nonbelievers ensured a spot in Paradise.

Although Americans believed Barbary leaders used the Koran to justify their actions and mobilize their supporters, they also understood that they did not consider themselves bound to its teachings. According to American observers, North African rulers, though swearing allegiance to Allah, did not always adhere to the teachings of the Koran. Thomas Barclay cited one instance when the emperor of Morocco, eager to increase trade throughout the Mediterranean, including with Christian Europe, allowed the exportation of corn, which was "prohibited by the Koran, [but] permitted by the King."[19] The Koran instructed Muslims to punish unbelievers by "cutting off trade and communication with them," trusting in God rather than commerce to supply their needs.[20] In short, in Morocco religious teaching was tempered by market realities. In some instances, the various treaties with Western powers made explicit references to "the Holy War," which suggested an ongoing struggle between Christians and Muslims dating from the Crusades rather than a specific declaration between the Barbary States and United States. Both Tunis and Algiers represented themselves as being frontier posts of "the Holy War." The designation *frontier* supported the notion of a long-standing struggle between the two religions, denoting the western outpost of the Ottoman push for dominance of the Mediterranean against Europe's Christian powers.[21] Barbary negotiators divided the world into "Christian" and "Muslim" nations and dealt with each differently. And Barbary leaders continually invoked their allegiance to Allah in signing treaties.[22]

On the other hand, American officials steered clear of any language that would suggest that their country's quarrel with Barbary had anything to do with religion. In fact, wishing to avoid any cultural conflicts that might jeopardize the commercial agreements they so eagerly sought, they went to some lengths to convince the Barbary States that this was not a religious war. Aware of the long history of enmity between Christians and Muslims in the Mediterranean, American negotiators assured Barbary leaders that religion was a nonissue. While Barbary draftsmen included in the treaties such boilerplate phrases as "in the name of Allah," U.S. negotiators made no reference to God or religion. Indeed, in its Tripoli Treaty of 1797 the United States explicitly declared that it was not a Christian state.[23]

Years later James Madison reflected on the religious clause in the Tripoli Treaty and thought it had had a favorable influence on America's relations with the Barbary States. By insisting that the United States was not a Christian state, the president and Congress had distanced themselves from European Christian powers that had a long history of religion-inspired animosity toward Muslims.[24] Madison hoped that America had succeeded in removing religion as an issue between the United and Barbary States. For him the two sides were not, nor had they ever been, engaged in a holy war.

While recognizing America's wisdom in steering clear of religion in the treaties, Madison overlooked the fact that religion was also not the central issue for the Barbarians. Richard O'Brien, the highest-ranking Christian official in Algiers, insisted that the driving force behind Algerine piracy was the quest for money. "Money is the God of Algiers & Mahomet their prophet," he declared.[25] Indeed, in all of the treaty negotiations, tribute, not theology, was the sticking point.

No aspect of the U.S. conflict with the Barbary pirates caused more outrage among the American public than the capture and enslavement of American citizens and news of the horrors of their ordeal. Reading letters from the captives in newspapers caused an outpouring of sympathy for the men and renewed efforts to relieve their suffering. In 1794 one group of Philadelphians solicited donations to fund the release of the captives. There was also an outcry of national humiliation that Americans were "enslaved at Algiers" and that others were at risk of being captured.[26]

The captives made the Barbary conflict a wrenching human story and reminded Congress and the American people of the limits of their independence. By the mid-1790s Algiers had captured more than a hundred Americans and sold them into slavery. At a time when most Americans were enjoying the "blessings of liberty" in a land where the "pursuit of happiness" was regarded as a natural right, the Algerine slaves labored under the hot Mediterranean sun, some building the fortifications that continued to impede their countrymen.

The captives complicated Congress's negotiations with the pirates because Barbary leaders wanted to use them to extort money from the United States. Thomas Jefferson hoped to remove the captives as bargaining chips by leading the dey of Algiers to believe that Congress would not redeem them. Upon learning of the strategy, the prisoners were understandably distressed, but foreign affairs secretary John Jay thought it best to continue it. Recognizing the captives' suffering, he thought that Congress and private citizens could send "little supplies" in "so indirect a Manner as not to be traced either by them or by the Algerines, and would tend greatly to the Comfort of these unhappy People."[27] Written in 1788, Jay's directive indicates that, while America was concerned for the captives' well-being, the nation's priority was to deceive the captors into thinking that Congress was prepared to sacrifice some of its citizens for the honor of the nation.

By 1794 public pressure caused Congress to abandon this ploy and make freeing the slaves a priority. Frustrated over delays in securing their release, an increasing number of Americans demanded that Congress free the hostages immediately.

In condemning the Barbary pirates for religious and political tyranny, Americans invoked the ideals of freedom and independence. In their telling, free America was a world apart from oppressive Barbary. But in denouncing slavery, Americans confronted atrocities committed by southern as well as Barbarian slaveholders, and any attack on slavery in North Africa invited a counterattack on the same institution that flourished in the United States.

Even as Americans grappled with these differences, no topic received more attention than the American slaves in Algiers, some of whom had languished for more than a decade. Indeed, the slave narrative, a literary form first made popular by seventeenth-century Puritans captured by Native Americans, became a powerful vehicle for condemning Barbary atrocities. The question of slavery posed a problem, because by 1800 Americans held more than three-quarters of a million Africans and persons of African descent in bondage while there were no more than a couple hundred American slaves in North Africa. Further, American slavery, as it had during the American Revolution, mocked the bold and noble language of the nation's Declaration of Independence that "all men are created equal." Throughout the War of Independence, republicans had characterized British tyranny as slavery over the colonies and regarded slavery as the denial of the republican ideal. Now, in the confrontation with the Barbary States, American slavery undermined America's claim to the moral high ground. How could the United States condemn the Barbary States for holding a few hundred enslaved Americans when Americans themselves owned hundreds of thousands of slaves? The irony was not lost on U.S. commentators who recognized that any condemnation of slavery on the Barbary Coast must also be leveled against the American South.

No popular works on the Algerine captives noted the hypocrisy of Americans condemning slavery in North Africa more poignantly than those written by Benjamin Franklin. Franklin had been in Paris when Algiers took the first Americans captive, and he had been intimately involved in trying to gain their release. Almost fifteen years after returning to the United States, he once again confronted the inhumanity of slavery and the slave trade. This time, however, he pointed the accusing finger at his own countrymen. In

1790, near the end of his long life, Franklin took up what would be his last great political cause: the abolition of slavery in the United States. As president of the Pennsylvania Society for Promoting the Abolition of Slavery, Franklin signed a petition urging Congress to use its power to discourage "every species of traffic in the persons of our fellow-men." The society invoked the same natural-rights argument that Americans had used to justify independence and that they continued to use in demanding free trade. The petition declared that the society wrote "from a persuasion that equal liberty was originally the portion, and is still the birthright of all men."[28]

The response to Franklin's petition was swift. Representatives from slaveholding states dismissed him as an old man who "ought to have known the Constitution better," pointing out that that charter protected slaves as property and that the matter was an issue for the states, not the federal government, to consider. James Jackson of Georgia went further, arguing that slavery was a positive good that introduced benighted Africans to Christian virtues and "lift[ed] them out of barbarism."[29] Franklin replied with a stinging parody that linked the holding of Africans by Americans with the holding of Americans by North Africans. Americans, he charged, not only betrayed their own citizens in Algiers, but within America they betrayed freedom itself.

The Barbary enslavement of Americans forced Americans to ask disturbing questions about the meaning of their revolution. Throughout the 1790s newspapers extolled the virtues of patriot leaders, especially George Washington, and reminded a new generation of the sacrifices that men and women had endured to throw off the tyranny of British rule. Reports of captured American ships and imprisoned American sailors on the same pages represented a jarring juxtaposition. In a 1797 poem written in the voice of an Algerine slave, one writer underscored the contrast.

> *While you enjoy prosperity and ease;*
> *Live without care and taste the sweets of peace,*
> *From me that birthright of Columbia's sons,*

Deserv'd by virtue and by valor won,
My much blov'd mistress, Liberty has flown
And with her all the sweets of life are gone.[30]

The fictional captive viewed the Algerine captivity as a test of American resolve to defend the lofty ideals of 1776. Thus, he wrote:

To rouse Columbia *from her torpid dream,*
And bid her every free-born son reclaim,
The fate of Slavery's hapless sons to scan,
And haste the triumph of the rights of man.

While laboring as a slave in North Africa, the fictional prisoner had two questions: Did Americans still claim him as one of their own, and did the United States have the means to "save her sons from slavery"?[31]

American captives echoed the sentiments of their fictive counterpart and made their enslavement a question of American independence. Captured aboard the *Maria* in 1785, James Leander Cathcart was at a loss to explain why a country founded on the principles of freedom and independence would allow its citizens to languish under a tyrant's absolute control. He asked, "Why are we left the victims of arbitrary power and barbarous despotism, in a strange land far distant from all our connections, miserable exiles from the country for which we have fought, forgotten by our co[n]temporaries who formerly used to animate us in all our expeditions with tales of liberty?" His ten-year captivity made him reflect on the meaning of republican rhetoric. Was it just talk, mere "tales of liberty"? In a moment of despair, he wrote that he and his fellow American prisoners were "the only victims of American Independence."[32] Cathcart's lament became the entire country's: Did the United States have the resolve to make independence a reality that would follow Americans even to the Barbary shores?

FIVE

THE TRIPOLITAN WAR: 1801-5

Thomas Jefferson called his election to the presidency the "Revolution of 1800." So he considered the country's bloodless switch from the Federalist Party's program of big, expensive centralized government to the noble ideals of his beloved Republicans. During the campaign, he and his fellow Republicans pointed out that Federalist extravagance had undermined liberty at home and had failed to ensure American independence abroad. Despite the growing size of its military, they noted, the United States was still "subjected to the spoliations of foreign cruisers" and shamefully paid "an enormous tribute to the petty tyrant of Algiers."[1] Jefferson vowed to change this. In his first inaugural address, he pledged that his Republican administration would pursue "peace, commerce, and honest friendship with all nations."[2] Having embraced religious and political tolerance, Americans, he believed, needed to be free to sell the fruits of their labor without prejudice or extortion in markets around the world.

Federalists, however, quickly dismissed Jefferson as a dreamy philosopher who lacked the mettle to advance American interests abroad. They pointed out repeatedly that he had behaved in a cowardly manner as governor of Virginia, fleeing his home at the first word of a British invasion. Moreover, he had opposed establishing a navy, the very instrument that could help protect American shipping. Federalists believed that a Republican White House would not possess spirit and vigor enough to guide the young republic in a dangerous world. While Jefferson talked tough about using force against the Barbary pirates, Federalists were dubious that as president he would deliver.

Before Jefferson even assumed the presidency in March 1801, the Barbary pirates once again attacked American interests and thereby challenged the incoming president's resolve. On February 26, 1801, the bashaw of Tripoli, Yusuf Karamanli, made good on his October 22, 1800, ultimatum that if the United States did not meet his demands for more tribute within six months, he would declare war and send his corsairs after American merchantmen. Jefferson's reaction was swift. Long a proponent of using military force against the pirates, he declared in a letter to Madison, "I am an enemy to all these doceurs, tributes and humiliations," adding, "I know that nothing will stop the eternal increase from these pirates but the presence of an armed force." Jefferson and Madison had opposed a naval buildup during the Quasi-War with France and had argued that a deep-water fleet was expensive and unnecessary. Though he preferred a defensive force that included gunboats to protect the American shoreline, Jefferson was now ready to dispatch a navy squadron to the Mediterranean. The frugal president reasoned that a naval deployment against Tripoli was more economical in the long run than continuing to pay tribute.[3]

Jefferson hoped to avoid actual warfare through an "awe and talk" strategy. He planned a display of overwhelming naval power that would close the harbor at Tripoli and so awe the Tripolitans that the bashaw would negotiate on the Americans' terms. Since the first Barbary attacks on American shipping seventeen years earlier, Jefferson had thought that the pirate republics could be easily defeated by a few modern warships. The European powers' unwillingness and the United States' inability to challenge the pirates alone had allowed the problem to continue. Now that the country had a fleet of frigates manned by sailors battle-hardened from the Quasi-War with France, the president was confident that he had the necessary power to defeat the Tripolitans. Secretary of State

James Madison confidently informed James Cathcart, U.S. consul at Tripoli, of the administration's strategy. Anticipating the negotiations that would follow decisive American action, the secretary instructed Cathcart "to stifle every pretension or expectation, that the United States will on their side, make the smallest contribution to him as the price of peace."[4] This war was to end America's tributary status in the Mediterranean.

But Jefferson's "awe and talk" policy foundered on the shoals of the Tripoli harbor. In the late 1790s Yusuf Bashaw harbored two grievances against the United States. First, he resented that America treated Tripoli as a subordinate of Algiers. Yusuf found offensive Article 12 of the U.S. treaty with Tripoli, which designated the dey of Algiers as the guarantor of the peace. His growing navy fueled his determination to assert Tripoli's economic and political independence. Second and more insulting, the United States denied Tripoli annual tribute, which it was willing to pay Algiers and Tunis. In lieu of tribute, Congress had agreed to pay Yusuf $40,000 and additional presents with the appointment of a consul at Tripoli. But this promise remained unfulfilled two years after the Senate had ratified the treaty. In a letter to the president in the waning days of John Adams's administration, the bashaw made his position clear: "treat us as you do the other Regencies, without any difference being made between us." When his demands were not met, he gave his ultimatum: meet our demands within six months or face war.[5]

After declaring war on the United States in March 1801, just before Jefferson's inauguration, Yusuf Karamanli indicated that Americans could "reestablish" the peace for a price. He demanded a prompt payment of $225,000 and $25,000 annually—the same terms that the Swedes had recently accepted and that the Danes were considering. William Eaton, American consul at Tunis, argued against accepting the terms on the grounds that, if Jefferson yielded, America could expect Tunis to make a demand of double that amount, and Algiers would expect even more. Eaton saw no alternative to war: "If the United States will have a free commerce in this sea they must defend it." He explained that since only American vessels were sailing in the Mediterranean at the time, they were the only targets available to satisfy the "restless spirit of these marauders."[6] To Eaton, Jefferson had no alternative but to defeat the Barbary pirates by force. Jefferson agreed, at least to the extent of approving the squadron of three frigates and a schooner to meet the threat. Left out were the gunboats that could penetrate Tripoli's shallow harbor and prevent pirate vessels from slipping around the blockade. It was an omission that he and his navy commanders would come to regret.

Though Jefferson had the squadron fitted out for service, he did not issue the order to sail for the Mediterranean until after he consulted his cabinet on May 15, 1801. While all agreed on the "expediency of a cruise," there was disagreement over the constitutionality of sending the squadron, which was a clear act of war. Article I, Section 8 of the Constitution invested Congress alone with the power to declare war, and as strict constructionists, Jefferson and his Republican colleagues wanted to ensure the constitutionality of their action. Attorney General Levi Lincoln advocated caution and maintained that American frigates should "repel an attack on individual vessels, but after the repulse, may not proceed to destroy the enemy's vessels generally." Treasury Secretary Albert Gallatin took a more aggressive approach, arguing that while the executive could not declare war, if another nation puts "us into that state," the president was authorized to use force to protect American interests. Secretary of the Navy Robert Smith and Secretary of War Henry Dearborn concurred, as did Secretary of State James Madison.[7] Jefferson lined up with Lincoln and close adherence to the letter of the Constitution. He instructed the navy to engage any enemy vessel that attacked American shipping, but not to pursue corsairs in offensive engagements nor to take them as prizes.

In May 1801 Madison wrote William Eaton: "The policy of exhibiting a naval force on the coast of Barbary, has long been urged by yourself and the other consuls." He and the president found the "present moment . . . peculiarly favorable" for the use of force, explaining, "not only is it a provision against an immediate danger, but as we are now at peace and amity with all the rest of the world, and as the force employed would if at home, be at nearly the same expence, with less advantage to our mariners."[8] In short, and in good Republican fashion, dispatching a squadron to the Mediterranean would protect American commerce at a reasonable expense.

Madison was hardly eager for war. Indeed, he first sent a good-faith gesture along with his formal protest of Algiers's treatment of the *George Washington*. None other than the *George Washington* was returning to Algiers laden with timber and other stores, which would satisfy "at least one annuity" of the two in arrears. Further its captain had in his possession $30,000, which President Jefferson hoped the dey would accept "as a commutation for the stores due for another" year's tribute. In addition, four hundred yards of cloth and "thirty pieces" of linen were offered up for the "biennial present."[9] Thus, the same ship that had been the focus of America's greatest national shame was returning with gifts to appease the perpetrator of that humiliation.

Also in May, Madison sent a circular letter to American consuls in the Mediterranean explaining the president's decision to dispatch the squadron. He announced that three frigates and a sloop of war would sail immediately under the command of Commodore Richard Dale. Madison restated America's preference for peace, but his announcement of the naval operation communicated the administration's firm resolve to end pirate depredations in the Mediterranean.

Jefferson had long considered the Barbary affair a sideshow. As participants in the Napoleonic Wars continued to ignore American neutrality in the Atlantic, European powers constituted a far greater threat to the United States. But by the time of his inauguration, events in the Mediterranean took center stage and would remain a nettlesome issue for the remainder of his presidency, as his annual messages to Congress convey.

Though Jefferson sounded more and more like a commander in chief determined to protect his nation's interest in hostile waters, his notice to the bashaw of Tripoli in summer 1801 struck a much more irenic note. He offered "assurances of friendship" and indicated that his country's "firm and unabated" desire was to enjoy relations of peace and commerce with Tripoli. He announced that he was dispatching a "squadron of observation" to the Mediterranean for two purposes: one, to protect American commerce, and two, "to exercise our seamen in nautical duties." Rather than an awesome display of naval power, this was, in Jefferson's depiction, simply a training exercise. He went so far as to express his hope that the squadron would give umbrage to no power. Commodore Dale followed up with a similar letter to the bashaw, again emphasizing friendship and respect.[10]

This veiled fist approach, however, did not work; Yusuf continued to insist on the payment of tribute. He replied to Dale's peace overture by restating why he had declared war in the first place: that America was delinquent in meeting the terms of the treaty and that the treaty itself was unjust when compared with the more generous pacts negotiated with Algiers and Tunis. Further, Yusuf had no intention of backing down to the Americans' show of force, because to do so would be political suicide. His declaration of war was popular in Tripoli, and he was not going to jeopardize his leadership by rushing to the bargaining table.[11]

Dale's fleet consisted of three frigates and a schooner: the *President*, the flagship commanded by James Barron; the *Philadelphia*, commanded by Samuel Barron; the *Essex*, commanded by William Bainbridge; and the schooner *Enterprise*, commanded by Andrew Sterrett. With its combined 126 guns, the fleet was fully capable of evoking the awe that Madison hoped would force the bashaw to the negotiating table. At more than a half million dollars, twice what the bashaw demanded in tribute, the costly enterprise underscored Jefferson's determination to eliminate the Barbary pirate scourge.[12]

Jefferson could not have scripted the early action better. On August 1, 1801, shortly after arriving in the Mediterranean, the schooner *Enterprise* encountered a Tripolitan corsair, the *Tripoli*, and defeated it with overwhelming firepower. Jefferson himself reported the triumph. "The arrival of our squadron," he optimistically wrote, "dispelled the danger" to American interests in the Mediterranean. Summarizing Sterrett's notable achievement, he reported that "one of the Tripolitan cruisers having fallen in with, and engaged the small schooner *Enterprise*, commanded by Lieutenant Sterret, . . . was captured, after a heavy slaughter of her men, without the loss of a single one on our part." Jefferson heralded the "bravery exhibited by our citizens" in defeating the pirates in the first major encounter.[13] His message was clear: unlike tribute-paying Europeans, freedom-loving Americans would rid themselves of the piratical pestilence.

Sterrett himself stirringly described the sea battle. Flying under a British flag, the *Enterprise* had hailed the *Tripoli* and asked what "business had brought her to sea." The corsair's reis replied "that he was hunting Americans but had not, alas, been able to find any." With that revelation, the *Enterprise* "took down the Union Jack and hoisted the American colors." Sterrett's men fired "their muskets across the Tripolitan deck, and the *Tripoli* answered with a ragged broadside."[14] In his full account of the battle to Commodore Dale, Sterrett described a decisive victory:

> I have the honor to inform you, that on the 1 of August, I fell in with a Tripolitan ship of war, called the Tripoli, mounting 14 guns, commanded by Rais Mahomet Rous. An action immediately commenced within pistol shot, which continued three hours incessantly. She then struck her colors. The carnage on board was dreadful; she having 30 men killed and 30 wounded, among the latter was the Captain and first Lieutenant. Her sails, masts and rigging were cut to pieces with 18 shot between wind and water. Shortly after taking possession, her mizzenmast went over the side. Agreeably to your orders, I dismantled her of everything but an old sail and spar. With heartfelt pleasure I add, that the officers and

men throughout the vessel [*Enterprise*], behaved in the most spirited and determined manner, obeying every command with promptitude and alertness. We have not had a man wounded, and we have sustained no material damage in our hull or rigging.[15]

Though the victory over the pirate ship *Tripoli* was a glorious moment for Americans, it revealed a flaw in the Constitution's allocation of war-making powers. Aware that he was not engaging the enemy under a congressional declaration of war, Lieutenant Andrew Sterrett, commander of the *Enterprise*, released the surviving pirates and their ship after the furious battle. Lacking orders to "take any defeated vessels as prizes," Sterrett "had the Tripoli's guns thrown overboard" and the boat abandoned as "a helpless hulk."[16] Nonetheless, Americans hailed the event as one of the most glorious triumphs in the navy's brief history. In an etching that appeared in *The Naval Temple* (1816), the caption under the battle scene boldly proclaimed: "Capt. Sterrett in the Schr. Enterprise paying tribute to Tripoli, August 1801."[17] The only tribute Tripoli could now expect from the United States was balls and shot.

Wanting to ensure future triumphs, Jefferson asked the legislature for greater war-making powers. Sanctioned by Congress to use force only for defensive purposes, Jefferson lamented that Sterrett had "disabled [the pirate vessel] from committing further hostilities" but then been forced to set it free. While respecting the constitutional requirement that the legislature declare and define war, Jefferson sought greater authority to defeat the Barbary States. He stated, "The legislature will doubtless consider whether, by authorizing measures of offence, also, they will place our force on an equal footing with that of its adversaries. I communicate all material information on this subject, that in the exercise of the important function considered by the constitution to the legislature exclusively, their judgment may form itself on a knowledge and consideration of every circumstance of weight."[18]

Though Congress was divided over whether to extend the president's war-making powers, it was united in recognizing Sterrett's feat as a great victory for America. Federalists joined Republicans in calling for a gold medal to be struck as "emblematic of that heroic action," noting that the Americans had overwhelmed a "barbarous enemy" but at the same time had also extended mercy.[19]

Congressional unity was short-lived. Though hailing the sailors' exploits, Federalists were quick to attack Jefferson for not taking the Tripolitan ship as a prize. Jefferson's longtime political enemy, Alexander Hamilton, led the opposition. While Jefferson hailed the defeat of the *Tripoli* as a tribute to American naval power, Hamilton saw it as evidence that Jefferson was unfit for office. Reacting to Jefferson's annual message, Hamilton refuted it point by point in a series of eighteen articles entitled "The Examination," which appeared in the Federalist newspaper the *New-York Evening Post*. He blamed the president for worrying too much about constitutional authority when as commander in chief he had the responsibility to defend Americans and American interests. "The Message of the President," he wrote, "by whatever motives it may have been dictated, is a performance which ought to alarm all who are anxious for the safety of our Government, for the respectability and welfare of our nation. It makes, or aims at making, a most prodigal sacrifice of constitutional energy, of sound principle, and of public interest, to the popularity of one man."[20] Hamilton was most outraged by Jefferson's decision to send sailors and marines into battle without full authority to engage and capture an enemy that had declared war on the United States. "When the newspapers informed us," he sarcastically noted, "that one of these cruisers, after being subdued in a bloody conflict, had been liberated and permitted quietly to return home, the imagination was perplexed to divine the reason."[21]

Conceding that the Constitution limited the executive's war-making powers "even in time of actual war," Hamilton charged Jefferson with going far beyond what was reasonable. He argued that Jefferson, not the Constitution, was guilty of "so great an absurdity," for "the framers of [the Constitution] would have blushed at a provision, so repugnant to good sense, so inconsistent with national safety and inconvenience."[22] It was foolhardy in the extreme, he noted, "that, without a declaration of war by Congress, our public force may destroy the life, but may not restrain the liberty, or seize the property of an enemy."[23]

Before delivering his second annual address to Congress, Jefferson asked Treasury Secretary Albert Gallatin to review a draft. Gallatin advised Jefferson to add a paragraph requesting "authority for our vessels to act offensively in case of war declared or waged by other Barbary powers." If Morocco or Tunis joined Tripoli in declaring war against the United States, Gallatin wanted to make sure that the navy would be allowed to attack aggressively. Echoing Hamilton's sentiments, Gallatin added, "I do not and never did believe that it was necessary to obtain a legislative sanction in the last case: whenever war does exist, whether by the declaration of the United States or by the declaration or act of a foreign nation, I think that the Executive has a right, and is in duty bound, to apply the public force which he may have the means legally to employ, in the most effective manner to annoy the enemy." Referring to Jefferson's strict constructionist position of the previous year, Gallatin acknowledged, "It is true that the message of last year adopted a different construction of the Constitution; but how that took place I do not recollect." Gallatin and the entire cabinet were clearly opposed to any restriction on U.S. war-making powers once an enemy had attacked.[24]

On February 6, 1802, Congress passed legislation authorizing the president to use all means necessary to defeat the Tripolitans. While not a formal declaration of war, it eliminated constitutional reservations and signaled America's determination to use its full force on the high seas. Styled "An Act for the protection of the Commerce and Seamen of the United States, against the Tripolitan Cruisers," it authorized naval commanders "to subdue, seize and make prize of all vessels, goods and effects, belonging to the Bey of Tripoli, or to his subjects, and to bring or send the same into port, to be proceeded against, and distributed according to law." Underlying the law was the recognition that America was in a state of war; thus there was no need to declare it. Further, because Tripoli had declared war on the United States, the act empowered the president "to cause to be done all such other acts of precaution or hostility as the state of war will justify, and may, in his opinion, require." In other words, Congress gave the president full authority to take whatever offensive as well as defensive measures necessary to defeat Tripoli and protect American interests.[25]

After Sterrett's spectacular victory, meanwhile, the American squadron took its position outside Tripoli's harbor and established a blockade. The objective, Jefferson said, was "to secure our commerce in that sea with the smallest force competent." This goal reflected Jefferson's primary objective: to secure independence for American merchants in the Mediterranean at the lowest possible cost. Although he spent an estimated half million dollars on the naval squadron, about twice what the bashaw of Tripoli had demanded in tribute and presents, he reasoned that until the Barbary pirates were defeated, American trade would be threatened and tribute demands would escalate.

America's bold action against the pirates earned the United States respect among European powers who had long paid tribute rather than fight. David Humphreys reported that Commodore Dale's circular letter to European consuls announcing America's intention to blockade the port of Tripoli had sounded just the right tone. The commodore's action was defensive, a response to the bashaw's declaration of war, and determined, a pledge to seal the port against all ships entering or departing. Humphreys boasted that "this is the first instance (within my recollection, during my residence in Europe) of any of the ports of the Barbary powers being put in a state of blockade, notwithstanding their multiplied piratical aggressions against the Christian nations." He added, "I cannot but flatter myself it will produce the happiest consequences, by being a commencement of the verification of the prediction which I made in print more than fifteen years ago, when not a single armed vessel, public or private, was owned in the United States, that the time would come when the United States would be the authors of the system for exterminating the piracies, for so long a time committed with impunity by the Barbary powers." As word of the blockade spread, it made "no inconsiderable sensation in Europe."[26] Humphreys could hardly contain his national pride, pointing out that republican Americans could no longer be regarded as part of the tribute-paying system that European monarchies and Barbary pirates had crafted.

The initial results of the American blockade were dramatic. First, American ships sailed through the Strait of Gibraltar and entered Mediterranean ports unimpeded by pirate attacks. The U.S. consul in Gibraltar reported that "the timely arrival of the squadron under the orders of Commodore Dale, has prevented at least twenty-five merchant ships, belonging to citizens of the United States, with rich cargoes, from falling into the possession of those pirates."[27] Second, the United States was able to offer naval escort services to neutrals. At a time when Sweden was negotiating a treaty with the bashaw of Tripoli with uncertain outcome, Humphreys offered the Swedish chargé d'affaires at Madrid "to engage the American squadron in the Mediterranean to furnish all possible protection to the commerce of that nation, in case of the renewal of hostilities." What a dramatic reversal from just a few years earlier! Rather than begging Europeans to assist American vessels, the United States now protected European ships. "These overtures were gratefully accepted," he wrote of the Swedish affair, "and afterwards happily reciprocated, and became the basis of making joint cause, and affording mutual convoy, as is actually the case."[28] Thus, by showing the way, America won allies in its battle with the Barbary States.

Although the naval blockade of Tripoli gave high hopes to those longing to defeat the Barbary pirates, the blockade was rendered less effective by the naval efforts of Admiral Murad Reis. Because U.S. warships could not patrol the rocky shoals of the harbor, three corsairs succeeded in capturing an American merchant ship practically under the navy's nose. The Tripolitans took the *Franklin*, bound from the West Indies to Marseilles, imprisoned her captain and crew of eight, paraded the captives in the streets of Tripoli, and forced the Americans to pay $5,000 ransom for their release. To Tripolitans, the successful raid underscored their independence in their own waters despite the American presence. Throughout 1802 the bashaw's navy penetrated the American blockade and maintained an "uninterrupted supply of food and ammunition between Tripoli and the rest of North Africa as well as the Levant."[29]

Commodore Dale conceded that the blockade was ineffective. Small shallow-draft pirate vessels easily entered and exited the port by hugging the shoreline, where the American frigates could not chase them. Dale knew that if the objective was "to Blockade Tripoli completely," he would need more resources and new tactics. He wanted several gunboats in the shoals in order to "prevent all the small craft from going in and coming out."[30] Armed with guns on the bow and stern and manned by thirty sailors, these vessels could prevent Tripolitan boats from coming out during a calm and harassing the frigates.

Doubting that the blockade alone sufficiently awed the bashaw, Dale began thinking about attacking Tripoli. He thought that a combination of "well fitted" gunboats and bomb boats could succeed in burning the harbor and destroying all shipping therein. A gunboat was a small vessel with an eighteen- or twenty-four-pound gun mounted on the bow and a nine- or twelve-pounder in the stern and a crew of about thirty men. Fast and maneuverable, it was designed to slip past enemy defenses and penetrate deep inside a harbor to attack enemy defenses. A bomb boat was of similar size but equipped for a different purpose. Commodore Dale described it as a small vessel constructed to "carry a Bomb to heave a few shells in the Town."[31] Early in 1802, however, he cautioned Rear Admiral Count Soderstrom, commander in chief of the Swedish navy in the Mediterranean, that no attack should be launched until there was near certainty of victory. An unsuccessful bombardment would only give the Tripolitans confidence and experience and make subsequent attacks more difficult.[32]

In spring 1802 Navy Secretary Smith replaced the first squadron under the command of Commodore Dale with a second under the command of Richard Morris, a thirty-four-year-old New Yorker who had been promoted to captain in 1798. The replacement squadron had greater firepower than the first, a total of 180 guns compared to 126, and higher costs, $900,000 compared to $555,000. Though a costlier squadron, the new force, Jefferson hoped, would prove to be economical by bringing the war to a quick end and restoring American trade in the Mediterranean. Perhaps the five frigates, instead of three, would convince Yusuf Karamanli that he could not prevail against American might. By summer James Cathcart, ex-consul to Tripoli, joined the growing number of critics of America's blockade. Explaining how easily the Tripolitan galleys slipped away at night, Cathcart criticized the blockade for being "6, & 8 leagues distance and oftentimes out of sight for days."[33]

Far from being cowed, the Barbary powers greeted the new squadron with confidence that the U.S. Navy, like European navies in the past, would make a great show and much noise but then withdraw in failure. Yusuf was optimistic and defiant. The blockade was not working. His pirates were able to come and go at will, keeping the home defenses well stocked. Moreover, the other Barbary States now presented threats that the Americans could not ignore. On June 19, 1802, after the United States refused to issue Morocco a passport for shipping a cargo of wheat to Tripoli, Emperor Muley Süleyman announced that he was at war with the United States and that he had directed his cruisers to attack American vessels. When Captain Morris heard the news, he wrote Navy Secretary Smith and requested additional ships, pointing out that the present squadron could not maintain the blockade of Tripoli, escort merchant ships, and protect merchantmen against Moroccan corsairs.[34] As if on cue, Tunis began to threaten hostilities because the American navy had threatened Tunisian vessels destined for Tripoli. Finally, Algiers continued its demands for tribute and voiced great displeasure at American delays in delivering it.

Such challenges would have taxed the ingenuity and resolve of the best naval commanders, and unfortunately Richard Morris fell short. Like Dale, he complained that he lacked the right vessels to completely close the harbor at Tripoli. He requested a number of small, swift ships that could chase down the enemy's galliots and galleys and even sought to procure them locally. His efforts to do so failed. Nations refused to part with the means of defending their own harbors. Further, they feared "giving umbrage, and involving themselves in war."[35]

In September William Eaton informed Madison with considerable alarm that he had observed the coast of Tripoli "totally abandoned by our ships of war," for Commander Morris had decided that it was more effective to protect American merchantmen by "frequent convoy" than by blockading the enemy's port. Eaton opined that "our present mode of warfare is not sufficiently energetic."[36]

While the Americans faltered, Yusuf and the Tripolitans flourished. Treaties with the Swedes and the Danes brought hundreds of thousands of dollars into the bashaw's coffers. Richard O'Brien reported on October 11, 1802, that new pacts with the Dutch, Spanish, Portuguese, Sicilians, French, and British would shortly follow. In addition, the French gave Tripoli a fourteen-gun corsair, and the Tripolitans purchased a sixteen-gun corsair from the British. Armed with greater firepower and able to evade the blockade, Tripoli's corsairs were in a good position to capture Americans and demand exorbitant ransom.[37] After a year and a half of blockading Tripoli, Americans, not Tripolitans, were fearful of what the enemy's fleet would do.

The view from the White House was as grim. In October Jefferson and his cabinet decided to treat with the emperor of Morocco, and although they refused to agree to annual tribute, they authorized American consul James Richard Simpson to pay as much as $20,000 for peace.[38]

As 1802 drew to a close, the Jefferson administration considered its options. Since Sterrett's initial victory, there had been little to cheer about from the Mediterranean. The blockade was by all accounts porous, and the bashaw was hardly awestruck by American naval might. The one bright spot was that, although the pirates had captured the merchantman *Franklin*, they had not captured an American frigate, but that success had come at a great cost. The Treasury Department reckoned the cost of keeping and provisioning the squadron in the Mediterranean at more than a half million dollars a year.[39] Jefferson decided to stay the course but reduced the force over the winter of 1802–3. He replaced the two largest frigates, the forty-four-gun *President* and the thirty-eight-gun *Chesapeake*, with smaller ships, the thirty-six-gun *New York* and the twenty-eight-gun *John Adams*.

When the president and his cabinet revisited the Tripolitan question the following spring, the mood had changed. A fiscal conservative, Jefferson worried about the war's strain on the budget, and influential Republican congressmen also voiced concern. In summer 1802, six months before the cabinet convened, John Randolph of Roanoke introduced a resolution calling for a reduction in the military establishment. His initiative was part of his effort to reduce the national debt by creating a sinking fund, which would receive revenues from certain duties for the purpose of paying the annual interest on the debt and redeem a portion of the principal until the debt was erased.[40] In addition to budgetary considerations, the blockade had proven ineffective, with Tripolitan vessels easily running around it. Thus the cabinet shifted toward seeking a peaceful solution. In a unanimous vote, the cabinet answered in the affirmative Jefferson's question: "Shall we buy peace of Tripoli?" Gallatin, Dearborn, and Lincoln thought that the United States should pay both a gross sum up front and an annual tribute and secure a peace treaty immediately. Madison and Smith objected to paying tribute, though they thought it would be necessary to promise the renewal of presents from time to time. Dearborn was willing to pay as much as $50,000 up front and $8,000 yearly, while Madison thought $10,000 should be the maximum gross payment with gifts totaling $5,000.[41]

By spring 1803 dissatisfaction with Morris's performance had reached Washington, and Jefferson asked his cabinet if sufficient grounds existed to recall Morris and institute an official inquiry into his conduct.[42] That June Navy Secretary Smith suspended Morris and ordered a board of inquiry to investigate charges against him. The panel concluded that Morris "might have acquitted himself well in the command of a single ship, under the orders of a superior, but he was not competent to the command of a squadron."[43]

Morris's replacement, Commodore Edward Preble, had spent many of his forty-three years at sea and had earned a reputation for courage and judgment as a lieutenant in the American War of Independence. After being promoted to the rank of captain, he protected U.S. merchantmen engaged in the Far Eastern or China trade, and he became the first American naval officer to display the flag east of the Cape of Good Hope. Now aboard the *Constitution*, he led a seven-ship, one-thousand-man squadron into the Mediterranean to blockade the ports of Tripoli and protect American commerce. After arriving off Tripoli in September 1803, Preble ordered his officers to establish a blockade that, unlike those of his predecessors, would completely close the port. Knowing that the lighter pirate corsairs sailed close to the shore and outflanked the blockade, he instructed his officers to give chase and run them down. He was confident that by spring 1804 his tactics would produce peace with Tripoli.[44]

Like his predecessors, Preble recognized the importance of gunboats in patrolling the Tripoli harbor. Fortunately for Preble, so did Jefferson. The president had asked Congress on February 28, 1803, to authorize the purchase or construction of four small warships, not to exceed sixteen guns each, and up to fifteen gunboats to be "armed, manned and fitted out for the protection of the seamen and commerce of the United States in the Mediterranean."[45] In his annual message of October 17, Jefferson said the new boats were on their way to the Mediterranean, where he expected them to transform the war. With their maneuverability, the gunboats could confine pirate cruisers to their harbors and eliminate the necessity of convoys for commercial ships. Always concerned with economy, Jefferson added that the tactical shift would "sensibly lessen the expenses" of the navy in the coming year.[46]

Before the gunboats arrived, however, the navy suffered its greatest setback of the war—a loss that emboldened the bashaw to raise his demands. While giving chase to a Tripolitan cruiser just to the east of Tripoli, William Bainbridge and the frigate *Philadelphia* ran aground on rocks in twelve feet of water. Trying every maneuver to get the ship off the rocks, Bainbridge and his crew came under heavy attack from gunboats that closed in on the helpless vessel. Bainbridge wrote in a report to Navy Secretary Smith that he had "no alternative but the distressing one of hauling our colours down."[47] With the ship's surrender, the bashaw now had the *Philadelphia*'s 307 crewmen in captivity, and he immediately pressed his new advantage by demanding $1,000 ransom for each, raising his total demand of ransom and tribute to $450,000 or twice what it had been three years earlier when he first declared war against the United States. Yusuf expected $307,000 to ransom the prisoners, $100,000 for a peace treaty, and $43,000 in presents at the signing.[48] The capture had far greater implications than escalating the cost of peace. The pirates now possessed a modern powerful naval ship for use against the United States. Americans began to speculate that the bashaw would sell the *Philadelphia* to the dey of Algiers for cash and military supplies, thus strengthening his ability to wage war. If that happened, the dey of Algiers would add the frigate to his formidable pirate fleet and increase tribute demands against all tributaries, including the United States.

Commodore Preble was well aware of what the loss meant. Upon hearing of the capture, he wrote, "This affair distresses me beyond description, and very much deranges my plans of operation for the present." Preble requested "another Frigate or two" to reconstitute the blockade and pursue Tripolitan vessels, and he vowed to "hazard much" to destroy the *Philadelphia*. He promised that the frigate would never be of service to Tripoli.[49]

In reporting the capture of the *Philadelphia*, American newspapers focused more on Jefferson's handling of the war than on Bainbridge's unfortunate accident. The account of the *Philadelphia*'s loss reached America at a time of intense partisan fighting. It was 1804, a presidential election year, and bad news from the Mediterranean could only help the Federalists unseat Jefferson. Partisan newspapers called upon the American people to place the blame where it belonged: on the "weak and pusillanimous administration." Reiterating their charges that Jefferson lacked the courage and spirit required of a commander in chief, the Federalists indicted the president for placing a frigate and more than three hundred sailors in the "power of the pirates of the Mediterranean."[50]

Republicans defended Jefferson by pointing to his actions upon hearing of the *Philadelphia*'s fate. Under a newspaper heading "Millions for Defence, but not a Cent for Tribute," Republicans reported that the president had immediately asked Congress to authorize the construction of a fleet of small ships and gunboats suited for fighting in the harbor of Tripoli. Lawmakers appropriated $1 million for the construction of two vessels of sixteen guns each and "as many gun boats as [the president] may think necessary." Republicans hailed Jefferson's actions as evidence of his "patriotism and energy" and added that such decisiveness should forever lay to rest the calumny that republican governments lacked "vigor and promptness."[51]

Acting U.S. consul at Tunis George Davis believed that America's future in the Mediterranean depended on a vigorous military response to the loss of the *Philadelphia*. In December 1803 Davis wrote Tobias Lear, consul general at Algiers, that "the idea of our naval force has been heretofore impressed on these Regencies, as being very trifling indeed." Far from awing the Barbary pirates, Lear believed American performance to date had demonstrated weakness and vulnerability. He suggested that America had three options. It could pay the price of peace demanded by Tripoli—

with the almost certain consequence that other states would increase their demands. It could withdraw American trade from
the Mediterranean. Or it could follow the "loss of the Phila. with
a force to reduce Tripoli."[52] Jefferson and Commodore Preble
moved toward implementing the third option.

The plan to destroy the *Philadelphia* started with its imprisoned captain. William Bainbridge's captivity at Tripoli enabled
him to assess the enemy's defenses and to determine how Americans could either retake the vessel or burn it. In an encrypted letter
to Preble dated December 5, 1803, he reported that the Tripolitans
had removed the ship from the rocks and moored it in twelve to
fourteen feet of water. He thought it "very practicable" that six to
eight "good Boats well manned" could slip into the harbor and destroy the frigate along with the pirate cruisers around it. The key
would be surprise. He observed that the pirates' gunboats were
hauled up on shore and that only one four-gun battery was aimed
at the harbor. Arguing that the city's guard was down after confidently capturing the *Philadelphia*, Bainbridge believed that the
Tripolitans were vulnerable to a daring attack. He suggested that
small American boats enter the harbor with enough powder and
shot to silence the harbor's battery and that a merchant vessel be
used to lead the raid, thus deceiving the Tripolitans into thinking
that it was a friendly trading ship. Because the *Philadelphia* could
not be removed quickly, Bainbridge thought it should be destroyed
by fire. He optimistically predicted that such a stealthy mission
could be executed "without any or a trifling loss."[53]

Preble approved of Bainbridge's daring plan and selected
Stephen Decatur of Philadelphia, a dashing twenty-five-year-old
lieutenant, to lead the raid. Commissioned as a midshipman in
1798, Decatur had served on the *United States* during the Quasi-
War against the French. Now he was called on to execute a dangerous expedition that, if successful, would destroy the bashaw's
trump card and turn disaster into new hope for an honorable
peace. But before the attempt could be made, the navy needed a
vessel that could be outfitted in such a way as to enter the har-

bor without arousing suspicion. On Friday, December 23, the schooner *Enterprise*, under the command of Lieutenant Decatur, captured the *Mastico*, a seventy-ton Tripolitan ketch, and towed it to Malta. There it was renamed the *Intrepid* and rigged "in a manner peculiar to the Mediterranean" so that it would not be suspected by the Tripolitans.[54]

On January 31, 1804, Commodore Preble ordered Lieutenant Decatur to destroy the *Philadelphia*. He instructed Decatur to secure seventy volunteers and lead the *Intrepid* into the harbor at Tripoli with the express purpose of "boarding and burning" the frigate. He was to enter at night in company with the *Syren*, commanded by Lieutenant Charles Stewart, whose mission was to provide supporting fire during and after the mission. Decatur carried ammunition for the frigate's eighteen-pound guns, which were to be fired at the pirates' ships as well as at the bashaw's castle. In addition, he brought enough combustibles to burn the *Philadelphia*. After successfully setting the captured ship on fire, he was to use two of his eighteen-pounders to sink her. That accomplished, he was to retreat and report to Preble at once.[55]

Decatur and his crew rehearsed the mission on the *Constitution* at Syracuse with each man boarding the frigate and descending to a designated spot on a lower deck to set the charges. On February 7, 1804, the *Intrepid* and the *Syren* sailed within sight of the minarets of Tripoli. But just as they prepared to launch their attack, a hard northward gale blew them back to sea, and they languished there for the next five days while their food grew rancid. Finally, on February 16, with favorable winds, they launched their mission under cover of darkness.[56]

Decatur ordered everyone to stay in the hold except for two men on deck, dressed in Turkish fashion. The *Intrepid* slipped past the rocks that protected the harbor from large warships and hailed the harbor pilot in the "*lingua franca* of the Mediterranean," explaining that he had run the blockade and was bringing provisions but in the process had lost both anchors and needed to tie to the frigate for the night. With that bit of deception, Decatur brought the ketch alongside the *Philadelphia* and took a rope aboard. As the crew then boarded the frigate, a shout went out from the watch, *Americanos!* After dodging a few pistol shots, the well-organized sailors overwhelmed the light opposition and began to load the combustibles onto the *Philadelphia*. The fort and pirate fleet remained silent as the Americans placed their charges and set fire to the frigate. When the crew reentered the *Intrepid* and pulled away from the burning ship, they came under fire. But as the flames rose aboard the *Philadelphia*, its stored powder exploded, and in the confusion the ketch made it out with no one injured or killed. In what British admiral Lord Nelson called "the most bold and daring act of the age," Decatur and his men executed the mission to perfection and reversed the tide of the Tripolitan War.[57]

The Danish consul at Tripoli, C. Nissen, reported that "the Bashaw Saw the whole business with his own Eyes." He had watched helplessly as the "Frigate was totally burnt" and the ketch escaped the reach of his batteries. Fearful of an impending assault on his capital, the angry bey ordered the American captives to be put under strong guard and held incommunicado. Further, he ordered "great preparations of defence."[58] The offensive had swung to the Americans. With no small amount of pride, George Davis, American consul at Tunis, wrote Tobias Lear that the destruction of the *Philadelphia* "has made much noise in Tunis, and is the only occasion, on which I have heard our Countrymen spoken of with due respect."[59]

In the United States, word of the daring feat fostered an outpouring of national pride while rekindling partisan rancor. While Federalists heralded the heroics of Decatur and his seamen, they gave no credit to the man they were trying to oust from the White House. For their part, Republicans sought to shame the Federalists for putting partisanship ahead of national pride. A reporter for the pro-Jefferson *National Intelligencer* opined that the "gallant conduct" of Americans in the Tripoli harbor should have produced a "common feeling" of patriotism across the country. But, the paper noted, the measure of applause was "either denied by the federalists, or is dealt out with a niggardly hand." Republican commentators were eager for the president to gain every advantage from his prosecution of the war against Tripoli.[60]

The importance of having burned the *Philadelphia* was not lost on Commodore Preble. Writing to U.S. minister to France Robert Livingston in March 1804, he reported that the bashaw was "extremely angry" at the loss of the ship and had confined the American prisoners within the walls of his castle and had forbidden the consuls to speak with them; the fact that Americans held a "sufficient" number of Tripolitan prisoners ensured their safety.[61]

As a result of the successful raid, the bashaw became much more reasonable in peace negotiations. Preble claimed that the bashaw's first demand for ransom and peace was "three Millions of Doll[ar]s!" But that had now "fallen considerably," and he had recently offered to make a truce "without Money" for five years.[62]

While delighted with the raid, Preble was eager to press his advantage by making direct assaults on Tripoli. He told Livingston that he planned to attack the coasts of Tripoli "on every part of it" and had requested the loan or hire of a few gunboats and mortar boats from the Neapolitan government. If he obtained those key assets, Preble stated as a matter of fact, "I will oblige the Bashaw to sue for Peace as a favour in three days after I reach his Coast."[63]

Fortuitously, in November 1803, Yusuf's brother Hamet Karamanli wrote to Thomas Jefferson and told him of his—Hamet's—plan to take Tripoli and requested U.S. assistance. Near the end of his rule, their ailing father, Ali Karamanli, had designated Hassan, the eldest of his three sons, as his successor; but before Ali died, Yusuf had shot and killed Hassan. Under the laws of primogeniture, Hamet was now heir to the throne, but upon Ali's death, Yusuf seized the throne and forced Hamet to flee to Tunis. In a short-lived reconciliation, Yusuf allowed Hamet to return as ruler of Derne, Tripoli's easternmost port. But as Hamet explained to Jefferson, he had been ousted from Derne because Yusuf had sent troops into the city and forced him to abandon it. In addition, Yusuf held Hamet's wife and five children hostage to ensure against any attempts Hamet might undertake to unseat Yusuf.[64] But with support from the United States, he planned to assemble a force of Arabs to retake Derne and then capture Tripoli. If America supported his efforts to take what he thought was legitimately his, he would enter into a peace treaty and guarantee peace between the United States and the other Barbary States. Hamet posed the question to Jefferson: Would it be better to support him with $40,000 plus some military supplies or to pay Yusuf's "unreasonable demand" of $3 million with no guarantee of a lasting peace?[65]

In the spring of 1804 Preble proposed to continue the blockade, attack Tripoli and the pirate fleet with gunboats and bomb boats, and support a land campaign led by the bashaw's brother, Hamet. So aggressive an attack would take far more assets than Preble currently had under his command, and he would have to watch his flanks against threats from Tunis and Morocco. Nevertheless, Jefferson approved the costly plan and dispatched a fourth squadron to the Mediterranean under the command of Preble's senior, Samuel Barron.

By far the largest, this final squadron had the mix of vessels that Preble requested: six frigates, six smaller ships, brigs and schooners, two bomb vessels, and ten gunboats. Costing $1.5 million, or three times that of the first squadron sent out in 1801, this formidable force reflected Jefferson's determination to end the war with a military victory.[66] Yet the resulting drain on the national treasury suggested that it would be the last great push. On May 26, 1804, Jefferson once again polled his cabinet over the question of negotiating with Tripoli and the terms to which the United States should agree. The conclusion: everything would depend on the outcome of Preble's strategy. If the joint sea and land offensive succeeded, then America would demand that Tripoli turn over all prisoners without ransom; the old treaty would be reestablished without paying tribute. If the campaign were unsuccessful, the cabinet advised that America pay $500 per prisoner, less an equivalent amount for the prisoners in American custody, plus "the sum in gross & tribute" previously agreed upon.[67] From partisan politics to the nation's finances to America's international standing, much depended on the success of Preble's strategy.

On August 3, before Barron's fleet arrived at Tripoli, Preble launched the first of a series of attacks that he hoped would destroy the Tripolitan fleet and shore defenses. Led by the "gallant Captain Decatur," six American gunboats entered the harbor and engaged nineteen Tripolitan gunboats, a brig, two schooners, and a galley. The enemy, Preble wrote in a hyperbolic damage assessment report, was "completely beaten." Three enemy gunboats were captured, one was sunk, and the remaining fifteen were damaged "considerably." The captured vessels were all new, and each carried a brass twenty-four-pound gun and a brass three-pounder. In all, fifty-two Tripolitans were killed and fifty-six taken prisoner. For two hours the American gunboats, positioned only five hundred yards from the shore batteries, pounded away at the city, and Tripoli "suffered very considerably" from the bombardment.[68] Finally able to maneuver gunboats within the harbor, the U.S. Navy delivered the outcome Jefferson had long predicted. The action also further secured Stephen Decatur's stature as America's foremost hero in the Tripolitan War.

As Decatur left the harbor, he learned that his brother, Lieutenant James Decatur, had been shot and killed while boarding an enemy vessel. Stephen immediately returned to the harbor to avenge his brother's death. According to Alexander MacKenzie, whose account of the event memorialized Decatur's feat that night, Stephen singled out the "treacherous commander" responsible for his brother's death and engaged him in hand-to-hand combat. Characterized as a Turk of "gigantic size," the pirate wielded a "heavily ironed boarding-pike," while Decatur had but a cutlass. In the fight, Decatur's sword broke at the hilt, leaving him without a weapon. The Turk capitalized on his advantage and thrust the pike into Decatur, but "tearing the weapon from the wound," Decatur grappled with his adversary and gained the topmost position as the two men fell to the deck in a struggle to the death. At that moment a Tripolitan officer rushed Decatur from behind and aimed a blow at his head, but an American named Reuben James, who had lost the use of both arms in the conflict, thrust himself between the attacker and Decatur, taking the blow on his own head. Meanwhile, the gigantic Turk had gained the upper hand. With a dagger drawn from his sash, he seemed certain to send yet another Decatur to his grave—when Stephen managed to pull a pistol from his pantaloon pocket and fire a fatal shot into the advancing Turk. MacKenzie concluded, "Decatur, disengaging himself from the heap of wounded and slain, which the struggle had gathered around him, stood again that day a victor on the enemy's deck."[69]

Over the next month Preble launched two more attacks, pounding the castle and its batteries and engaging the pirate fleet deep within the harbor. American sailors and diplomats were certain that the raids would force the bashaw to the bargaining table and make his demands more reasonable. And there was some evidence they did. One sailor noted that before the attacks, French and Russian ministers had interceded on the United States' behalf in arranging for the release of American prisoners but that the bashaw had insisted on a payment of $500,000. After the second attack, the sailor boasted, Yusuf came down to $150,000 for ransom and peace. Preble shared the sailor's belief that further attacks, especially after the arrival of the big guns of Barron's frigates, would force the bashaw to come to terms. Accordingly, in August 1804, Preble offered $80,000 for ransom and $20,000 for peace.[70]

The view from inside the bashaw's palace, however, was quite different. Monsieur Beaussier, French chargé d'affaires, indicated that the Tripolitan leader's spirit was hardly broken. Tripolitan minister of foreign affairs Sidi Muhammad Dghies told Beaussier that "since the Effusion of blood had already commenced, his country was bent upon continuing the war."[71] Supported by his people's patriotic fervor, the bashaw vowed to "wait the event, unless the sum is considerably augmented." Dghies thought that peace was impossible for "less than two or three hundred thousand dollars."[72] Of the American bombardment, Beaussier noted that a few rounds had landed in the castle, one in the sailors' prison, and another had struck some houses, but that overall the result was hardly devastating. He opined that "the Bashaw seems to care little about the injure done to the houses by the Shot, which is easily repaired," adding that such "Menaces have no other effect than to inflame the mind of the Prince."[73]

Frustrated by the failure of Barron's powerful fleet to arrive on time and anxious about the deteriorating weather and less favorable seas, Preble decided to launch one final attack on the harbor. On September 4 he sent a fire-ship loaded with explosives into the harbor, intending to detonate it under the walls of the castle. The ketch *Intrepid*, which Decatur had commanded while capturing and burning the *Philadelphia*, was the instrument chosen for this "daring and highly dangerous enterprise." This time she was under the command of Richard Somers who, along with one other officer and four volunteer seamen, carried out the mission. They loaded fifteen thousand pounds of powder in the hold of the ketch and placed atop the explosives 250 thirteen-inch fused shells. At nine o'clock the *Intrepid* began working its way into the harbor, and an hour later an "awful explosion took place." According to one American sailor aboard the frigate *Constitution*, "the flash illumined the whole heavens around, while the terrific concussion shook every thing far and near." Over the next several hours Preble learned that the *Intrepid*'s crew had chosen to blow themselves up rather than be captured by the enemy. Further, the explosion had occurred several hundred yards short of the point where the detonation had been calculated to do maximum damage, inflicting no casualties on the Tripolitans and causing no damage to pirate ships.[74]

Since it was already early September, a disappointed Commodore Preble decided to end his attacks on Tripoli and wait for Barron's relief squadron. Preble was in need of supplies, reporting that fresh water and ammunition were running dangerously low. Summer's favorable sailing conditions were also ending.

Thankfully, in September 1804 Barron's relief squadron arrived and brought with it naval firepower, instructions for supporting a daring land attack, and the man who would lead it. William Eaton, an ex–army captain and former consul to Tunis, had long believed that the United States should assist the bashaw's brother, Hamet Karamanli. Now Eaton returned to the Mediterranean with approval to direct a "concerted operation" by the United States and Hamet's forces against Yusuf. Jefferson authorized Commodore Barron "to enter into an understanding with Hamet" and to supply him with arms, ammunition, and money "to a moderate extent." The president gave Eaton the vague designation of agent for the navy to facilitate the joint venture. The navy, primarily through Eaton, was to coordinate operations with Hamet to "attack the common enemy by land and sea at the same time."[75]

With Eaton's arrival, the American war effort was left to the discretion of three individuals, a division that almost guaranteed conflict. First, Jefferson invested Tobias Lear with "full power and authority to negociate a Treaty of Peace with the Bashaw of Tripoli."[76] The critical decisions of when to negotiate and under what terms rested with Lear. Second, Jefferson placed Commodore Samuel Barron in charge of the naval squadron with overall responsibility for military affairs. He was to continue the blockade of Tripoli and keep the pressure on the bashaw to negotiate. And he was to cooperate with William Eaton "in all such measures as may be deemed the best calculated to effectuate a termination" of the war.[77] Third, Eaton had a great deal of latitude from the president and full cooperation from Barron to proceed with his scheme to join forces with Hamet Karamanli and reestablish him as bashaw of Tripoli. Having been driven from Tripoli by Yusuf, Hamet maintained that he was the country's legitimate ruler.[78]

After arriving in the Mediterranean in the late summer of 1804, Eaton boarded the brig *Argus* under the command of Isaac Hull and sailed for Alexandria to meet Hamet, who was in Egypt recruiting Arabs for his expedition against Yusuf. On February 23,

1805, Eaton and Hamet signed an agreement that Eaton forwarded to Secretary of State Madison. In the pact, Eaton pledged that the U.S. forces would use "utmost exertions, so far as comports with their own honor and interest," to reestablish Hamet as bashaw of Tripoli. Specifically, the United States would supply cash, ammunition, and provisions to aid Hamet's land operations against Yusuf. Once installed as bashaw, Hamet would repay America by consigning all tribute from Sweden, Denmark, and the Batavian Republic to the United States. In order to carry out the operation, it was agreed that Eaton would be designated "General and Commander in Chief" of all land forces, including the Arabs Hamet had recruited in Egypt, those loyal Tripolitans who remained with him, and ten United States volunteers, including eight marines and two navy midshipmen.[79] Though never ratified by the U.S. Senate, the agreement defined relations between Hamet and Eaton and the mission they planned to undertake.

On March 8 Eaton and his force of about five hundred men left Alexandria for Derne, the strategic Tripolitan port about four hundred miles east of Tripoli, where Hamet had formerly ruled. Hamet convinced Eaton that an overland march five hundred miles across the Libyan Desert was preferable to bringing the army by sea. This would prove an early indication of Hamet's less-than-sure control over his own troops. Meanwhile Captain Hull would sail for a rendezvous point near Derne in order to provide Eaton's men with provisions and reinforcements.[80]

With an optimism matched by determination, Eaton led the expedition on its long, arduous trek that would take six weeks to reach the outskirts of Derne. But he soon confronted a series of obstacles that threatened to abort the mission. First, he characterized the "hordes of Arabs" that Hamet had assembled as "a rabble [rather] than an Army," lacking military firmness and discipline. Second, he had serious reservations about Hamet's leadership abilities. Low on supplies, at one point the motley army revolted against Eaton, with Hamet participating in the attempted mutiny.

Through personal courage, perseverance, and resolve, Eaton held the force together, and on April 27 it arrived outside the walls of Derne.[81] On the next day the assault on the city began.

Derne was vulnerable to a well-coordinated land-sea attack, but its defenders were confident that the Americans could not launch such an assault. They did not think that the navy could mount a successful bombardment from the sea because the harbor was shallow, and American warships could not approach close enough to do serious damage. Consequently, the port was lightly defended by a "small fortification" with "8 or 10 Guns."[82] The defenders were equally certain that the Americans could not attack the city by land, because such an assault would require a march of hundreds of miles through the Libyan Desert, a feat only a madman would attempt.

Derne's defenders underestimated the resourcefulness and daring of the American-led forces. After providing Eaton with arms and ammunition, Captain Hull lightened the *Argus*, the *Hornet*, and the *Nautilus* so that they could maneuver within firing range of Derne's outer fort, then commenced to pour a "heavy fire" upon it. For about an hour, the Tripolitans returned fire from the fort, but with shot "flying thick about them," the defenders quit their posts and withdrew into the town. Then the cruisers turned their guns onto the beach and cleared the way for the handful of Americans in Eaton's force to enter the fort. At the same time Hamet's recruits attacked from the landward side. At about three o'clock in the afternoon, the two midshipmen and eight marines led by Lieutenant Presley O'Bannon stormed the fort from the seaward side, "haul[ed] down the Enemys flag, and plant[ed] the American Ensign on the Walls of the Battery." The Americans turned the guns of the battery onto the fleeing defenders. At the same time Hamet's forces had forced their way into the landward side of the fort, and the Tripolitans were caught in the middle of a deadly crossfire, which "silenced them." By four o'clock, Eaton and his forces had "complete possession of the Town and Fort."[83]

When Hull sent boats ashore bringing ammunition and provisions and retrieving the wounded, he discovered that one marine, John Wilton, had been killed in action, and two others wounded, along with ten of Hamet's recruits. In addition, William Eaton suffered a musket shot through his left wrist.[84]

Undeterred by his wound, Eaton turned his thoughts to attacking Tripoli. In a letter to Captain Barron, he expressed confidence that his army could easily proceed to the port some four hundred miles to the west, but he expressed apprehensions, "grounded on experience," about Hamet's Arabs. During the Derne assault the Arabs had sought out "safe positions" until an area was secure, and only when given an opportunity to plunder did they become "at once brave." Eaton voiced another concern. He feared that the United States would use Hamet only to take Tripoli and then abandon his interests at the peace talks. Eaton thought it only fair that the United States should at minimum return Hamet to his status ante bellum plus restore to him his family, whom Yusuf was holding. Despite his misgivings, Eaton stated that Derne should "not be abandoned, nor terms of peace precipitately embraced." Land-sea operations were poised to deliver a "death blow to the Barbary System," and to withdraw and settle too quickly would be "a wound to the National honor."[85]

As he planned his attack on Tripoli, Eaton, recently buoyed by reports of reinforcements, received word that on June 4 Tobias Lear had concluded a peace agreement with Tripoli that called for Eaton and his garrison to leave Derne immediately. While granting the treaty to be "more favorable—and, separately considered, more honorable than any peace obtained by any Christian nation with a Barbary regency at any period within a hundred years," Eaton worried that the United States had left Hamet and his Arab fighters to a fate that Yusuf would decide. Reflecting on the significance of what he regarded as a premature departure, Eaton penned that Derne was being "thrown from proud success and elated prospects into an abys of hopeless wretchedness."[86]

In a letter to Eaton, Lear explained why he had made the peace. In late May he had received intelligence from foreign consuls at

Tripoli and from American prisoners that "the present was a favorable moment" for negotiations. Soon thereafter he received an offer from the bashaw, who demanded $200,000 for peace and ransom plus the return of all Tripolitan prisoners and property, a demand that Lear rejected "*in toto*." Lear countered with an ultimatum: $60,000 for ransom "but not a cent for peace." Lear told Eaton that his forces' "heroic bravery" had made a "deep impression" on the bashaw. Lear exploited that military triumph in negotiating with the bashaw, in particular with regards to Hamet. In the end Yusuf accepted Lear's terms: if the United States withdrew all forces from Derne and Hamet peacefully left the kingdom, he would restore Hamet's family to him.[87]

Several factors explain why Yusuf agreed to a treaty whose terms were far less favorable than those the United States extended to the other Barbary States. The growing U.S. naval force outside his harbor finally gave Yusuf "the greatest anxiety for peace," especially since his funds were dwindling and disaffection for him among his people was growing.[88] Moreover, Yusuf apparently read American newspapers sent to the prisoners and learned that the Mediterranean Fund would raise more than half a million dollars each year for the war effort. According to one American, that report made the bashaw realize that the United States had the resources to press its attack on Tripoli. In addition, William Bainbridge suggested that reports of Eaton's attack on Derne had weighed heavily on the bashaw, and that Lear had exploited that concern by pointing out that if a handful of Americans could take Derne, then a more robust force could topple Tripoli.[89]

Upon hearing news of the peace, Jefferson applauded both Eaton's land campaign and Lear's negotiations. He credited Eaton's assault on Derne with forcing Yusuf to accept a peace without tribute and reduce his original ransom demands by almost 90 percent. The president underscored the significance of restoring the American prisoners to the "life and liberty" that he believed to be the sacred right of every American citizen. Evoking language from the Declaration of Independence, Jefferson exulted in the fact that the United States had won a significant battle and had secured a sense of American independence in a place where it had been denied for more than twenty years. He was about to learn, however, that the treaty with Yusuf would be subjected to a highly partisan critique at home and that the Barbary pirates were still far from being awed into submission.

SIX

AN UNEASY PEACE:
PARTISAN DEBATE AND BRITISH HARASSMENT

For some Americans, the victorious outcome of the Tripolitan War represented an extension of the glory of 1776. The revolutionary generation knew the cost of independence and believed that it should never be taken for granted. In early 1806, in what was billed as a "Patriotic Celebration," the producers at one New York theater linked the recent sacrifice of American sailors in the Mediterranean with American revolutionary hero General Joseph Warren. The first part of the evening's bill was *The Historical Tragedy of Bunker Hill, or the Death of General Warren.* The second half was a two-act musical called *The Tars of Tripoli, or, A Tribute of Respect to the Mediterranean Heroes.* The latter concluded in dramatic fashion with the unveiling of a "Triumphant Naval Pillar," which was inscribed to the American sailors who fought the Tripolitans and was adorned with trophies from their victory. As the final dance terminated, Columbia descended to the stage supported by "LIBERTY AND JUSTICE," after which the defeated Tripolitans knelt before her decree.[1]

America's victory in the Mediterranean contributed to the growing sense of nationalism fostered by the War of 1812. Even before the Tripoli Treaty was signed in 1805, Americans celebrated the defeat of the pirates as an important battle in the march toward national prosperity. An 1804 song credited the Tripolitan War and the Louisiana Purchase (1803) with advancing the nation's "highest ambition" of "freedom and trade." The latter doubled the size of the country and represented a new "link in the Union," while the former promised that the Tripolitan pirates would soon be forced to abandon tribute demands and to give Americans justice.[2]

Americans expressed nationalist sentiments by comparing and contrasting the United States and its feats on the world stage with those of more established powers. In 1804 residents in several large American cities viewed a large painting of Britain's victory over the French in the naval Battle of the Nile (1798). The following year an American painter produced a similar painting that celebrated America's defeat of Tripoli. Clearly intended to depict America's naval triumph as being as glorious as Britain's, the huge canvas, entitled *Tars in Tripoli*, showed the American fleet in the Tripoli harbor bombarding Yusuf's defenses and thereby shattering his despotic power.[3] In the next year, 1806, Joseph Hanson expanded the theme in verse: "The Musselman Humbled, or a Heroic Poem in Celebration of the Bravery Displayed by the American Tars, in the Contest with Tripoli." In his patriotic salute, Hanson contrasted Tripolitan tyranny and American freedom: the pirates fought for oppressive and lawless masters in quest of plunder, while Americans defended personal freedom and strove for free trade.[4]

While Americans paid tribute to the Mediterranean heroes and basked in national pride, Washington politicians squared off in a heated contest over who should receive credit for the war's successes and who should be blamed for its setbacks. Republicans regarded the outcome as a glorious victory attributable to the sage policies of President Jefferson, but Federalists charged the commander in chief with indecision, deceit, and betrayal. Throughout the war Federalists had criticized Jefferson's conduct, from his hesitancy to pursue the enemy without a congressional declaration of war to the negotiation of a peace treaty before total military victory had been achieved. Though the opposition joined in the outpouring of gratitude to the brave officers and men who defeated the Barbary pirates, they mounted a withering offensive against the president on three fronts: his slighting of the real war hero, William

Eaton; his exploitation and abandonment of the ex-bashaw Hamet Karamanli; and his complicity in Tobias Lear's premature and dishonorable treaty.

Debate over the administration's conduct of the war occurred within a Congress deeply divided by political ploys aimed at settling old scores and by policy initiatives that were directed toward defining the nation's place in the world. Guaranteeing a partisan debate over the Tripolitan war and peace was the Republican impeachment of Federalist judges Samuel Chase and John Pickering. Still smarting from Federalist imprisonment of Republican newspaper editors during the presidential election of 1800, Jeffersonians were determined to exact political revenge. On December 30, 1803, House Republicans impeached Pickering on charges of high crimes and misdemeanors, and on March 12, 1804, the Senate convicted him by a vote of 20 to 6. The House impeached Chase in March 1804, but the Senate acquitted him a year later. When the Tripoli Treaty arrived on the Senate floor in December 1805, lingering ill will from the impeachment battles ensured that the debate over its terms would occur within a bitter partisan atmosphere.

More important for the nation's future, the treaty debate became part of the larger debate over America's place in the world. While agreeing that U.S. political independence must be accompanied by economic independence, Federalists and Republicans disagreed over how best to achieve the goal. America's international aspirations were expressed in the country's trade policy, and the 1803 expiration of the commercial provisions of Jay's Treaty had sparked heated discussions over such questions as access to markets, the introduction of tariffs and duties, and retaliation for trade discrimination. Viewing domestic manufactures as the basis of national economic independence, Federalists advocated a protectionist trade policy that would shield American industry while the country maintained close commercial ties with its most important trading partner, Britain and British colonies. Republicans, on the other hand, regarded America's agricultural surplus as the foundation of a prosperous future and feared that protectionist tariffs would result in retaliation by other countries, leading to a decline in demand for U.S. exports. Moreover, Republicans advocated retaliation for British discrimination against American goods and interference with American shipping.

While the Tripoli Treaty inspired celebrations and sparked partisan debate at home, it hardly caused a ripple in Europe. The Tripolitan War was a minor affair in a centuries-old conflict with the Barbary powers, not unlike numerous earlier bombardments of North African strongholds by England, France, Spain, Portugal, and Venice. After seemingly successful attacks that had initially been hailed as victories, Europeans had seen the corsairs quickly reconstitute themselves and continue their raids on merchant vessels; so they were not about to consider the American feat as a "victory" until the peace held over time. But more important, the Tripolitan War failed to make headlines in European capitals because the Napoleonic Wars eclipsed it. By 1799 Europe was ablaze in a struggle between Napoleon's armies and those of a coalition headed by Britain. Indeed, American as well as European newspapers regarded the struggle between Europe's titans as the top story of the day, relegating America's clash with Tripoli to a sidebar. At issue in Europe were such big questions as the balance of power, the future of monarchies, and the course of democratic revolution. The Napoleonic Wars had direct effects on U.S. affairs, reminding the Jefferson administration that Europe, not America, still controlled the Atlantic world. While European attention was diverted, Americans in 1801 to 1805 had had a relatively free hand to fight Tripoli with little outside interference, but Britain and France decided in 1805 and 1806 that neutral shipping, including that of the United States, must not be allowed to reach each other's ports.

Much of the patriotic celebration of the victory over Tripoli centered on the exploits of a few individuals. While the New York play honored all seamen who fought the corsairs, three individuals in particular were singled out for public acclaim: Commodore Edward Preble, Captain Stephen Decatur, and Captain William Eaton. More than any of the several squadron commanders dispatched to the Mediterranean, Preble successfully carried out Jefferson's order to blockade the port of Tripoli. Despite delays in receiving reinforcements, he sealed off the harbor and took the war to the Tripolitans with a series of bold raids. He won the admiration of the officers who served under him; they memorialized it in a scroll that every man signed expressing their "very high esteem" for Preble as an officer and a commander. Pope Pius VII sent Jefferson a letter declaring that the American navy had done more "for the cause of Christianity" than had "the most powerful nations in ages," a tribute that belonged to Preble and his squadron. When Preble arrived in the United States, he was given a hero's welcome: feted with dinners in New York, honored at a White House reception, and granted a sword and gold medal by a grateful Congress. President Jefferson wanted to make him secretary of the navy, but the commodore's declining health rendered the appointment impossible. He died of cancer two years after returning home.[5]

While Preble was the persevering commander credited with winning the Tripolitan War, Stephen Decatur's daring exploits gave him celebrity status. Everyone knew of his courageous forays deep into Tripoli's harbor, first to burn the captured *Philadelphia*, and second to destroy and capture Tripolitan gunboats. When he arrived at Norfolk, the entire town seemed to want a glimpse of the conquering hero. And when he reached Washington, "the whole government seemed his to command." Congress presented him with a commemorative sword and awarded him, along with each of the other officers and crew of the *Intrepid*, two months' pay for destroying the *Philadelphia*. Decatur had expected as much as $15,000, hoping Congress would declare the captured ship a prize, but that was not to be. Though disappointed, he traveled home to Philadelphia, where he received another hero's welcome, including a sparkling round of celebratory dinners and a warm reunion with his commander, Commodore Preble.[6]

Republicans hoped that Preble and Decatur would inspire Americans to similar exertions of greatness and foster a stronger sense of national unity. In Tripoli they had demonstrated what all Americans were capable of doing, and with similar courage and purpose Americans could not only stand up to foreign threats but could also overcome domestic factionalism. The Philadelphia *Aurora* expressed the hope that the Tripolitan War, which had rid the country of Barbary depredations, would stir the nation to unite at home as Americans embraced with an "undivided spirit, the virtues and the valor of her heroes and statesmen, exerted in the maintenance of her rights, and the assertion of her independence and her honor." If so, "national joy" would replace partisan strife.[7]

Like the homecomings of Preble and Decatur, the arrival of the third returning hero, William Eaton, sparked celebration, but it also ignited a partisan battle. Unlike the two naval officers, Eaton was not at all pleased with the way the war had ended. He believed that if Jefferson and the navy had continued to support his land forces after they had taken Derne, he would have been able to capture Tripoli and win a much more glorious victory for America. As he sailed for home, Eaton poured out his bitterness in a long letter to the secretary of the navy, setting forth his interpretation of a war brought to a premature and dishonorable conclusion. He blamed Commodore Samuel Barron for betraying Hamet, and he blamed Tobias Lear for betraying America. Eaton insisted that Barron had repeatedly and firmly endorsed the plan of restoring Hamet to the throne of Tripoli, and he blamed Lear for lamely accepting Barron's subsequent denial that he had made any such commitment to Hamet. In Eaton's words, Lear's treaty was the "work of a Machevellian Commissioner into whose influence the Commodore had yielded his mind through the infirmity of Bodily weakness." Further, Eaton believed Barron's "debilitated state" explained why the commodore endorsed Lear's negotiating a peace treaty before Eaton could finish the job with a land attack on Tripoli.[8]

Federalists had long held that military leadership was Jefferson's political Achilles' heel. In the presidential elections of 1796 and 1800, they had accused Jefferson of cowardly behavior during the War of Independence, pointing in particular to his fleeing his post as Virginia governor when the British invaded the state in 1780. Federalist senators now saw an opportunity to exploit that image. Eaton's analysis of Jefferson's peace treaty with Tripoli as a sellout provided Federalist senators with an arsenal in the partisan battle over ratification. Eaton was particularly incensed that the treaty obligated the United States to pay $60,000 to ransom the *Philadelphia*'s officers and crew. Lear justified the payment by arguing that Tripoli held two hundred more prisoners than the number of Tripolitans in U.S. custody. Eaton thought that such reasoning was preposterous. In capturing Derne, Eaton had taken between twelve and fifteen thousand Tripolitans prisoner. He asked, "Could not [these have] been exchanged for 200 Prisoners of War?" Eaton found it disgraceful that no attempt was made to make such an exchange, concluding that "Tripoli was in our power and with no very extraordinary effort it might have been also in our hands. The enemy felt a conviction of this and did not hesitate to acknowledge it in the presence of commissioner."[9] Upon returning to the United States, Eaton was eager to tell his side of the story and found in the Federalists a party willing to give his version full exposure.

Members of both political parties agreed that Eaton's daring expedition against Derne was heroic and, more important, had hastened the end of the war. His return to the United States in late 1805 occasioned an outpouring of admiration by Americans everywhere. On December 2 he was feted at a dinner at Stelle's Hotel in Washington in appreciation for his "gallantry and heroism" in America's "glorious successes" in Tripoli. Toasts following the dinner extolled Eaton's spirit, energy, and courage. But very quickly the feting took on political overtones. The same issue of the *National Intelligencer* that reported on the dinner carried a scathing Federalist attack on Jefferson's conduct of the war and asserted that "the expense and procrastination of the Barbary War [should be] charged to the imbecile measures of the executive," as well as the "premature and dishonorable" peace.[10] The juxtaposition was damning: Eaton was portrayed as decisive and vigorous, Jefferson as hesitant and timid.

The subsequent jousting began over a sword. On December 16 Congress opened debate on a resolution calling for the president to present Eaton with a sword as testimony to his "gallantry and good conduct." The wording of the resolution reflected a partisan edge. While assigning Jefferson's navy but a "small part" in a supporting role, it extolled the Federalist champion Eaton for leading a small band across the Libyan Desert and successfully defeating the Tripolitans at Derne. Federalist representative Barnabas Bidwell of Massachusetts thought that Eaton's heroics merited more than a sword, and he proposed that a gold medal be given instead. Republican Joseph Clay of Pennsylvania opposed, on the grounds that only on "extraordinary" occasions should Congress recognize a citizen's contribution to the nation with a gold medal. He noted that a medal had been struck commemorating the service of Commodore Preble, who had directed naval operations in the war, but that the individual officers who served under him had received only swords. The implication was that Eaton was no Preble. Federalist James Elliott of Vermont expressed surprise at Clay's objection, given what he believed to be the magnitude of Eaton's accomplishment. He pointed out that Eaton's objective had been nothing short of ending the war and that he had met that goal despite an inadequate supply of men and arms. Elliot concluded that the "brave Preble" had received a gold medal and Eaton should also. Federalist hyperbole reached its height when Elliot pronounced Eaton's feat to be a "phenomenon in military history," undertaken in the "general interest of mankind," restoring freedom to a part of the world where it had been extinguished since Cato's senate was toppled at Utica.[11]

With the deep split between Federalists and Republicans widened by the impeachment of the Federalist judges, unanimity over Eaton's achievement and its just merits was politically impossible, and after a week's postponement, debate over the motion to award Eaton a gold medal resumed with even greater intensity. Representative Clay opposed the measure on the grounds that prior to the Tripolitan War only three gold medals had ever been struck by the United States: one commemorating the victory at Saratoga, one for the capitulation at Yorktown, and a third on Washington's resignation of military power to civilian authority. In Clay's reckoning, Eaton's accomplishment did not rise to this standard. Indeed, Clay thought that Eaton's heroics did not even match those of Stephen Decatur during the Tripolitan War, and Decatur had been recognized with simply a sword, despite having "captured, and burnt the frigate *Philadelphia*, and was afterwards the first man, who took a gunboat from the enemy." Republican John Randolph of Virginia weighed in against Eaton receiving a medal with an acerbic tongue. Belittling Eaton's achievement, Randolph referred to it as "a skirmish between a few of our countrymen and a handful of undisciplined, half armed barbarians."[12]

The Republicans won the debate, but the Eaton affair was hardly put to rest. When Congress failed to pass any of the various Federalist proposals to recognize Eaton, including awarding him a sword, a medal, a tract of public land, or simply a resolution of thanks, Eaton became determined to vindicate his action in the desert at the expense of Jefferson and Lear. He put out the word that he had information that Federalists could use to discredit the Republican administration. Senator William Plumer of New Hampshire was eager to learn what Eaton had to say concerning Jefferson's mismanagement of the war and Lear's betrayal of American interests. But after interviewing Eaton at his hotel in Washington and listening to a torrent of invective, Plumer confessed that while Eaton was "a bold, brave, enterprising man," he was at the same time "imprudent and not fit to command."[13] But the unstable Eaton also had information about the administration's conduct during the war that the Federalists could not resist.

The most explosive item that Eaton provided his congressional allies concerned the American commitments to Hamet Karamanli. According to Eaton, Jefferson and Madison had always known that in exchange for the ex-bashaw's assistance in defeating his brother's regime, the United States had promised to restore him to the throne of Tripoli. When the administration insisted that the agreement was restricted to military cooperation with no political strings attached, Eaton charged Jefferson with deceit and dishonor; he had lured Hamet into an alliance, used him to achieve a military victory, and then discarded him.

The matter formally came before Congress in early 1806, when Hamet petitioned for monetary relief and assistance in securing the release of his family, who were still in Yusuf's custody. On January 13 Jefferson sent Congress a letter explaining the United States' commitment to Hamet. He reported that when the idea of a joint action had been first presented to him, he had deemed "concerted operations by those who have a common enemy [to be] entirely justifiable," adding that such operations "might produce effects favorable to both without binding either to guarantee the objects of the other." Jefferson wrote that he had informed Commodore Samuel Barron to spend a moderate amount on arms and ammunition to support a land assault on Derne if he thought the "utility" of the enterprise justified it. But, the president added, "the instructions of June 6 to Commodore Barron shew that a co-operation only was intended, and by no means an union of our object with the fortune of the ex-bashaw [Hamet]; and the Commodore's letters of March 22 and May 19, prove that he had the most correct idea of our intentions."[14] With that testimony, Jefferson contradicted Eaton's claim that he had had authorization to restore Hamet to the throne.

Jefferson then addressed Eaton's charge that Tobias Lear had negotiated a premature treaty. He had never intended a land attack against Tripoli, the president explained; "we certainly had never contemplated, nor were we prepared to land an army of our own, or to raise, pay, or subsist, an army of Arabs to march from Derne to Tripoli, and to carry on a land war at such a distance from our resources. Our means and our authority were merely naval." Jefferson added "that such were the expectations of Hamet, his letter of

June 29th, is an unequivocal acknowledgment." In response to Eaton's insistence that Barron had given him "verbal instructions" that amounted to a commitment by the United States to place Hamet on the throne, Jefferson called such a stipulation "so entirely unauthorized, so far beyond our views, and so onerous, [that it] could not be sanctioned by our government." Jefferson further contended that an assault on Tripoli was unnecessary. Eaton's capture of Derne had been sufficient to make Yusuf seek terms, and Lear had seized the moment to negotiate the treaty. Jefferson concluded his defense by insisting that Lear had not ignored the ex-bashaw's plight, pointing to article 3 of the signed treaty that demanded the restitution of Hamet's family.[15]

To counter the president's interpretation, Federalists offered Eaton's version of events, which cast Hamet as a freedom fighter and Jefferson as an ungrateful coward. Federalist newspapers carried the congressional debates over the relief bill with commentary that left no doubt in readers' minds about who was the hero and who the villain. In a typical account, the *New-York Evening Post* of March 24 sarcastically invited the "admirers of every thing Jeffersonian" to read Senator Stephen R. Bradley's committee report on Hamet's treatment. Drawing on Eaton's recollection and interpretation of events, Bradley's committee claimed that beginning in 1801 the United States had entered into an agreement with the ex-bashaw to obtain a permanent peace with Tripoli and place Hamet on the throne. Hamet, Bradley reported, had received repeated assurances that the United States would "persevere" in the joint venture until he was restored to his rightful place. The committee asserted that Hamet, assisted by a few Americans, had defeated Yusuf's forces at Derne and "would have marched to the throne of Tripoli, had he been supported by the co-operation of the American squadron, which in honor and good faith he had a right to expect."[16] Once again the implication was that, but for Jefferson's withholding naval support, Hamet would have retaken Tripoli and, once restored to the throne, negotiated a more honorable, and more favorable, treaty with the United States.

In his report, Bradley cast Tobias Lear as the villain. With Commodore Barron "debilitated by sickness," it was Jefferson's appointee Lear who had determined the timing of the treaty and, thus, the early withdrawal of troops from Derne. Bradley said the committee found no basis in fact for Lear's expressed desire to end the war out of concern for "the danger of the American prisoners in Tripoli, the unfitness of the ships for service, and the want of means to prosecute the war." Rather, the committee found Lear's explanation to be "a veil to cover an inglorious deed." Given Eaton's success at Derne, the committee concluded that had he been supported by the navy, Hamet clearly could have assumed the throne, the prisoners could have been safely returned, and a peace could have been secured without expending $60,000. Indeed, with Hamet in power, peace with the other Barbary States would have followed. Bradley closed the committee report by urging the Senate to make restitution through the remuneration bill before it.[17]

After reprinting the committee's report, the editors of the Federalist *New-York Evening Post* offered damning commentary on Jefferson's conduct during the war. They asked if, after reading the report, there was any "man in the United States weak enough to justify the conduct of the government's agent? Is there a print profligate and mercenary enough, after this, to tell us that the Tripolitan Treaty is a good treaty?" Attacking such Republican newspapers as the *Richmond Enquirer*, the *Aurora*, the *Citizen*, and the *Boston Chronicle*, the editors could not imagine that even diehard Jeffersonians could persist in saying that Lear had made a "good, and a cheap, and an honest, and an honourable treaty." The *Post* article ended with a charge that Eaton had made and forwarded to the committee: that Lear, with the administration's knowledge, had absolved the bashaw from compliance with the treaty's article promising delivery of Hamet's family to him.[18]

The Federalists tried to hold ratification of the peace treaty hostage to providing Hamet with financial relief. On April 8, 1806, they also proposed that further consideration of the treaty be postponed until June in order to make certain that the Jefferson administration forced Yusuf to return Hamet's family to him. That proposal was defeated in a vote that revealed a growing split among Federalists, with Bradley and Pickering supporting the measure and Adams and Plumer opposing it. On April 12 the Senate voted to ratify the Tripoli Treaty by a vote of 21 to 9.[19] With ratification, the Senate approved a treaty of historic significance, not only for the United States but for all nations treating with the Barbary powers. By waging a determined, sustained war, the Americans had forced Tripoli to accept a pact with neither annual tribute nor the customary presents to the bashaw. At a time when other tributaries were paying hundreds of thousands of dollars at the signing of agreements and tens of thousands each year, the United States paid neither. But the treaty was tainted by the Tripolitan demand for $60,000 in ransom, a payment that many Americans regarded as a form of tribute to merciless pirates.

As Americans celebrated and debated peace with the Barbary pirates, ominous new threats to U.S. commerce loomed on the Atlantic horizon. Locked in a war of epic scale, Britain and France redrew the rules of navigation on the high seas and reminded Americans that their victory in the Mediterranean did not fundamentally alter the Atlantic world as a tribute-demanding arena. Regarding the Tripolitan War as a sideshow to the main event of the Napoleonic Wars, the colossal European powers, not the United States, ruled the seas and dictated the terms of commerce. In a struggle for the future of Europe, England and France mobilized their entire societies in a war whose scale eclipsed the conflict in the Mediterranean. Just as Americans defeated the Tripolitan corsairs and anticipated free trade in the Mediterranean, the Atlantic became a much more dangerous place as the European combatants imposed new restrictions on ships of neutral countries, including those of the United States.

Centering on Jefferson's conduct of the war, the debate over ratifying the Tripoli Treaty had masked the larger, equally divisive issue of American trade policy. Since 1789 Federalists and Republicans had debated the commercial terms under which Americans should do business with nations around the world. Controlling the presidency and Congress throughout the 1790s, Federalists adopted a protectionist stance, though one with relatively low tariffs, averaging about 20 percent on imports. While the Republicans maintained a similar schedule of duties after winning the White House and majorities in the House and Senate in 1800, they voiced opposition to protectionism and insisted that tariffs should be levied for revenue only. In 1803, when Jefferson asked for a Mediterranean Fund to finance the war against Tripoli, Congress enacted a tariff schedule that would generate the necessary income.[20]

The commercial clauses of the Tripoli Treaty of 1805 reflected the Republican Party's vision of an independent America trading on the basis of reciprocity in markets around the world. Under that agreement, U.S. merchants would have access to Tripoli markets under the terms granted to the most favored nation trading with Tripoli at the present or in the future. But the importance of the Tripoli Treaty was not its trade provisions but its commitment to peace. American imports and exports with Tripoli were minuscule. The real significance of the accord was the right of free navigation whereby American merchantmen could sail past Tripolitan territory without interference.

Far more important was the commercial treaty that Jefferson was seeking with Britain. Indeed, while the Senate ratified the Tripoli Treaty, Jefferson instructed James Monroe, U.S. emissary in London, to negotiate a trade agreement with Britain that would replace the commercial terms of Jay's Treaty. Jefferson had opposed the ratification of Jay's Treaty in the mid-1790s. At the time he had spoken out against the pact's mercantilist policies, including Britain's granting only limited U.S. access to West Indies markets and the Royal Navy's continued harassment of American ships trading with France, then locked in combat with the British. Now Jefferson sought a commercial treaty based on the same principles

embodied in the Tripoli Treaty: access to all markets on a most favored nation basis, trade reciprocity between Britain and America,
and cessation of British interference with American neutrality. A favorable agreement with Britain was at the top of Jefferson's trade
priorities because of the current and potential trade between the
two nations. Unlike Tripoli, Britain provided a rich market for U.S.
agricultural surpluses and supplied American consumers with
manufactured goods.

But alas, Jefferson failed to get the terms he sought because
Americans and Europeans pursued diametrically opposed goals.
While Jefferson sought to expand American access to European
markets, British and French leaders were determined to constrict
neutral shipping. In 1805 a British judge permitted British warships and privateers to seize and condemn merchant vessels sailing
to French ports. And the next year Napoleon responded to the
British blockade of the European coast with the Berlin Decree,
which forbade all commerce and communication with the British
Isles. America's response was to restate its neutral rights and to insist that U.S. merchant vessels had a right to ship nonmilitary
goods to both Britain and France.

Throughout 1806 Monroe gamely pursued a commercial
agreement, but Britain had greater priorities than a bilateral trade
agreement with the United States. Britain was at the head of a coalition to stop Napoleon's march across Europe. Jefferson followed
the widening conflict, commenting on one occasion that war had
"lighted up Europe" and on another that the nations of Europe
were "in commotion and arming against each other." To deny
Britain war matériel, Napoleon devised a strategy known as the
Continental System, barring Britain from trading with France,
French allies, and neutrals, including the United States. Britain
countered this commercial warfare with a naval blockade of its
own. Thus British negotiators utterly refused to consider Jefferson's free-trade proposals, regarding them as patent violations
of the war effort against Napoleon. Impatient with Monroe's
progress, Jefferson named William Pinkney of Maryland as a spe-

cial envoy to assist in the negotiations, but his presence at the bargaining table made little difference: the British remained adamant in their insistence that the Royal Navy reserved the right to keep American merchantmen within bounds that suited Britain's war interests, including the right to forbid U.S. ships from sailing to French ports, the right to board and search American vessels for contraband cargo, and the right to impress American sailors into the Royal Navy. When Jefferson received the treaty signed by Monroe and Pinkney on December 31, 1806, he was so indignant that he refused to submit it to the Senate for ratification.

Britain's refusal to allow American vessels to sail freely in the Atlantic had a direct bearing on Jefferson's plans to enforce the Tripoli Treaty. Peace with Tripoli, the president knew, did not mean American independence in the Mediterranean. Past experiences had proven that the Barbary pirates would resume depredations at the slightest breach of the treaty or at any alleged provocation. Therefore he instructed Navy Secretary Smith to draw up a "naval peace establishment," specifying the number and types of vessels and the number of officers and men needed to keep the peace in the Mediterranean and secure America's home waters. As the country shifted from wartime to peace, the president wanted to restructure the navy. The effectiveness of American gunboats in the Tripolitan War had reaffirmed his long-held belief that the United States would be better served by a navy of small warships and gunboats suited for defending harbors than by a deepwater navy.

Included in Smith's restructured navy were warships designated for service in the Mediterranean. Secretary Smith ordered Captain James Barron to take command of a squadron that would patrol the region, protect American commerce, and remind the Barbary pirates that any raids on American shipping would be met by overwhelming force. Barron was ordered to take command of his flagship, the frigate *Chesapeake*, at Hampton, Virginia, and sail for the Mediterranean on or about June 1, 1807.[21]

But in March, while the *Chesapeake* was being outfitted for its cruise, the British consul in Norfolk, Virginia, Colonel John Hamilton, sent a letter to Stephen Decatur stating that four British sailors had been recruited into the *Chesapeake*'s crew and demanding their immediate return. Though he was commander of the Norfolk Navy Yard, Decatur replied that the matter lay outside his jurisdiction. With tensions between the two nations already running high, Decatur had no intention of aiding the British; he suggested that Colonel Hamilton take up the matter through diplomatic channels. Hamilton found Decatur's reply unacceptable. British warships were stationed outside the Chesapeake because two French ships that had been damaged by a hurricane had sought refuge at Norfolk and were undergoing repairs. Vice Admiral Sir George Cranfield Berkeley, commander of His Majesty's North American operations, was determined to remain in the area until the French ships weighed anchor, at which point the Royal Navy could pounce on them. But the waiting took its toll on the morale of his seamen, and some of them deserted. At least five of the deserters accepted enlistment bonuses offered by the U.S. Navy for qualified hands to man the *Chesapeake*.[22]

The question of returning the deserters to the British soon escalated into a dramatic confrontation that had profound implications for the American mission to the Mediterranean. To the British, desertions were intolerable breaches of naval discipline and had to be dealt with accordingly. Moreover, locked in an ongoing war with France, British ships could ill afford to be shorthanded. But to the Americans, desertions raised the vexing question of impressments. Some of the deserters might be American citizens who had been illegally impressed or forced into the Royal Navy. Accordingly, Navy Secretary Smith ordered Captain Barron to look into the matter, specifically stating, "You will be pleased to make full inquiry relative to these men (especially if they are American Citizens) and inform me of the result." Upon conducting his investigation, Barron determined that at least three of the deserters were indeed American citizens, and he refused to hand them or any of the sailors over to the British. Barron considered the matter closed and prepared his squadron to sail for the Mediterranean.[23]

On June 22, 1807, the *Chesapeake* and a squadron of American ships set sail for the Barbary Coast. While still in Chesapeake Bay, the Americans passed a British squadron lying at anchor off Lynnhaven Bay, among which was the HMS *Leopard*, a fifty-five-gun double-decker frigate recently arrived from Halifax. Shortly after the *Chesapeake* sailed beyond Cape Henry and into the Atlantic, sailors reported that the *Leopard* seemed to be shadowing the American frigate. By mid-afternoon, the *Leopard* pulled within sixty yards of the *Chesapeake* and signaled the Americans. On boarding the American ship, a British officer informed Captain Barron that Admiral Berkeley had directed the commanders of any British vessel that met the *Chesapeake* in international waters to search it for deserters. Furious that a British officer would presume to possess such authority over an American vessel, Barron told the messenger that he knew of no British deserters aboard his ship and that in no case would he allow British officers to search it. With that reply, the officer returned to the *Leopard*, and Barron ordered his crew to make the *Chesapeake* ready for battle. Upon hearing Barron's response, the *Leopard*'s commander once again pulled alongside and again hailed the American ship. When Barron asked him to repeat the message, the *Leopard* fired a shot across the bow of the American frigate followed within minutes by a broadside that ripped into the *Chesapeake*'s masts and hull. Damaged to the point that it was unable to return fire, the American ship took three more broadsides, the last coming even as Barron ordered the flag lowered in surrender.[24]

As a result of the *Leopard*'s attack, the administration scrapped its plan for providing American merchant ships with a naval escort in the Mediterranean. The British boarded the *Chesapeake* and forcibly reimpressed the sailors who had deserted in Norfolk, but they refused to take the American ship as a prize because the two nations were not officially at war. In reality, America was at war, in a war similar to the Barbary Wars but against a much more powerful enemy. While Barbary pirates captured unescorted American merchantmen that sailed too close to North African ports, the British had taken an American warship just off the U.S. coast. The U.S. Navy in the early nineteenth century was powerful enough to defeat the Tripolitan corsairs, but it was no match for the Royal Navy.

A comparison of naval engagements during the Tripolitan War and those of the Napoleonic Wars shows the relative power of the United States and Britain. When Commodore Preble arrived in 1803 to blockade Tripoli, he had under his command a squadron of 150 guns; by contrast, in 1798 Admiral Horatio Nelson engaged the French in the Battle of the Nile with a fleet carrying about 900 guns. Then, in the Battle of Trafalgar off Cádiz in 1805, Nelson defeated a combined Franco-Spanish fleet boasting 2,640 guns.

Jefferson knew that the Royal Navy outgunned America's relatively small fleet. Yet after the *Leopard* affair, he faced demands for revenge from indignant citizens with a "unanimity never exceeded." He confided in Attorney General Caesar Rodney that in case of war with Britain, the United States would be "unable either to protect our commerce or to meet their fleets." The British interdiction of neutral ships in the Atlantic, he knew, would deny America the fruits of its victory in Tripoli. "Under the new law of the ocean," he wrote in October 1807, "our trade in the Mediterranean has been swept away by seizures and condemnations," not by Barbary pirates but by His Majesty's Navy.[25]

Rather than engage in a military conflict that the United States could not win, Jefferson responded to the *Leopard*'s attack by bringing economic pressure against the British, and he recommended an embargo against foreign trade to Congress. He had long held the view that America should retaliate against powers that refused to trade on a reciprocal basis, and he had specifically deemed the cessation of trade as the republic's most potent weapon against Britain. In 1785, after Britain's refusal to sign a commercial treaty on terms favorable to the United States, Jefferson had suggested to Madison that only "physical obstruction" of trade would bring the British to reason. He reasoned that once America demonstrated that it could forgo commerce with Britain, the British would then be eager to consent to an "equal commerce."[26] Again in 1794, as Americans debated Jay's Treaty, Jefferson advocated "distressing their commerce" to Washington as a means of convincing the British to accept trade terms more favorable to the United States.[27] Now, in 1807, he viewed embargo as an alternative to war, and though he was uncertain that it would force Britain to recognize American neutrality, he thought it wise to give it a trial of one year.

Predictably, opposition came from seaboard states engaged in overseas trade. In particular, New England Federalists fought the measure on economic grounds, predicting that the region's shipping industry would be devastated and thousands of seamen idled. But Jefferson also encountered attacks from within his own party, most notably from John Randolph of Roanoke, leader of a splinter group of Republicans known as the Tertium Quids. Once a staunch Jefferson supporter, Randolph thought that the president's policies, especially the annexation of Louisiana and the embargo, trampled on the principles of 1776. While Jefferson called the embargo "peaceable coercion," Randolph called it unconstitutional. Invoking the "Spirit of '76," he thought that Jefferson, while seeking independence from British tyranny on the seas, was engaging in tyranny at home.[28]

Despite opposition, Congress passed the Embargo Act on December 22, 1807. Unlike an earlier measure that forbade the importation of specified British goods into the United States, this was a total ban on all foreign trade, both imports and exports. Jefferson and his Republican colleagues in Congress were confident that American trade was so important to the British economy that the embargo would force Parliament to honor U.S. neutrality and allow merchant vessels to sail unmolested to European ports. But alas, they overestimated the significance of American trade to Britain and underestimated British resolve to control shipping in the Atlantic.

While the Embargo of 1807 failed to bring England to its knees, it brought New England to a virtual standstill. Ships remained moored in ports, and ships' captains and seamen were idle. Heavily dependent on Atlantic commerce, New England merchants saw their livelihoods imperiled. Economic distress soon translated into political outrage. Republicans from New York and Pennsylvania joined New England Federalists in protesting the embargo.

In addition to facing mounting political opposition, Jefferson had to scrap his plans for ensuring a lasting peace in the Mediterranean. After the *Chesapeake* incident he ordered American warships in the Mediterranean to return home and ended the plan for a "Peace Establishment" intended to check the Barbary powers. Soon after Commodore Hugh Campbell learned that Captain Barron and the *Chesapeake* would not be relieving his Mediterranean squadron, he received orders to bring all American warships home, including the frigates *Constitution* and *Hornet*. The *Constitution* departed on September 8 after four years in the Mediterranean. Even before it arrived at Boston on October 14, Algerine pirates once again began roaming the sea. With no U.S. naval threat, the corsairs soon took three American vessels captive. Claiming that the United States had not fully remitted tribute payments for the past two years, the pirates captured the *Eagle* of New York, the brig *Violet* of Boston, and briefly the schooner *Mary Ann*, also of New York. After spending millions of dollars on defense to eliminate piratical depredations, America once again faced demands for tribute.[29]

With military power withdrawn from the Mediterranean, the administration relied on diplomacy to defuse renewed Barbary intimidation. Tobias Lear, still U.S. consul general at Algiers, negotiated with the new dey, Achmet, who after a successful coup had succeeded Dey Mustapha in 1805. Achmet was particularly angry because Captain Ichabod Shiffield and his crew of the *Mary Ann* had managed to overpower the prize crew that had captured the schooner, retake the vessel, and escape. The dey demanded

$16,000 in reparations for the prize crew and threatened to imprison Lear if he did not pay. Lear agreed to pay the sum and to remit the two years of past-due tribute in exchange for a pledge by Achmet to cease molesting American commercial ships.[30] Once more, despite the promise of the Treaty of Tripoli, American commercial independence rested on the word of the Barbary pirates.

SEVEN

THE ALGERINE WAR OF 1815 AND AMERICAN INDEPENDENCE IN THE ATLANTIC WORLD

Thomas Jefferson had long thought James Madison would be a good president. In the mid-1790s, when both men believed the ship of state to be off course under Federalist direction, Jefferson told Madison that, in his view, there was no one else in the country better fitted "for the fortunes of our political bark." According to French minister Louis-Marie Turreau, Jefferson claimed that he would not have sought the presidency without Madison's pledge to act as secretary of state and direct his cabinet. Thus, when the 1808 presidential election began, there was no doubt among Republicans that Madison was Jefferson's hand-picked successor. The Tripolitan and Napoleonic Wars had pushed foreign affairs to the forefront of the nation's attention, and Madison as secretary of state was unmatched in knowledge and experience of the major issues. Though opposed by John Randolph and the Tertium Quids for his role in the embargo, Madison defeated his Federalist opponent Charles C. Pinckney by a vote of 122 to 47, carrying all the southern states, the new states of Vermont, Kentucky, and Tennessee, and the mid-Atlantic states of New Jersey and Pennsylvania. He split votes in New York with Quid candidate George Clinton, who represented the party's opposition to the embargo.[1]

To Republicans, the election of 1808 was a referendum on Jefferson's performance as president. As one pamphleteer put

it, the party's candidate would likely "pursue that wise and virtuous policy which Mr. Jefferson has pursued, and in which Madison has so honorably participated." Clearly Madison represented
continuity in foreign policy, pledging ongoing retaliation against
Britain's violation of America's commercial and shipping rights
and vowing to end "ruinous depredations," whether perpe-
trated by European or Barbary powers.[2] He called Britain's
blockade of Europe "a system of monopoly & piracy" and regarded it as an outrage against legitimate shipping as much as that
existing "on the shores of Africa."[3] Without retaliation, the United
States would never take the place it aspired to in international affairs. So despite Federalist and Quid opposition, Madison vowed
to persist in economic warfare against the British and French on
the grounds that nothing short of "national independence" was
at stake.[4]

Even as Madison expressed his determination to extend American independence beyond the United States, events in the Mediterranean and the Atlantic warned that formidable opposition stood
in the way. While Tripoli remained at peace, Algiers once again
posed a threat to American shipping. In late 1808 a cabal of Turkish soldiers assassinated Dey Achmet, who had by and large honored the Algiers Treaty with the United States. The Turks replaced
him with a figurehead named Ali, creating uncertainty in Washington about future relations with Algiers. At minimum, there would
be demands for presents and cash payments, as was customary in
Barbary upon a change of regimes. The immediate threat to American shipping was minimal because U.S. merchantmen continued
to be bottled up in American harbors by the Embargo Act of 1807.
Thus, once more, Europe's maritime powers established America's
place in the Atlantic world. Without being able to sail freely in the
Atlantic, U.S. merchants who had hoped to benefit from the
Tripolitan War were cut off from Mediterranean markets. Any mili-
tary victory against the Barbary pirates was hollow unless the
United States' stature in the Atlantic world improved, and, given

Britain's overwhelming naval superiority, that was unlikely to happen unless Britain deemed it important.

Upon taking office in March 1809, President Madison determined that economic warfare was America's best hope to pressure Britain into honoring neutral rights, despite mounting evidence that the embargo was riddled with problems. First, a brisk smuggling trade had emerged across the Canadian border as New England merchants transported large quantities of goods by land. Moreover, when the embargo was put into effect in late 1807, many U.S. merchantmen continued to operate in foreign waters and engage in trade with the warring nations. These mavericks found favor with the British government, who employed American merchants in the fight against Napoleon. All in all, Britain suffered little. South American countries supplied it with many of the raw materials no longer available from the United States. And with the removal of a commercial rival, British merchants increased their market share of the carrying trade.[5]

Hoping for greater compliance, the Republican-led Congress repealed the Embargo Act in March 1809, just before Madison's inauguration, and replaced it with the Nonintercourse Act, which opened American trade with all nations but Britain and France. Though he supported the measure, Madison's unsteady administration of the policy over the next three years raised questions about the character of his leadership during a crisis. On April 19, on the unauthorized word of David Erskine, British minister to the United States, that the Orders in Council of 1807 would be lifted on June 10, 1809, Madison proclaimed that trade with Britain would be reopened. On August 9, however, he revived nonintercourse against Britain when British foreign secretary George Canning disowned Erskine's statement and recalled the diplomat to London.[6]

With mounting criticism by Federalists and disaffected Republicans, especially John Randolph's Quids, Congress took the initiative in the commercial war by passing a measure aimed at enticing the belligerents to stop harassing American ships. North Carolina's Nathaniel Macon, chairman of the Foreign Affairs Committee, offered a ploy, known as Macon's bill number 2, that repealed nonintercourse, reopened trade with Britain and France, and promised to reimpose an embargo against either Britain or France if the other rescinded its attacks on American shipping. With no intention of complying, Napoleon nevertheless saw the bill as a chance to gain an advantage over Britain and ordered the Duc de Cadore, France's foreign minister, to write a letter suggesting that France would exclude the United States from its decrees against neutral trade. Though Napoleon meant to ensure American goods never reached British ports, Madison took the Cadore letter at face value and reimposed nonintercourse against Britain. Naïvely, he hoped that his action would force the British to suspend their Orders in Council, but he miscalculated. When Congress in March 1811 passed a second nonintercourse act that gave Madison's action against Britain the full force of law, the British ordered their minister home, a move suggesting that the long conflict was moving toward a military encounter.[7]

Like Jefferson, Madison had pinned his hope for peace on a series of bilateral trade agreements. If the United States became an important trading partner with each of the great European powers, then mutual interests in protecting profitable relationships would lessen the likelihood of warfare. Conversely, Madison was confident that economic coercion would force Britain to cease its violations of American trade. Both Jefferson and Madison overestimated the importance of American goods and markets to the British economy, at least in the short term. From the Embargo of 1807 to the second Nonintercourse Act of 1811, Britain suffered little. But while American actions alone did not have the desired effect, when combined with Napoleon's Continental System they began to pinch the British by 1812. Able to circumvent American trade restrictions in the larger Atlantic world, Britain could not long prosper when both U.S. and European ports were closed to it. In 1812 the cumulative toll was grim: widespread unemployment, closed factories, and rising prices. Responding to the growing economic crisis, Parliament voted in June to rescind the Orders in Council and recognize American commercial independence. But the action was too late; before learning of the measure, Madison had requested and received a declaration of war from a Congress led by a vocal group of Republican war hawks.[8]

In his war message Madison viewed the conflict as America's defense of what it had won in 1776. Britain, he asserted, had trampled on rights that "no independent nation can relinquish."[9] Though recognizing the United States' political independence in 1783, Britain had not embraced America as an equal trading partner; nor had it endorsed American free-trade aspirations in the Atlantic world. The War of 1812, Madison hoped, would complete American independence.

While the war was fought on American soil and in American waters from 1812 through 1814, it must be considered within a broader context. To Britain, it was, like the Tripolitan War, of secondary importance. Mobilized to defeat Napoleon, the British were leading a coalition that included Britain, Prussia, Russia, and Austria in what they hoped would be a decisive final battle. Thus, at the outbreak of hostilities in America, most of Britain's military assets were committed to the Napoleonic Wars.

Meanwhile, with the assistance of the British, the Barbary pirates seized on America's war preparations at home to extract more tribute. In July 1812, a month after America declared war against Britain, Algiers refused to accept America's annual tribute. Dey Hadji Ali declared the quality of the goods delivered by the *Allegheny* inferior and demanded an immediate cash payment of $27,000 in lieu of the rejected naval stores. When American consul Tobias Lear refused the demand, Ali expelled all Americans, but a condition of their safe departure was the payment of the tribute.

Lear borrowed the sum at 25 percent interest, made the remittance, and departed on July 25. Within a month Algerine corsairs captured the Salem brig *Edwin* and imprisoned its captain and ten-member crew.[10] Though a minor irritant when considered in the context of the impending war with Britain, the Algerine extortion illustrated anew the challenges facing the United States if it were to achieve its goal of free trade in all parts of the Atlantic world. Once more a "petty" pirate state had stopped American commerce in the Mediterranean.

As had often been the case since 1785, British complicity lay behind the new pirate attack. An 1812 letter from Whitehall assured Dey Ali that he could count on British support in any action taken against "enemies of Great Britain," including the United States. The prince regent, writing in the name of his father George III, promised naval protection of Algiers if the two countries worked in concert. Always eager for more tribute, Ali agreed. This alliance between "the two strongest naval powers in the Mediterranean" brought American trade in the region to a halt for the duration of the War of 1812.[11]

The British-backed Algerine attack coincided with the beginning of hostilities in America. The U.S. strategy was to take advantage of Britain's preoccupation in Europe and mount an attack against Canada. Hoping for a quick war, the United States launched a major offensive in July 1812 aimed at defeating the British in their North American stronghold. But inexperienced, poorly trained American militiamen were no match for British regulars who forced first the surrender on July 17 of the U.S. fort at Michilimackinac in the Straits of Mackinac and then the capitulation of General William Hull's invading army of twenty-two hundred soldiers. The defeat ended prospects for a swift victory and prompted Secretary of State James Monroe to make peace overtures to British foreign minister Lord Castlereagh, who rejected them. Both sides had major problems to surmount, and the inability of each to do so resulted in a war that dragged on for more than two and a half years without a decisive outcome. For most of the conflict, the British lacked sufficient forces to mount a major offensive, but the Americans were unable to exploit that weakness because they were badly divided. The Federalist stronghold of New England condemned the war, and the governors of Massachusetts and Connecticut refused to supply militiamen to the federal government.

The small U.S. Navy acquitted itself well in several single-ship battles but was unable to challenge Britain's control of the seas. In the fall of 1812 the British established a blockade along the Atlantic seaboard that by late 1813 extended from New England to Spanish Florida. As a result, both foreign trade and the coasting trade fell sharply. "Commerce is becoming very slack," complained one Baltimore resident in early 1813. By the end of that year, transatlantic traffic had become so perilous that an oceangoing vessel's insurance premiums soared to half of the ship's value. With trade disrupted, the American economy and war effort suffered from shortages and inflation. In addition to attacking U.S. commerce, the British waged devastating raids against coastal cities and towns, especially in the Chesapeake. While Admiral Sir George Cockburn sought out and destroyed American warships and military depots, he also ordered the burning of three Maryland towns in the Upper Chesapeake—Havre de Grace, Georgetown, and Fredericktown—in order to impress upon Americans the futility of resisting British might.[12]

Individual commanders in the U.S. Navy, hardened by war in Tripoli, were able to score victories that stung British pride and spurred American hope. The *Constitution*, the *Constellation*, the *President*, the *Essex*, the *United States*, and the repaired *Chesapeake* engaged the Royal Navy. And "Preble's Boys," captains William Bainbridge, Isaac Hull, Stephen Decatur, and David Porter, distinguished themselves in the ensuing combat just as they had in the Mediterranean.[13] The British were taken aback by the performance of the U.S. Navy in the opening months of the war, when American ships scored a series of single-ship victories. The editors of Britain's leading naval journal, *The Pilot*, were appalled by the defeats.

Can these statements be true; and can the English people hear them unmoved? Anyone who would have predicted such a result of an American war this time last year would have been treated as a madman or a traitor. He would have been told, if his opponents had condescended to argue with him, that long ere seven months had elapsed the American flag would be swept from the seas, the contemptible navy of the United States annihilated, and their maritime arsenals rendered a heap of ruins. Yet down to this moment not a single American frigate has struck her flag. They insult and laugh at our want of enterprise and vigour. They leave their ports when they please, and return to them when it suits their convenience; they traverse the Atlantic; they beset the West India Islands; they advance to the very chops of the Channel; they parade upon the coast of South America; nothing chases, nothing engages them but to yield them triumph.[14]

Though an embarrassment and nuisance, the U.S. Navy's success was limited mainly to single-ship victories. The Royal Navy's blockade continued to be effective, and in August 1814 British warships overcame coastal gunships and assisted the army in capturing and burning Washington. Neither side, however, was able to deliver a decisive blow, and the war dragged on in a costly stalemate. Therefore in March, when Andrei Dashkov, the Russian minister in Washington, offered his government's assistance to broker a peace treaty, Madison quickly accepted, appointing Albert Gallatin, John Quincy Adams, and James Bayard as peace commissioners even before the British accepted. In May the British appointed negotiators, and talks got under way in August in Ghent. Responding to mounting protests at home over the rising cost of the war in America and wishing to rid itself of distractions from defeating Napoleon, the British were eager for a peace settlement.

For the American negotiators, nothing was more important than to settle the maritime issues that had led to war in the first place. Americans insisted on freedom of navigation, which meant that the British had to forswear the capture of merchantmen, the confiscation of cargo, and impressments of sailors. Instructions to the American negotiators explicitly made the end of impressments essential to any peace settlement.[15]

For the British, the negotiations at Ghent were a distraction. Far more important were the discussions at the Congress of Vienna (September 1814 to June 1815) to punish Napoleonic France, secure boundaries in Europe, and establish a basis for lasting peace. British diplomat Jonathan Russell summed up the general European attitude when he compared the "Great Congress at Vienna" to the "little congress at Ghent." The two congresses overlapped, with Vienna's opening discussions coming about a month after those in Ghent. British and European attention was trained on Vienna, with its prospects for a general European settlement that would end fifteen years of untold bloodshed and loss of treasure, a prospect that overshadowed talks to settle the skirmish in America.[16]

For much of the almost five months of talks at Ghent beginning on August 8, 1814, the two sides made little progress. The sticking point was impressment. British officials were as adamant against giving up the right to impress sailors as the Americans were for ending the practice. James Monroe voiced the American view: "This degrading practice . . . must cease, our flag must protect the crew, or the United States, cannot consider themselves an independent Nation." Eager to get a settlement, however, the Madison administration dropped impressment, reasoning that the end of the European war would in fact bring an end to the practice. With that thorny issue removed, the two sides were able to reach an agreement that was signed on December 24, 1814. But the Treaty of Ghent decided little. Most significantly, it was silent on the maritime issues that had led to war in the first place. And each side agreed to return territory taken during the fighting, thus restoring the status quo ante bellum.[17]

Before news of the peace reached the United States, Americans registered their most glorious victory of the war. At the Battle of New Orleans, General Andrew Jackson with a colorful collection of about five thousand militiamen, slaves, Indians, and pirates defeated General Edward Pakenham's seventy-five hundred veterans in a lopsided battle that resulted in almost two thousand losses for the British and only about twenty for the Americans. That victory fostered a new wave of fervent nationalism that overshadowed the peace treaty's failure to secure American maritime rights. At the end of the war Republican orators across the country spared no rhetoric in transforming the war from a stalemate to a glorious victory. "Never did a country occupy more lofty ground," said Supreme Court justice Joseph Story; "we have stood the contest, single-handed, against the conqueror of Europe." The New York *National Advocate* hailed the war as the "second war of independence," whose achievements were more splendid than those of the American Revolution.[18]

With peace secured, Madison turned his attention to the Algerine corsairs who had taken advantage of America's preoccupation with the war against Britain to prey on American interests in the Mediterranean with impunity. During the war the United States had needed all available naval vessels in American waters, and even if Madison had wished to send a squadron to the Mediterranean, the British blockade would have prevented its passage. The end of hostilities in America, and more important the defeat of Napoleon, gave America freedom of navigation in the Atlantic. No longer concerned with neutral countries supplying France, Britain ceased to interfere with American shipping. Thus in 1815 Madison turned his attention once again to the Barbary pirates, determined to end forever the menace of those "petty" tyrants.

Led primarily by the Algerine dey, Hadji Ali, and encouraged by the British, the Barbary States had taken advantage of America's inability to retaliate during the War of 1812. They had captured American merchantmen as prizes and imprisoned their crews. The best the Madison administration could do was to rely upon the good offices of American merchants in the Mediterranean to seek release of the prisoners. On one such occasion in 1813, an American businessman with commercial interests in Spain traveled to Algiers under the guise of a Spanish subject to negotiate with the dey. There he found unexpected support from the British consul, who agreed to help secure the sailors' freedom. But the dey would not hear of it, informing the consul that "my policy and my views are to increase, not to diminish the number of my American slaves, and not for a million dollars would I release them."[19] Thirty years after the first Americans were enslaved by Algiers, another group of prisoners languished in North Africa and the United States was helpless to rescue them.

James Madison was furious, and one week after the ratification of the Treaty of Ghent on February 17, 1815, ended hostilities with the British, he asked Congress to declare war on Algiers. In his war message, he reviewed events on the Barbary Coast, beginning with the dey's expelling the American consul general in 1812. Madison told Congress that the dey had committed "acts of more overt and direct warfare against the citizens of the United States trading in the Mediterranean, some of whom are still detained in captivity, notwithstanding the attempts which have been made to ransom them, and are treated with the rigor usual on the coast of Barbary." He noted that the United States had not been able to take hostile action against Algiers at the time, but peace with Great Britain now "opens the prospect of an active and valuable trade of their citizens within the range of the Algerine cruziers." Therefore he recommended that Congress declare "the existence of a state of war between the United States and the Dey and Regency of Algiers" and provide all means "as may be requisite for a vigorous prosecution of it to a successful issue."[20] On March 3 Congress authorized hostilities against Algiers.

The naval force that Madison deployed reflected his determination to end all harassment against American ships and American citizens not only by Algiers but by all of the Barbary States. As secretary of state under Jefferson, he had witnessed firsthand the futility of purchasing peace through the payment of tribute. Barbary leaders were never satisfied with the amount or nature of the tribute and at the slightest excuse would send their corsairs out to capture more American vessels in order to extort additional payments. As president, he meant to stop the payment of tribute once and forever. Two squadrons would sail to the Mediterranean, each under the command of a battle-hardened commodore familiar with the Barbary pirates and their tactics. Captain Stephen Decatur led the first squadron of ten warships, the largest naval fleet ever assembled by the U.S. Navy. On March 20 three frigates, a sloop, four brigs, and two schooners sailed from New York, presenting a magnificent sight as they slipped out through the Narrows. Decatur's flagship, the *Guerrière*, was one of America's new ships of the line, a seventy-four-gun frigate capable of delivering devastating broadsides. Also in the squadron was the *Ontario*, a British sloop that Decatur had taken prize. No doubt he appreciated the irony of attacking British allies with one of the Royal Navy's own warships. A couple of months after Decatur departed, the second, and even larger, squadron under the command of William Bainbridge set sail. Bainbridge had experienced the humiliation of having the *Philadelphia* captured and its entire crew imprisoned by the Tripolitans. Now he returned to the Mediterranean with a powerful squadron of seventeen warships.[21]

The squadron's mission was to win a lasting peace with the Barbary powers, and Decatur and Bainbridge, along with Consul William Shaler, were designated peace commissioners. Their instructions from Secretary of State James Monroe cautioned them against rushing into an agreement with the dey, recognizing that the Algerines had a long history of signing treaties that they had no intention of keeping. Rather, negotiations should accompany the "dread or success" of American naval power. "If a just punishment should be inflicted on those people for the insult and injuries we have received from them," Monroe reasoned, "the peace might be more durable than if it should be concluded at the first approach of our squadron." Monroe was confident that the dey knew about Britain's failure to defeat America in the War of 1812 and that, when he saw the "formidable force" arrayed before Algiers, he would quickly agree to terms. The commissioners were to reject all demands for tribute and biennial presents.[22] And they were to negotiate a treaty that would give them equal footing to that of the great European powers, namely, England, France, and Russia. Madison and Monroe, like Jefferson before them, insisted that the Atlantic world be a free-trade zone in which equal trading partners exchanged goods in markets open to all, replacing mercantilism and all its monopolies, exclusions, regulations, tariffs, and tribute.

Decatur's arrival in the Mediterranean made an immediate impression. At Cádiz he learned that the Algerine pirates had been prowling the Atlantic but had recently returned to the Mediterranean. He also learned that the Algerine admiral Reis Hammida had just two days earlier sailed for Cape de Gatte on Spain's southeastern coast awaiting Spain's tribute payment of a half million dollars. From Cádiz, Decatur sailed through the Strait of Gibraltar and entered the port of Gibraltar, where he received fresh intelligence confirming Hammida's intention to lie off the Spanish coast until Spain's tribute was assembled and ready for him to take possession.

Two days after leaving Gibraltar Decatur spotted a large sail about twenty miles off the Spanish coast, and as the Americans drew closer, they determined that it was Reis Hammida's flagship, the *Mashouda*. To conceal the identity of his own ships, Decatur, in keeping with standard wartime practice, ordered an English flag displayed. Hammida saw through the ruse, however, and attempted to elude the attackers by taking a southerly course toward Algiers. With an entire squadron at his command, Decatur soon overtook the Algerine cruiser and surrounded it. After enduring twenty-five minutes of broadsides that rendered the corsair helpless and killed many of its crew, Hammida surrendered. Decatur ordered a prize crew to board the *Mashouda*, secure it for sailing, and take the more than four hundred prisoners to Cartagena, where they would be held. Two days later the Americans overwhelmed a twenty-two-gun Algerine brig, the *Estedio*, and took another eighty prisoners, who were also taken to Cartagena. Within a week of beginning operations against the enemy, Decatur had captured two warships and taken almost five hundred prisoners. With those bargaining chips, he sailed for Algiers.[23] There is no record that Hammida had received the Spanish tribute before the capture.

On June 28, just thirty-nine days after leaving New York, the American squadron arrived off Algiers. The following day Decatur delivered the president's message demanding peace. The *Guerrière* sailed into the Bay of Algiers with the Swedish flag at the main. Around noon the consul of Sweden and the captain of the port came out on a boat to meet the Americans and request confirmation that the U.S. Navy had in fact captured an Algerine frigate and a brig. It was clear to Decatur that the American naval victory made a "visible and deep" impression on the port captain, who asked the commodore to "state the conditions on which we would make peace." Decatur responded by handing over a copy of the president's instructions to the dey. The current dey was Omar the Agar, who was attempting to restore some semblance of order and stability to a country that had over the past two years witnessed a series of coups and assassinations. In 1814 Hadji Ali had been assassinated and replaced by his prime minister, who was also assassinated after serving as interim dey for only two weeks. Thus it was to Omar that Decatur addressed his demands. The port captain accepted the messages and then requested "that hostilities should cease pending the negotiation, and that persons authorized to treat should go on shore," adding that the Algerine minister of marine had "pledged himself for our security and return to our ships when we pleased." Decatur rejected both propositions and informed the emissary that the "negotiation must be carried on board the fleet, and that hostilities, as far as they respected vessels, could not cease."[24]

On the following day the Swedish consul and the port captain returned to the *Guerrière* with the dey's reply. They informed Decatur that the dey had authorized them to "treat with us on the proposed basis," and the commodore noted that "their anxiety appeared extreme to conclude the peace immediately." Thereupon the Americans produced the model of a treaty, declaring that it would not be "departed from in substance," explaining in particular that, although the United States would not under any circumstances agree to pay tribute, it would offer customary gifts to the dey and his officers upon the presentation of consuls.[25]

The dey's negotiator examined the proposed treaty and stated that the dey would not agree to it in its present form, particularly the demand requiring Algiers to return all American property that the regency had captured and distributed among government officials, privateer investors, and ships' crews. The port captain and the Swedish consul pointed out that such a demand "had never before been made upon Algiers."[26] Decatur accepted that claim, finding it just. Further, he agreed to return the two captured Algerian vessels as a goodwill gesture, noting that the current dey had not initiated the war against the United States. He insisted, however, that this concession not appear in the treaty but would be considered a "favor." Decatur also refused the port captain's request for a truce "to deliberate upon the terms of the proposed treaty," even when the latter asked for just three hours. Decatur replied, "Not a minute; if your squadron appears in sight before the treaty is actually signed by the Dey, and the prisoners sent off, ours will capture them." Within three hours the port captain returned with the signed treaty and the American prisoners. Decatur noted privately that the Algerines "now show every disposition to maintain a sincere peace with us, which is, doubtless, owing to the dread of our arms." He concluded by declaring that the treaty "places the United States on higher grounds than any other nation," because only the United States had a treaty with the Barbary powers without any pledge to pay tribute or ransom.[27]

After obtaining a treaty at Algiers, Decatur sailed for Tunis to make similar demands of the Tunisians. During the War of 1812 the British had captured two U.S. merchantmen and brought them to Tunis, where they were held as prizes. In addition to securing peace, Decatur was determined to get satisfaction for those vessels. According to an American lieutenant aboard one of the squadron's warships, the U.S. "difficulties" with Tunis were settled quickly, with Decatur dictating the terms. Under the agreement, the American flag would be able to "pass unmolested through the Mediterranean, without tribute." Decatur received $60,000 for the two vessels held by Tunis.[28] Thus, instead of the United States paying tribute to a Barbary power, as had been customary for thirty years, a Barbary power made financial restitution to the United States.

From Tunis, the American squadron sailed to Tripoli, where the United States' old foe, Yusuf Karamanli, was still the ruling bashaw. Again, Decatur made demands for a peace treaty that would guarantee the safe passage of American ships without the payment of tribute. Also, he demanded from Yusuf an indemnity of $30,000 for vessels taken by the British in the late war and held in the port of Tripoli. Then, in an action sure to gain widespread approval in Europe, Decatur demanded the release of prisoners from various nations. A sailor recording the historic moment noted that it would not be lost on those hearing of the event that Europeans "long enslaved" were "released by the American government."[29] One American eyewitness offered a similar expression of national pride that no doubt prompted similar sentiments among Americans who read his account at home: "I need not say how gratifying this cruise must be to every American soul, how delightful it was to see the stars and stripes holding forth the hand of retributive justice to the barbarians, and rescuing the unfortunate, even of distant but friendly European nations, from slavery."[30] An American squadron had done what no European power had ever done: force the Barbary pirates to disavow tribute and forgo ransom.

Before Decatur's departure to the Mediterranean, Secretary of State James Monroe had predicted that the European powers would take notice of the American expedition against Algiers. He thought that the "honorable manner" in which the United States had concluded the war against Britain and the stand that it had made against French violations of its neutrality had resulted in "immense advantages" for America in Europe. At a minimum, he thought, Europeans would be less likely to attack Americans and more likely to trade with American vessels. If, then, Decatur's squadron succeeded in its mission, U.S. prestige among Europeans, especially the English, could only rise.[31] Monroe's concern with the European reaction reflected his understanding that America's ability to trade in the Atlantic world on an equal footing with the great powers depended on winning their respect.

From his post in London as minister to Great Britain, John Quincy Adams monitored European reaction. In a letter to his mother, Abigail, Adams wrote, "Our naval campaign in the Mediterranean has been perhaps as splendid as anything that has occurred in our annals since our existence as a nation." But he noted that "it has excited little attention in Europe," eclipsed by the defeat of Napoleon at Waterloo within days of the signing of the Algiers Treaty. Though America's success against the Barbary pirates was not headline news, Adams believed that American influence over the Barbary powers would "sink deep into the memory" of cabinets all across Europe. He told American envoy William Shaler that the United States' refusal to pay tribute to the Barbary pirates would reshape British and European policy as well, jettisoning one of the linchpins of mercantilism. Americans had extirpated tribute, which had prevailed for centuries in the Mediterranean, and insisted on trading freely. He predicted that the British would soon demand the same privilege for themselves.[32]

Europeans in the Mediterranean did take notice, albeit reluctantly, of America's achievement. An officer aboard the U.S. brig *Enterprise* described a newfound respect for America in the Mediterranean after its young navy had defeated the Algerines. Sailing with Commodore Bainbridge when the U.S. squadron sailed into the British port of Gibraltar, the officer wrote, "It was a proud sight for an American to see in a British port just at the close of a war with her, which the English thought would have been the destruction of our navy, a squadron of seventeen sail, larger perhaps than our whole navy at the commencement of that war." His observation captured one of the key links between the War of 1812 and the Algerine War: because of the tremendous expansion of the U.S. Navy to fight the former, America was able to win the latter and, indeed, to subdue all of Barbary. But according to the officer, the British were unaccustomed to showing proper respect to a navy that had recently defeated them. "On our arrival at Gibraltar," he continued, "the Commodore Bainbridge fired a salute of *seventeen* guns, which was returned with *fifteen*." An American officer was immediately sent on shore to inform the lieutenant governor that he had fired seventeen guns and expected his salute "to be returned *gun for gun*, and he therefore *demanded* that *two* more guns should be immediately fired." After apologizing for the slight, the lieutenant governor fired the other two guns. The officer concluded in a letter to a friend, "Thus you see, my dear____, that an American Commodore can now *demand* respect from those who formerly would scarcely have noted us." He added,

> You have no idea of the respect which the American character has gained by our late Wars. The Spanish especially think we are devils incarnate—as we beat the French, who beat them, whom nobody ever beat before—and the Algerines, whom the devil himself could not beat.[33]

On November 12 the *Guerrière* returned to New York to a tumultuous reception. As had been the case after the Tripolitan War, the public, press, and president gave Stephen Decatur a hero's welcome. The *National Intelligencer* hailed him as a "chivalric commander" who gave the Algerines, Tunisians, and Tripolitans such an "*electric shock*" that they accepted the "humiliating terms" of a treaty without tribute. The reference to "shock" echoed the Jeffersonian strategy during the Tripolitan War (1801–5) of confronting the enemy with overwhelming force sufficient to bring him to the bargaining table. Then Yusuf Bashaw and his forces had hardly been awed and had instead put up stiff resistance for four years. But in 1815 the United States was able to present a much greater display of power. It fought an enemy that could no longer count on assistance from Britain or any other European power. And at least in the case of Algiers, the Barbary powers had been weakened by a series of bloody coups that left Dey Omar unwilling to risk a military defeat.

The arrival of Bainbridge's squadron at Newport two weeks later caused more celebration. The fleet was the largest ever fitted out by the United States, and as one reporter explained, although Decatur's cometlike victory in the Mediterranean had left Bainbridge with little to do, the very display of American power was important. The rapidity with which the squadron was mobilized and the power that the seventeen ships represented "will most powerfully render our character as a nation respectable."[34]

Unlike the aftermath of the Tripolitan War, the end of the Algerine War transcended partisan wrangling and contributed to the sense of national identity fostered by the successful outcome of the War of 1812. And just as Andrew Jackson and his forces at the Battle of New Orleans had given a badly needed boost to an otherwise embarrassed army, so too did Stephen Decatur's exploits on the Barbary Coast. Stephen Chatham, the American consul at Marseilles, provided his countrymen with enduring descriptions of the American squadron at Tripoli receiving a twenty-one-gun salute from the bashaw as the American colors were hoisted and a full band played the "President's March" and "Yankee Doodle." As another observer noted, the United States had finally made "free trade" a reality in the Atlantic world. After thirty years of humiliation at the hands of the Barbary pirates, the United States was no longer at the mercy of the corsairs.[35] As Madison put it, American commercial vessels could now safely pass "within reach of the Barbary cruisers."[36] To make certain that that continued to be the case, Madison ordered the frigates *Constellation* and *United States*, along with two sloops, to maintain patrols in the Mediterranean.

On December 5, 1815, President Madison laid the Algiers Treaty before the Senate. The war, he reported, had allowed the United States to attain the long-sought goal of extending its independence to the high seas. He stated, "I have the satisfaction, on our present meeting, of being able to communicate to you the successful termination of the war which had been commenced against the United States by the regency of Algiers." He declared that the rights and honor of the American republic had been vindicated by the Barbary pirates' "perpetual relinquishment . . . of all pretensions to tribute."[37] He extolled the brilliance and gallantry of Decatur and his men in bringing the war to a swift and satisfactory conclusion.

At the same time Madison gave the Senate an optimistic report on commercial negotiations with the British that would put American trade on a more independent footing. "It is another source of satisfaction that the treaty of peace with Great Britain," he stated, "has been succeeded by a convention on the subject of commerce, concluded by the plenipotentiaries of the two countries." The tone of the discussions made Madison hopeful that "liberal arrangements" would now define trade between the United States and Britain. For him, the crowning achievement would be a treaty placing "American navigation" in the hands of "American seamen; a measure which, . . . would have the further advantage of encreasing the independence of our navigation, and the resources for our maritime defence."[38]

For the first time since the United States won its War of Independence, American vessels operated in the Atlantic world without being molested. Americans remembered British predictions that the United States would be locked out of the Mediterranean trade because European powers would not find it in their interests to protect a commercial rival from the depredations of the Barbary pirates. The British editor of the New York journal *Cobbett's Weekly Political Register* reflected on how events in 1815 defied predictions made in 1783. A critic of British mercantilism, William Cobbett published an open letter to Lord Sheffield, who had insisted that the newly independent United States would find itself without any European allies in the Mediterranean and would, consequently, be devoured by the Barbary pirates. Cobbett recalled Lord Sheffield's assertion that America would not likely become a powerful commercial and manufacturing nation or a naval power. Indeed, to make sure that America remained weak, Sheffield had called on Parliament "to employ all the means in our power, among which means was the *withholding of all protection* of American vessels FROM THE BARBARY POWERS, and the inducing of the other great marine powers to do the same." Cobbett delighted in pointing out to Lord Sheffield that in 1815, thirty-two years later, the United States, with no assistance from Britain or any European power, had dispatched a squadron of ships across the Atlantic and chastened the pirates.[39]

The Algerine War ended America's thirty-year effort to rid itself of Barbary pirate depredations and establish free navigation in the Mediterranean. From the first captures of American vessels in 1784 and 1785, corsairs, understanding that the United States no longer enjoyed British naval protection, had challenged American independence. The pirates had prevailed in the mid-1780s because America was disunited at home under a weak central government that lacked both resolve and resources. Under the Articles of Confederation, Congress had no authority to levy taxes and consequently was unable to build a navy sufficient for suppressing the pirates. While the Constitution produced by the 1787 convention created a federal government with sole authority over national defense and foreign policy along with the means of establishing a navy, deep sectional disagreements over trade emerged within that government. Favoring federal regulation of commerce, the northern states, which had suffered most when Britain refused to sign a commercial treaty in 1783, wanted the power to defend their trade against foreign regulations. Southerners envisioned an enlightened world where free trade fostered peace between equal trading partners and thus there was no need for a large, expensive navy. Northerners saw a more dangerous world in which competing states sought advantage over their rivals; they believed a navy was essential to protect American interests overseas. Unable to reach an agreement, Congress was unable to establish a navy until the mid-1790s, and the Barbary pirates took advantage of the inaction by capturing more Americans and escalating demands for tribute.

Though every American president regarded the Barbary powers as petty states, each was forced to deal with the pirates. From Washington through Madison, all had to seek the release of imprisoned and enslaved Americans; all had to pay tribute; and all struggled for an honorable and permanent solution. Through numerous humiliating attacks and demands, the pirates had mocked American claims to independence. In 1801 and again in 1815 Barbary States declared war against the United States, forcing America to fight two wars in the Mediterranean. American presidents were hampered by lack of military resources and by European machinations. Washington, having no navy, chose to negotiate and in 1795 agreed to tribute and ransom payments amounting to 15 percent of the national budget. John Adams had a navy capable of defeating the Barbary pirates, but in 1799 French violations of American neutrality in the Atlantic forced him to deploy warships against France in the so-called Quasi-War. In 1801 Thomas Jefferson, a consistent advocate of the use of force against the pirates from the first Algerine captures in 1785, dispatched a naval squadron to the Mediterranean when Tripoli declared war against the United States over the demand for more tribute. And in 1815 James Madison sent an even more powerful fleet to force Algiers to cease raiding American vessels and coercing more tribute.

The struggle between America and Barbary pitted two marginal players in the Atlantic world against each other as each sought to better its position vis-à-vis Europe's maritime powers. Each in its own way had tried to determine an independent course, and both had met the opposition of those who wished to keep them in their place. Their efforts met with different outcomes. After 1815 the

Barbary powers lost their independence. Following the humiliating U.S. treaty that refused tribute, the Algerines tried to rebuild their military forces, only to be crushed by a joint British-Dutch bombardment in August 1816. Then in 1830 the French invaded Algiers and after a bloody war made the once-feared leader of the Barbary States a colonial dependent. Over the course of the nineteenth century, Morocco, Tunis, and Tripoli met similar fates, each becoming a dependent of either France or Spain.

By contrast, in 1815 the United States was much closer to realizing its goal of free trade in a mercantilist world. With the defeat of the Barbary powers, American merchantmen could sail the Mediterranean without wondering if a corsair would pounce on them from hidden coves. And after the Peace of Paris in 1815, Britain no longer harassed American ships crossing the Atlantic. For much of the new republic's short history, American commerce had been caught in the crossfire of conflict between Britain and France. By declaring neutrality in 1793, the United States had tried to avoid entanglement in the war of titans, but the belligerents refused to allow American vessels access to the enemy's ports. Now, with the long Napoleonic Wars over, Britain emerged as the Atlantic world's superpower, and no longer facing France's Continental System, it recognized America's shipping rights.

Moreover, America in 1815 was an emerging, though junior, power in the Atlantic world. With its rapidly growing population and its expanding commerce, it represented an attractive trading partner, especially for the British. Its population more than doubled from 1785 to 1815, when it exceeded eight million people, becoming a consumer market that could not be ignored.[40] And its rapidly expanding cotton production provided valuable raw materials for Britain's textile mills. In addition to becoming more important to British merchants, the United States after 1815 found favor with British investors, who poured millions of pounds sterling into developing American factories. Thus, thirty years after the War of Independence, Britain and America found a mutual interest in forging a strong economic partnership. That new reality found formal expression in a bilateral commercial treaty agreed to in 1815 that aimed at rendering Anglo-American trade "reciprocally beneficial and satisfactory."[41] Trade statistics bear out the optimism: American imports of British goods increased more than sevenfold from 1815 to 1860, and American exports to Britain kept pace.[42] By opening British markets to American ships and guaranteeing most favored nation status, the agreement meant that U.S. merchants could finally trade in the Atlantic on free and equal terms.

The nationalist fervor following the Algerine War of 1815 gave U.S. actions in the Mediterranean an inflated role in America's new independence. In newspaper editorials and Fourth of July orations, Americans convinced themselves that by standing up to Barbary, and then British, tyranny, the United States had ensured free trade in the Atlantic. In an 1818 speech in Detroit, one of Michigan's proud patriots, Andrew Griswold Whitney, boasted that Europe had witnessed America's "chastisements and humiliation of the PIRATIC states of Barbary." He declared that "our naval flag has also been equally triumphant" over Britain as commanders "Hull—Decatur—Jones—Bainbridge—Lawrence have demonstrated our superior skill and prowess." What a change in America's fortunes: "pirates dread punishment"; captives are delivered from servitude; and the "Star-spangled banner" waves freely in "every port of the civilized world."[43]

Nationalist hyperbole notwithstanding, America's rise was the result of changes in the Atlantic world more than in the country's military exploits. With peace in Europe, merchantmen replaced warships and privateers, transforming the Atlantic from a dangerous battleground into a beehive of commerce. Instead of draining national treasuries in fighting wars, the Atlantic brought in millions through trade. As a result of peace, reciprocity replaced retaliation, and America gained time to grow in wealth and power until its place in the world matched its nationalist boasts.

NOTES

INTRODUCTION

1. *Boston Gazette*, December 15, 1783.
2. Ibid.
3. *The Revolutionary Diplomatic Correspondence of the United States*, ed. Francis Wharton, 6 vols. (Washington, D.C., 1889), 6:781.
4. For the idea of the Atlantic as a "tribute-demanding" system, see Immanuel Wallerstein, *The Modern World-System I: Capitalist Agriculture and the Origins of the European World-Economy in the Sixteenth Century* (New York, 1974), 348.
5. Philip Corrigan and Derek Sayer, *The Great Arch: English State Formation as Cultural Revolution* (Oxford, 1985), 83.
6. *Journals of the Continental Congress 1774–1789*, ed. Worthington C. Ford et al. (Washington, D.C., 1904–37), 3:479–81.
7. *Articles of Peace & Commerce Between the most Serene and Mighty Prince Charles II. By the Grace of God, King of Great Britain, France and Ireland, Defender of the Faith, etc. And the Most Illustrious Lords, The Bashaw, Dey, Aga and Governours of the Famous City and Kingdom of Algiers in Barbary* (London, 1682), 4–11.
8. Robert J. Allison, *The Crescent Obscured: The United States and the Muslim World, 1776–1815* (New York, 1995). After September 11, 2001, Allison's theme is supported in Richard Parker, *Uncle Sam in Barbary: a Diplomatic History* (Gainesville, Fla., 2004).
9. See, for example, A.B.C. Whipple, *To the Shores of Tripoli: The Birth of the U.S. Navy and Marines* (New York, 1991), 5. One post-9/11 work views the Tripolitan War as the "First War on Terror." See Joseph Wheelan, *Jefferson's War: America's First War on Terror, 1801–1805* (New York, 2003).
10. Whipple, *Shores of Tripoli*, 5.
11. See Rick Forcier, "The Tales of Terrorism," *Newsletter of the Christian Coalition of Washington State*, November 2001. For similar interpretation of Barbary Wars

as primarily religious wars, see David Barton, *Original Intent: The Constitution, the Court and Religion* (Aledo, Tex., 1996).

12. *Washington Post*, October 15, 2001.

13. For more on the Atlantic world, see David Armitage and Michael Braddick, *The British Atlantic World, 1500–1800* (New York, 2002).

ONE: THE AMERICAN REVOLUTION CHECKED

1. *Revolutionary Diplomatic Correspondence of the United States*, ed. Francis Wharton, 6 vols. (Washington, D.C., 1889), 4:277.

2. For a fuller treatment of how the American motto influenced public policy in the Mediterranean, see James Field, *America and the Mediterranean World: 1776–1882* (Princeton, N.J., 1969).

3. *The Papers of Thomas Jefferson*, ed. Julian Boyd and Lyman Butterfield, 30 vols. (Princeton, N.J., 1953), 8:231.

4. Ibid., 7:556.

5. Philip Corrigan and Derek Sayer, *The Great Arch: English State Formation as Cultural Revolution* (Oxford, 1985); 83.

6. Stephen Saunders Webb, *1676: The End of American Independence* (New York, 1984), 224–25.

7. Ibid., 235.

8. Ibid., 30–31.

9. *Pennsylvania Gazette*, November 14, 1765.

10. For works on republicanism, see J.G.A. Pocock, *The Machiavellian Moment: Florentine Political Thought and the Atlantic Republican Tradition* (Princeton, N.J., 1975); Gordon Wood, *The Creation of the American Republic, 1776–1787* (Chapel Hill, N.C., 1969); Caroline Robbins, *The Eighteenth-Century Commonwealthman* (Cambridge, Mass., 1959); Bernard Bailyn, *The Ideological Origins of the American Revolution* (Cambridge, Mass., 1967).

11. Willard Sterne Randall, *Alexander Hamilton: A Life* (New York, 2003), 82.

12. *The Annals of America*, 18 vols. (Chicago, 1968), 2:242.

13. Ibid., 2:278.

14. *Pennsylvania Gazette*, February 20, 1766.

15. *Thomas Paine's Common Sense*, ed. Isaac Kramnick (1776; repr., New York: Penguin, 1976), 86.

16. For Jefferson's reworking of Locke, see Garry Wills, *Inventing America: Jefferson's Declaration of Independence* (New York, 1978).

17. *Revolutionary Diplomatic Correspondence*, ed. Wharton, 2:226–30.

18. *Journals of the Continental Congress, 1774–1789*, ed. Worthington C. Ford et al. (Washington, D.C., 1904–37), 11:426–27.

19. *Revolutionary Diplomatic Correspondence*, ed. Wharton, 4:423.

20. Ibid.

21. *Independent Chronicle and Universal Advertiser*, September 5, 1782.

22. Ibid.

23. Ibid.

24. *The Writings of George Washington*, ed. John Fitzpatrick, 39 vols. (Washington, D.C., 1940), 28:520.

25. *The Correspondence and Public Papers of John Jay*, ed. Henry Johnston, 4 vols. (1890; repr., New York, 1970), 3:85.

26. Ibid., 3:153–54.

27. *Writings of Washington*, ed. Fitzpatrick, 28:520.

28. Ibid.

29. Michael Palmer, "The Navy: The Continental Period, 1775–1800," Naval Historical Center website, www.history.navy.mil/history/history2.htm.

30. Gardner Allen, *A Naval History of the American Revolution*, 2 vols. (New York, 1962), 2:615.

31. *Naval Documents Related to the United States Wars with the Barbary Powers*, 6 vols. (Washington, D.C., 1939), 1:22.

32. H.J.A. Sire, *The Knights of Malta* (New Haven, Conn., 1994), 63.

33. William Spencer, *Algiers in the Age of the Corsairs* (Norman, Okla., 1976), 14–17.

34. Ibid., 12–14.

35. Ibid.

36. Ibid., 66.

37. Sire, *Knights of Malta*, 90.

38. Ibid., 89.

39. Christopher Hill, *God's Englishman: Oliver Cromwell and the English Revolution* (New York, 1970), 166.

40. Daniel Defoe, *The Life and Strange Surprising Adventures of Robinson Crusoe* (1719; repr.: Boston, 1923), 23–24.

41. *Pennsylvania Gazette*, May 10, 1759.

42. Spencer, *Algiers*, 13.

43. Ibid., 14.

44. Ibid., 16.

45. *United States Chronicle*, October 30, 1785.

46. Spencer, *Algiers*, 16.

47. Ibid., 16–17.

48. Ibid., 18.

49. Stanley Lane-Poole, *The Story of the Barbary Corsairs* (New York, 1890), 221.

50. John Wolf, *The Barbary Coast: Algiers Under the Turks, 1500–1830* (New York, 1979), 149–50.

51. *Naval Documents Related to Barbary Powers*, 1:2–3.

52. *United States Chronicle*, April 28, 1785.

53. Wolf, *Barbary Coast*, 139.

54. Lane-Poole, *Story of the Barbary Corsairs*, 224.

55. Ibid., 224–25.

56. For slave population figures, see Richard Morris, ed., *Encyclopedia of American*

History (New York, 1953), 513; and *Naval Documents Related to Barbary Powers*, 1:29.

57. *United States Chronicle*, May 5, 1785.

58. Mathew Carey, *A Short Account of Algiers, Containing a Description of the climate of That Country, of the Manners and Inhabitants . . . with a concise View of the Origins of the Rupture Between Algiers and the United States* (Philadelphia, 1794), 44.

59. *Journals of the Continental Congress*, ed. Ford et al., 26:357–61.

60. *Pennsylvania Gazette*, October 8, 1783.

61. Ibid.

62. *Papers of Thomas Jefferson*, ed. Boyd and Butterfield, 7:231.

63. Ibid., 4:278–79.

64. *Pennsylvania Gazette*, October 8, 1783.

65. *Boston Gazette*, July 5, 1784.

66. *United States Chronicle*, July 15 and August 26, 1784.

67. *Boston Gazette*, October 11, 1784.

68. *United States Chronicle*, September 9 and October 7, 1784, and March 17, 1785.

69. *Boston Gazette*, October 21, 1785.

70. *United States Chronicle*, March 17, 1785.

71. John Lord Sheffield, *Observations on the Commerce of the American States* (London, 1784), 200, 217–18.

72. Ibid., 204–5.

73. *Naval Documents Related to Barbary Powers*, 1:149.

74. *United States Chronicle*, March 31, 1785, and April 21, 1785.

75. Ibid., April 21, 1785.

TWO: TRIBUTE OR ARMS?

1. *Letters of the Delegates to Congress, 1774–1789*, ed. Paul Smith et al., 25 vols. (Washington, D.C., 1976–2000), 4:356.

2. Jack Greene, ed., *Colonies to Nation, 1763–1789: A Documentary History of the American Revolution* (New York, 1975), 515.

3. *Naval Documents Related to the United States Wars with the Barbary Powers*, 6 vols. (Washington, D.C., 1939), 1:23.

4. Ibid., 7:6.

5. Ibid., 1:7.

6. *Journals of the Continental Congress, 1774–1789*, ed. Worthington, C. Ford et al. (Washington, D.C., 1904–37), 26:362.

7. Sherrill Wells, "Long-Time Friends: Early U.S.-Moroccan Relations, 1777–87," *Department of State Bulletin* 87 (September 1987), 8.

8. *The Correspondence and Public Papers of John Jay*, ed. Henry Johnston, 4 vols. (1890; repr. New York, 1970), 3:153–54.

9. *The Papers of Thomas Jefferson*, ed. Julian Boyd and Lyman Butterfield, 30 vols. (Princeton, N.J., 1950), 8:61–62.

10. Ibid.

11. Ibid., 8:70–72.

12. Ibid., 7:511.

13. Cited in ibid., 8:611.

14. Ibid., 7:511.

15. Ibid.

16. Ibid., 9:167.

17. *The Works of John Adams*, ed. Charles Francis Adams, 10 vols. (Boston, 1854), 8:92.

18. Ibid., 8:217–18.

19. Ibid., 8:218.

20. Ibid.

21. *Papers of Thomas Jefferson*, ed. Boyd and Butterfield, 8:347.

22. Ibid.

23. Ibid., 8:613–14.

24. Wells, "Long-Time Friends," 9.

25. Ibid.

26. Ibid., 10.

27. *Journals of the Continental Congress*, ed. Ford et al., 33:392–93.

28. Randall's report is found in his report to the American commissioners, May 14, 1786. See *Papers of Thomas Jefferson*, ed. Boyd and Butterfield, 9:525–36, 551.

29. *Works of John Adams*, ed. Adams, 8:406.

30. *Naval Documents Related to Barbary Powers*, 1:10.

31. *The Adams-Jefferson Letters: The Complete Correspondence Between Thomas Jefferson and Abigail and John Adams*, ed. Lester Cappon (1959; repr., New York, 1971), 133–34.

32. Ibid., 142–43.

33. *Works of John Adams*, ed. Adams, 7:407.

34. Ibid., 8:400–1.

35. Ibid., 8:381.

36. *Papers of Thomas Jefferson*, ed. Boyd and Butterfield, 8:334.

37. *Journals of the Continental Congress*, ed. Ford et al., 29:834.

38. Ibid., 842–43.

39. Ibid., 843.

40. *Papers of John Jay*, ed. Johnston, 3:198.

41. Ibid., 3:70.

42. Ibid., 3:90.

43. Ibid., 3:299–300.

44. Rufus King to Jonathan Jackson, *Letters of Delegates to Congress*, ed. Smith, 23:352–53.

45. *Works of John Adams*, ed. Adams, 8:219.
46. *Papers of Jefferson*, ed. Boyd and Butterfield, 9:13–14.
47. *Letters of Members of the Continental Congress*, ed. Edmund Burnett, 8 vols. (Washington, D.C., 1921–36), 8:360.
48. Ibid., 8:414.
49. Ibid., 8:433.
50. Ibid., 8:471.
51. *Papers of Thomas Jefferson*, ed. Boyd and Butterfield, 8:426–28.
52. *Works of John Adams*, ed. Adams, 8:407.
53. Jack Greene, ed., *Colonies to Nation, 1763–1789: A Documentary History of the American Revolution* (New York, 1975), 516.
54. *Naval Documents Related to Barbary Powers*, 1:34–40.
55. Ibid., 1:84–85.
56. *United States Chronicle*, May 5, 1787.
57. *Naval Documents Related to Barbary Powers*, 1:46.
58. Ibid., 1:51.
59. Ibid., 1:54–55.
60. Mathew Carey, *A Short Account of Algiers, Containing a Description of the climate of That Country, of the Manners and Inhabitants . . . with a concise View of the Origins of the Rupture Between Algiers and the United States* (Philadelphia, 1794), 40.
61. *Boston Gazette and the Country Journal*, December 30, 1793.
62. *Naval Documents Related to Barbary Powers*, 1:67.
63. *The Writings of George Washington*, ed. John Fitzpatrick, 39 vols. (Washington, D.C., 1940), 33:331.
64. Samuel F. Bemis, *Jay's Treaty: A Study in Commerce and Diplomacy* (New Haven, Conn., 1962), 256.
65. *[Boston] Mercury*, March 18, 1794.
66. Ibid., February 21, 1794.
67. *Naval Documents Related to Barbary Powers*, 1:69.
68. Ibid., 1:71–74.

THREE: TRIBUTARY TO THE BARBARY STATES

1. *The Papers of Thomas Jefferson*, ed. Julian Boyd and Lyman Butterfield, 30 vols. (Princeton, N.J., 1953), 28:49–50.
2. *[Boston] Mercury*, February 21, 1794.
3. *Naval Documents Related to the United States Wars with the Barbary Powers*, 6 vols. (Washington, D.C., 1939), 1:82–83.
4. Ibid., 1:60.
5. For Algiers Treaty, see ibid., 1:107–11.
6. Ibid., 1:192.
7. Ibid., 1:148–49.

8. *Boston Price-Current and Marine-Intelligencer*, November 30, 1795.

9. *Gazette of the United States*, April 21, 1796.

10. *Massachusetts Mercury*, May 16, 1796.

11. *The Writings of John Quincy Adams*, ed. Worthington C. Ford, 7 vols. (New York, 1913), 1:468–69.

12. *Naval Documents Related to Barbary Powers*, 1:139, 150.

13. *Claypoole's American Daily Advertiser*, Philadelphia, June 10, 1796.

14. Ibid., February 20, 1797.

15. Ibid., January 16, 1797.

16. Ibid., September 19, 1796.

17. *Naval Documents Related to Barbary Powers*, 1:144.

18. *The Writings of George Washington*, ed. John Fitzpatrick, 39 vols. (Washington, D.C., 1940), 35:137.

19. Ibid., 35:138.

20. *Naval Documents Related to Barbary Powers*, 1:223.

21. Ibid., 1:239.

22. Ibid., 1:140.

23. Ibid., 1:140–42.

24. Kola Folayan, *Tripoli During the Reign of Yusuf Pasha Qaramanli* (Ile-Ife, Nigeria, 1979), 26.

25. Indeed, a Scotsman, Peter Leslie, who had converted to Islam, was Yusuf Bashaw's admiral of the navy.

26. Folayan, *Tripoli During the Reign*, 29.

27. Ibid., 31.

28. *Naval Documents Related to Barbary Powers*, 1:158–59.

29. Ibid., 1:324.

30. *The Papers of Alexander Hamilton*, ed. Harold Syrett, 27 vols. (New York, 1961–87), 20:536.

31. *Senate Journal*, 5th Cong., 1st sess., June 24, 1797, 246.

32. *Writings of George Washington*, ed. Fitzpatrick, 35:272–73.

33. *Senate Journal*, 5th Cong., 2nd sess., February 5, 1798, 434.

34. *Journal of the House of Representatives*, 5th Cong., 2nd sess., June 12, 1798, 333.

35. *Naval Documents Related to the Quasi-War Between the United States and France*, 7 vols. (Washington, D.C., 1935), 2:113–14.

36. *Senate Journal*, 5th Cong., 2nd sess., July 7, 1798, 531.

37. *Naval Documents Related to Barbary Powers*, 1:329.

38. *Naval Documents Related to the Quasi-War*, 2:388–89.

39. *Writings of John Quincy Adams*, ed. Ford, 2:448.

40. *Naval Documents Related to Barbary Powers*, 1:374–75.

41. Ibid., 1:379.

42. *National Intelligencer*, May 4, 1801.

43. Ibid., May 4, 1801.

44. *Naval Documents Related to Barbary Powers*, 1:459.

45. Ibid., April 27, 1801.

46. Ibid.

47. *Naval Documents Related to Barbary Powers*, 1:397-98.

FOUR: THE CULTURAL CONSTRUCTION
OF THE BARBARY PIRATES

1. J. Franklin Jameson, ed., *Privateering and Piracy in the Colonial Period: Illustrative Documents* (New York, 1970), ix.

2. Alan Taylor, *American Colonies: The Settling of North America* (New York, 2001), 65.

3. *Naval Documents Related to the United States Wars with the Barbary Powers*, 6 vols. (Washington, D.C., 1939), 1:64.

4. *The Papers of Thomas Jefferson*, ed. Julian Boyd and Lyman Butterfield, 30 vols. (Princeton, N.J., 1953), 18:401-2.

5. *The Works of Thomas Jefferson*, ed. Paul L. Ford, 12 vols. (New York, 1904), 10:346-47.

6. *Naval Documents Related to Barbary Powers*, 1:66; *The Writings of George Washington*, ed. John Fitzpatrick, 39 vols. (Washington, D.C., 1940), 29:85.

7. *Journals of the Continental Congress, 1774-1789*, ed. Worthington C. Ford et al. (Washington, D.C., 1904-37), 22:93-94.

8. Mathew Carey, *A Short Account of Algiers* (Philadelphia, 1794), 19.

9. *Naval Documents Related to Barbary Powers*, 1:316-17.

10. Ibid., 1:317.

11. John Adams, *A Dissertation on the Canon and Feudal Law*, in *The Works of John Adams*, ed. Charles Francis Adams, 10 vols. (Boston, 1851), 3:449-50.

12. Frank Lambert, *The Founding Fathers and the Place of Religion in America* (Princeton, N.J., 2003), 238, 246.

13. *An American in Algiers, or the Patriot of Seventy-Six in Captivity* (New York, 1797), 15.

14. [Peter Markoe], *The Algerine Spy in Pennsylvania: Or, Letters Written by a Native of Algiers on the Affairs of the United States of America, From the Close of the Year 1783 to the Meeting of the Convention* (Philadelphia, 1787), 62, 88, 126-29.

15. Robert Allison, *The Crescent Obscured: The United States and the Muslim World, 1776-1815* (New York, 1995), 48-49.

16. Ibid., 54.

17. Ibid., 73-74.

18. Abdrahaman's comments are found in the American commissioners' report to John Jay, in *Works of Thomas Jefferson*, ed. Ford, 9:358.

19. Ibid., 10:346.

20. George Sale, *The Koran: Commonly Called the Alcoran of Mohammed* (London, 1825), 151.

21. See truce with Tunis, *Naval Documents Related to Barbary Powers*, 1:158–59.
22. See Tripoli Treaty, ibid., 1:179.
23. Ibid.
24. Ibid., 2:485.
25. Ibid., 1:3.
26. Cited in Martha Rojas, " 'Insults Unpunished': Barbary Captives, American Slaves, and the Negotiation of Liberty," *Early American Studies* 1 (Fall 2003), 160.
27. *Journals of the Continental Congress*, ed. Ford et al., 34:523.
28. Cited in Allison, *Crescent Obscured*, 102–3.
29. Ibid., 103.
30. *An American in Algiers*, 5–9.
31. Ibid., 5, 16.
32. Paul Baepler, ed., *White Slaves, African Masters: An Anthology of American Barbary Captivity Narratives* (Chicago, 1999), 15–16.

FIVE: THE TRIPOLITAN WAR: 1801-5

1. Cited in Arthur Schlesinger, Jr., *History of American Presidential Elections, 1789–1968*, 4 vols. (New York, 1971), 1:136.
2. For Jefferson's First Inaugural Address, see *The Annals of America*, 18 vols. (Chicago, 1968), 4:145.
3. Joseph Ellis, *American Sphinx: The Character of Thomas Jefferson* (New York, 1996), 203.
4. *Naval Documents Related to the United States Wars with the Barbary Powers*, 6 vols. (Washington, D.C., 1939), 2:126–27.
5. *The Papers of James Madison: Secretary of State Series*, ed. Robert Brugger et al., 6 vols. (Charlottesville, Va., 1986), 1:197–98.
6. Ibid., 1:78–79.
7. *The Works of Thomas Jefferson*, ed. Paul L. Ford, 12 vols. (New York, 1904), I:365–66.
8. Madison's letter to Eaton, dated May 20, 1801, was reprinted in the *National Intelligencer*, January 4, 1802, as part of the administration's making its case for war.
9. *Papers of James Madison*, ed. Brugger, 1:213.
10. *Naval Documents Related to Barbary Powers*, 1:470–71.
11. Ibid., 1:560–61.
12. For details of the squadron, see ibid., 6:30.
13. Thomas Jefferson, First Annual Message, in *Journal of the House of Representatives*, 7th Cong., 1st sess., December 8, 1801, 8.
14. Alexander Laing, *American Sail: A Pictorial History* (New York, 1961), 42.
15. *Naval Documents Related to Barbary Powers*, 1:537.
16. Laing, *American Sail*, 42.

17. The painting of Sterrett's victory originally appeared in *The Naval Temple: Containing a complete history of the battles fought by the Navy of the United States. From its establishment in 1794, to the present time; including the wars with France, and with Tripoli, the late war with Great Britain, and with Algiers* (Boston, 1816). It is reproduced as the frontispiece of volume 1 of *Naval Documents Related to Barbary Powers*.

18. Jefferson, First Annual Message.

19. *Journal of the House of Representatives*, 7th Cong., 1st sess., January 28, 1802, 74.

20. *The Papers of Alexander Hamilton*, ed. Harold Syrett, 27 vols. (New York, 1961–87), 25:454–57.

21. Ibid.

22. Ibid.

23. Ibid.

24. *The Writings of Albert Gallatin*, ed. Henry Adams, 3 vols. (New York, 1960), 1:105.

25. *Naval Documents Related to Barbary Powers*, 2:51.

26. David Humphreys, *The Miscellaneous Works* (Gainesville, Fla., 1968), 73–74.

27. Ibid., 74.

28. Ibid.

29. Kola Folayan, *Tripoli During the Reign of Yusuf Pasha Qaramanli* (Ile-Ife, Nigeria, 1979), 35–36.

30. *Naval Documents Related to Barbary Powers*, 2:46.

31. Ibid., 1:553.

32. Ibid., 2:46.

33. Ibid., 2:177–78.

34. Ibid., 2:185–86.

35. Ibid., 2:297.

36. Ibid., 2:272.

37. Ibid., 2:290.

38. See Madison's instructions to Simpson in ibid., 2:246.

39. Ibid., 6:30.

40. Hugh Garland, *The Life of John Randolph of Roanoke*, 2 vols. (1859; repr., New York, 1969), 1:192.

41. *Works of Thomas Jefferson*, ed. Ford, 1:371–72.

42. Ibid., 1:371.

43. *Naval Documents Related to Barbary Powers*, 2:526–31.

44. Ibid., 3:257.

45. Ibid., 2:366.

46. Jefferson annual message in *Senate Journal*, 8th Cong., 1st sess., October 17, 1803, 298.

47. *Naval Documents Related to Barbary Powers*, 3:171–72.

48. Ibid., 3:292.

49. Ibid., 3:256–57, 258.
50. *National Intelligencer*, March 23, 1804.
51. Ibid.
52. *Papers of James Madison*, ed. Brugger, 6:261.
53. *Naval Documents Related to Barbary Powers*, 3:253.
54. Ibid., 3:288, 295, 376.
55. *Papers of James Madison*, ed. Brugger, 3:376–77.
56. For Decatur's account of the mission, see *Naval Documents Related to Barbary Powers*, 3:414–15.
57. Fletcher Pratt, *Preble's Boys: Commodore Preble and the Birth of American Sea Power* (New York, 1950), 94–95.
58. *Naval Documents Related to Barbary Powers*, 3:421–22.
59. Ibid., 3:483.
60. *National Intelligencer*, May 28, 1804.
61. *Naval Documents Related to Barbary Powers*, 3:498.
62. Ibid., 3:498–99.
63. Ibid., 3:499.
64. A.B.C. Whipple, *To the Shores of Tripoli: The Birth of the U.S. Navy and Marines* (New York, 1991), 67–68, 129.
65. *Naval Documents Related to Barbary Powers*, 4:222.
66. Ibid., 6:30.
67. *Works of Thomas Jefferson*, ed. Ford, 1:382.
68. *Naval Documents Related to Barbary Powers*, 4:340.
69. Cited in ibid., 4:347–48.
70. Ibid., 4:355.
71. Ibid., 4:393.
72. Ibid.
73. Ibid., 4:482.
74. Ibid., 4:508–9.
75. *National Intelligencer*, January 20, 1806.
76. Ray Brighton, *The Checkered Career of Tobias Lear* (Portsmouth, N.H., 1985), 225.
77. Ibid.
78. Ibid., 237, 243.
79. *Naval Documents Related to Barbary Powers*, 5:367–68.
80. Ibid., 5:351.
81. Ibid., 5:552.
82. Ibid., 3:228.
83. Ibid., 5:547–48.
84. Ibid., 5:548.
85. Ibid., 5:552.
86. Ibid., 6:116–17.
87. Ibid., 6:92.

88. Brighton, *Checkered Career of Tobias Lear*, 251–52.
89. See Robert Allison, *The Crescent Obscured: The United States and the Muslim World, 1776–1815* (New York, 1995), 32.

SIX: AN UNEASY PEACE: PARTISAN DEBATE AND
BRITISH HARASSMENT

1. *New-York Evening Post*, February 28, 1806.
2. Robert Allison, *The Crescent Obscured: The United States and the Muslim World, 1776–1815* (New York, 1995), 189.
3. Ibid., 194.
4. Ibid., 188–89.
5. Fletcher Pratt, *Preble's Boys: Commodore Preble and the Birth of American Sea Power* (New York, 1950), 38–39.
6. James de Kay, *A Rage for Glory: The Life of Commodore Stephen Decatur, USN* (New York, 2004), 72–76.
7. Allison, *Crescent Obscured*, 191–92.
8. *Naval Documents Related to the United States Wars with the Barbary Powers*, 6 vols. (Washington, D.C., 1939), 6:216.
9. Ibid., 6:217.
10. *National Intelligencer and Washington Advertiser*, December 2, 1805.
11. Ibid., December 16, 1805.
12. Ibid., December 30, 1805.
13. Louis Wright and Julia Macleod, *The First Americans in North Africa: William Eaton's Struggle for a Vigorous Policy Against the Barbary Pirates, 1792–1805* (Princeton, N.J., 1945), 191–94.
14. *Senate Journal*, 9th Cong., 1st sess., January 13, 1806, 19–20.
15. Ibid.
16. *New-York Evening Post*, March 24, 1806. For the full text of Bradley's report, see *Naval Documents Related to Barbary Powers*, 6:391–93.
17. Ibid., 6:392.
18. *New-York Evening Post*, March 24, 1806.
19. *Senate Journal*, 9th Cong., 1st sess., April 12, 1806, 31.
20. For an evaluation of free-trade thought and its early formulation in United States trade policy, see Douglas Irwin, *Against the Tide: An Intellectual History of Free Trade* (Princeton, N.J., 1996).
21. *Naval Documents Related to Barbary Powers*, 6:419–20.
22. De Kay, *Rage for Glory*, 83–84.
23. Ibid., 84–85.
24. Ibid., 86–89.
25. *The Works of Thomas Jefferson*, ed. Paul L. Ford, 12 vols. (New York, 1904), 10:503–05, 512, and 516.

26. *The Papers of Thomas Jefferson*, ed. Julian Boyd and Lyman Butterfield, 30 vols. (Princeton, N.J., 1953), 8:40.

27. Ibid., 4:106.

28. For a summary of Randolph's views, see *The Annals of America*, 18 vols. (Chicago, 1968), 4:248-50.

29. A.B.C. Whipple, *To the Shores of Tripoli: The Birth of the U.S. Navy and Marines* (New York, 1991), 262-63.

30. Ibid., 263-64; *Naval Documents Related to Barbary Powers*, 6:583.

SEVEN: THE ALGERINE WAR OF 1815 AND AMERICAN INDEPENDENCE IN THE ATLANTIC WORLD

1. Arthur Schlesinger, Jr., ed., *History of American Presidential Elections, 1789-1968*, 4 vols. (New York, 1971), 1:186, 246.

2. Ibid., 1:231-33, 239.

3. Merrill Peterson, ed., *James Madison: A Biography in His Own Words* (New York, 1974), 279-80.

4. Schlesinger, ed., *History of Presidential Elections*, 1:233.

5. Richard Morris, ed., *Encyclopedia of American History* (New York, 1953), 136.

6. See Donald Hickey, *The War of 1812: A Forgotten Conflict* (Urbana, Ill., 1989), 22.

7. Ibid., 22-24.

8. For a discussion of the declaration of war, see ibid., 29-51.

9. A.B.C. Whipple, *To the Shores of Tripoli: The Birth of the U.S. Navy and Marines* (New York, 1991), 276-77.

10. Louis Wright and Julia Macleod, *The First Americans in North Africa: William Eaton's Struggle for a Vigorous Policy Against the Barbary Pirates, 1792-1805* (Princeton, N.J., 1945), 202-3.

11. William Spencer, *Algiers in the Age of the Corsairs* (Norman, Okla., 1976), 139.

12. Hickey, *War of 1812*, 152-53.

13. Spencer, *Algiers*, 276.

14. James de Kay, *A Rage for Glory: The Life of Commodore Stephen Decatur, USN* (New York, 2004), 131.

15. Hickey, *War of 1812*, 284.

16. Ibid., 287.

17. Ibid., 288-96.

18. Ibid., 299.

19. Wright and Macleod, *First Americans in North Africa*, 203.

20. Madison's war message in *Senate Journal*, 13th Cong., 3rd sess., February 23, 1815, 687.

21. De Kay, *Rage for Glory*, 155.

22. *The Writings of James Monroe*, ed. Stanislaus Hamilton, 7 vols. (1901; repr., New York, 1969), 5:377-79.

23. De Kay, *Rage for Glory*, 156-57.

24. Letter of July 5, 1815, William Shaler and Stephen Decatur explaining negotiations that led to the treaty with Algiers, in *Senate Journal*, 14th Cong., 1st sess., Foreign Relations, vol. 4, 6.

25. De Kay, *Rage for Glory*, 158.

26. *Senate Journal*, 14th Cong., 1st sess., Foreign Relations, vol. 4, 6.

27. Ibid.

28. *New-York Evening Post*, November 27, 1815.

29. Ibid.

30. *National Intelligencer*, November 20, 1815.

31. *Writings of James Monroe*, ed. Hamilton, 5:331.

32. *The Writings of John Quincy Adams*, ed. Worthington C. Ford, 7 vols. (New York, 1913) 5:427-28, 453-54.

33. *Daily National Intelligencer*, November 24, 1815.

34. Ibid., November 29, 1815.

35. Ibid., November 29 and 30, 1815.

36. Ibid., December 6, 1815.

37. Ibid.

38. *Senate Journal*, 14th Cong., 1st sess., December 5, 1815, 12.

39. *Daily National Intelligencer*, November 21, 1815.

40. Population figures are found in *The Statistical History of the United States from Colonial Times to the Present* (Stamford, Conn., 1965), 7.

41. The Anglo-American treaty is found in Charles Bevans, compiler, *Treaties and Other International Agreements of the United States of America, 1776-1949*, 12 vols. (Washington, D.C., 1974), 12:49-53.

42. *Statistical History of the United States*, 538, 553.

43. Cited in Henry Hawkins, ed., *Trumpets of Glory: Fourth of July Orations, 1786-1861* (Granby, Conn., 1976), 340.

ACKNOWLEDGMENTS

From its conception this book has been a true collaborative effort. When Thomas LeBien, publisher of Hill and Wang, first raised the idea of a work on the Barbary Wars, I readily accepted. I had benefited from his editorial expertise while writing *The Founding Fathers and the Place of Religion in America* and looked forward to another project together. Once again, I have benefited from his inestimable skill as he deftly shepherded this project with constructive criticism, insightful suggestions, and timely encouragement. I have also profited from the talent of Thomas's superb staff, in particular that of his assistant editor, Kristina McGowan. The book is better for her close reading and text editing. I, of course, am fully responsible for any errors that might remain.

I have incurred personal debts as well. My sons Talley and Will accompanied me on a delightful and informative trip to the Barbary Coast, where we visited many of the sites that played pivotal roles in the narrative. Standing on the battlements of Rabat's Kasbah des Oudaias overlooking the walled city of Salé, we imagined the Sallee Rovers as they slipped into the Atlantic in fall 1784 seeking an American prize. And standing atop Cape St. Vincent, the soaring promontory of southern Portugal that gave cover to the Rovers, we pictured them pouncing on the American brig *Betsey* just a few miles off shore. In addition to stimulating my historical imagination, the trip, with hours of lively repartee, helped clarify my thinking about the project. Most important, I got to spend a couple of weeks with two great guys.

As always, my wife, Beth has been a wellspring of love, support, and encouragement.

INDEX

DATE			